PRAISE FOR

How to Have a Fabulous Wedding for $10,000 or Less

"How nice to finally discover that the most important day of your life no longer means taking on a lifetime of debt! Sharon Naylor's eight easy steps save you thousands of dollars while still allowing you the wedding of your dreams."

—**Beth Reed Ramirez**, publisher, *Bride Again*

"Even if you don't want to save money (not likely!), Sharon Naylor makes wedding planning easier than imagined. Her smart tips and practical advice will save time, money, *and* your sanity!"

—**Diane Forden**, editor in chief, *Bridal Guide*

"Practical and to the point. Everything a bridal couple wants to know, and more importantly, needs to know. Congratulations!"

—**Bettie Bradley**, editor, *Today's Bride*

"Full of friendly, practical advice, with hundreds of creative ideas for planning a wedding that won't take you to the cleaners!"

—**Sarah Francis**, managing editor, *Rhode Island Monthly* and *Rhode Island Monthly's Bride*

How to Have a

FABULOUS WEDDING

for

$10,000 or Less

Creating Your Dream Day with
Romance, Grace, and Style

Sharon Naylor

PRIMA PUBLISHING

Copyright © 2002 by Prima Publishing, a division of Random House, Inc.

Published by Prima Publishing, Roseville, California. Member of the Crown Publishing Group, a division of Random House, Inc., New York.

PRIMA PUBLISHING and colophon are trademarks of Random House, Inc., registered with the United States Patent and Trademark Office.

Library of Congress Cataloging-in-Publication Data
Naylor, Sharon.
    How to have a fabulous wedding for $10,000 or less : creating your dream day with romance, grace, and style / Sharon Naylor.
        p.   cm.
    Includes index.
    ISBN 0-7615-3597-7
    1. Weddings—Planning. I. Title.
HQ745 .N3875   2002
395.2'2—dc21   2002025306

03 04 05 06 DD 10 9 8 7 6 5 4 3 2
Printed in the United States of America

First Edition

Visit us online at www.primapublishing.com

For D.

Contents

Acknowledgments

My deepest thanks go across the miles to my editors, Denise Sternad and Michelle McCormack of Prima Publishing, for making the creation of my books—from start to finish—a pure joy. I owe you both a lemon martini. My publicist, Jennifer Dougherty Hart, gets a big hug from me for always going the extra mile to get the word out and for her extraordinary consideration.

As always, I must thank the many wedding-industry professionals who answered my phone calls and gave their best advice even during the most difficult and trying of times: Rich Penrose of Dean Michaels Studio; Sarah Stitham of Charmed Places; Linda Zec-Prajka of An Invitation to Buy—Nationwide; Michelle Orman of Jewelery Information Center; Andrea Rotundo of GetawayWeddings.com; Kimberly Aurora Kapur of RomanticFlowers.com; and the rest of the wonderful, helpful wedding professionals who contributed to this book.

Thank you, thank you, thank you to all of my family; my Madison and my Kevin; and my dearest friends, who—now more than ever—mean the world to me. Jill, Susan C., Jen, Pam, and Susan D., . . . you are all part of my heart.

Introduction

Congratulations on your upcoming wedding! By now, you've been hugged and kissed by everyone you know with their best wishes, you've flipped through more than one bridal magazine, and at least one person has ogled your engagement ring with pure envy. Your mind may be filled with visions of your dream wedding—the beautiful princess gown, the seven-tiered cake, the champagne toast, a sea of white roses gracing every inch of your reception hall, all of your guests dancing until the wee hours at your reception, the honeymoon in Maui. The gorgeous images keep coming until reality screeches its tires and brings up the big issue: *Wait a minute . . . What's all this going to cost?*

Facing the money issue is a sobering thought for most brides and grooms. Every one of those white roses, cake layers, and beads on your gown *costs* something, and the grand tally can knock your socks off. Weddings are expensive. While the Association of Bridal Consultants pins the national average wedding budget at $20,000, I've spoken to many brides who spent $20,000 on the reception alone! It's not unusual to find brides in certain areas of the country, where prices are naturally inflated, spending an average of $40,000 on their weddings, and celebrities might easily spend as much as a million. These are the Checkbooks-of-Gold brides, and this book isn't for them. This book is for you, the person who wants to plan a gorgeous, elegant wedding within a modest, realistic, responsible budget. I assure you, you can have a beautiful wedding for half the national average cost, without the savings being obvious to your guests and without being disappointed with the outcome.

You're about to find out that $10,000 can stretch further than you think, even in the high-priced wedding world, where a $32-billion bridal sales industry encourages big spending for "the most important day of your life." You're about to plan your own wedding on a budget, so that after it's over, you'll have the financial freedom to create a wonderful married life. You just have to have a plan and a good understanding of the "rules" that determine the prices of each of your wedding's elements.

Let's get started.

Where Will You Marry?

A 100-guest formal wedding taking place in New York City is going to cost a lot more than a 100-guest formal wedding in Mississippi. Like it or not, price tags vary tremendously depending upon the region of the country in which you'll be married, just as the *styles* of weddings vary from state to state. While glitzy formal weddings can be held in any state, there are fundamental price differences between the average wedding in the pricey Northeast and West Coast, the laid-back Midwest, and the deep South. Later in the book, you will see some comparison charts that show vast price ranges depending upon the state in which the wedding item or service is offered, and the style of wedding itself. It's a fact of life that location does play a role in planning your expenses, so take your region's price levels into consideration when planning your wedding. If you wish to marry in a higher-priced, higher-income area, you will run into more expensive wedding packages. If you'll marry in a more moderately priced area, your $10,000 will generally stretch a bit further. It's difficult to generalize, but your location *will* determine the price quotes you'll receive for all of your choices.

When and How Will You Marry?

A wedding held in "high wedding season" in your area—that is, during the most popular months for weddings—will cost more than one held during months of lower demand. This is why the date and time you choose for your wedding will also affect your budget. As you will see in the chapters on choosing a date, time of day, and wedding style, price differentials of 10% to 25% are available when you choose a less-in-demand time. The same goes for the style of your wedding, whether it be a full-fledged reception with cocktail hour and five-course dinner or a simple but elegant cocktail party.

What Kind of Wedding Can You Plan at This Price Level?

The simple answer is . . . *all* kinds of weddings are affordable. The arrangement of a budget is a purely individual process. You can plan a full, elegant wedding with all of those roses and that dazzling cake, but to lower the total budget, you will invite fewer guests. Or, you can plan an elegant cocktail party, a champagne and dessert affair, a wonderfully informal backyard wedding, an afternoon brunch, or a classy garden tea to varying degrees of size and elements, all within that $10,000 boundary.

I've spoken to many, many wedding coordinators and bridal couples across the country and heard about every style of wedding pulled off for $10,000 without any disappointment. The vast majority of wedding coordinators do strongly agree that a smaller, less formal wedding is far more realistic for a $10,000 budget. In other words, *bigger isn't always better,* and all of these coordinators warn that brides are certainly going to reach the inevitable conclusion that the 250-person guest list just isn't going to be possible, except in rare, homespun cases. These experts just want you to be aware that planning a wedding in any geographic area for $10,000 will be a challenge and may require scaling down the size of the wedding . . . but it is entirely possible. These coordinators all subscribe to the following general rules of the beautiful budget-wedding:

• While we see many traditional formal weddings with 250 guests on a much larger budget, the $10,000 formal weddings we see are just as lovely, but on a much smaller scale. In some areas, you're looking at having only fifty or so total guests in order to fit that size budget.

• Among brides on a budget, there is a movement toward weddings held at nontraditional locations that offer the guests something other than the same old formal wedding in a banquet hall. These nontraditional weddings are more affordable, and guests are thrilled at the novelty of an outdoor or backyard celebration, or one held on a boat, at the beach, or even in a museum. These are all realistic options on a $10,000 budget, depending upon your additional plans and choices.

• In many ways, the smaller, more intimate wedding for $10,000 is actually more rewarding to the bride and groom. They will, after all, have more time to enjoy the celebration with fewer tables to visit and fewer hands to shake.

These wedding coordinators and the couples I spoke to said that the most important key to planning a wedding on a budget—and I urge you to hear this now and remember it as you go through this book—is to keep your expectations realistic. While there's certainly plenty of room for prioritizing your expenses, a practice which may allow you to buy that $3,000 gown and make up for the price differential by shaving expenses in other areas, you must keep a grounded approach to your wedding plans. Throughout this book, you'll learn exactly how to do that, how to fit many of your dream wedding images into a real-world budget, where to make necessary alterations to your plans, and how to avoid disappointments along the way.

The Very First Steps

Before any major undertaking, such as planning a wedding for half the national average cost, it's always best to do a little preparation, to set the foundation under you. Before you look at your first dress, scout out your first reception hall, or hire a wedding planner, think about and discuss the following guidelines. Anyone can save money by choosing a $5 favor rather than a $25 favor—those kinds of choices are basic. But to truly create a gorgeous wedding on a budget, you couldn't take better first steps than these:

1. Prioritize where you want your money to go. Let's say that you definitely want that $1,500 dream gown. No negotiation, no tailored knockoffs. You. Want. That. Gown. Period. Some brides feel this strongly, and indeed they have a right to. So, that means that 15% of your entire budget goes to the gown. That's a done deal. Your task now will be to lower the amounts you spend in other areas of your wedding. Perhaps you'll spend less on your flowers, or you'll skip the limousines in favor of your groom's decorated convertible. The art of prioritizing a wedding budget—and it is an art—lies in your ability to move a little extra here and take a little extra from there. Done well, you can bring to life the most important elements of your dream wedding. In chapter 2, you'll learn all about prioritizing and managing your budget to achieve the best outcome.

2. Be realistic about what your budget will buy. This bears repeating. You will only frustrate yourself if you insist on having exotic stephanotis in your floral arrangements, a designer gown, and a

five-course meal for 250 guests. These items may not fit into your budget, depending on where you live. So, always keep realistic numbers and conditions in mind. If you fail to do so, you will not enjoy this process, and few people will enjoy planning it with you.

3. Discuss what you can do without. You might wish to cut some elements out of your wedding altogether. Most couples find they're happy with the basics when the basics are done well. Spending extra to release doves after the ceremony, or hiring a horse and carriage, or giving guests expensive gifts as favors just isn't realistic. So sit down and chat about what's *not* necessary for your day and then shift that part of the budget to where you'd really like to shine.

4. Focus on the bigger picture, not just the money. The most important part of your day, obviously, is the fact that you're getting married. You're taking vows in front of your loved ones and making a lifelong commitment. Would your commitment be any less important if you were to carry a smaller bouquet? Absolutely not. Remember, a wedding is a celebration of your union, and there's no price tag on what your love and your promises mean to your future. Don't fall into the trap of thinking a bigger wedding means you love each other more. A more expensive wedding only means that you took vows and spent a fortune doing it.

5. Don't compete. Sure, your cousin may have just had a $50,000 wedding, but what does that mean to you? The surest way to waste money on a wedding is to compete to impress others or to live up to a family standard of some sort. Throughout the planning process, you will certainly hear either directly or in some implied form the whine, "But what will people think?" Ignore that. Don't worry what others will think. Don't compete. You will not be able to plan your wedding on your budget, and enjoy it, with that kind of mind-set. The only wedding you need to think about is your own.

6. Don't rip yourself off. In an effort to save money on their weddings, some brides cut too deep. They reluctantly agree to do without

the dance band or the Viennese dessert table out of a sense of have-to. Because they don't look to save money or scout out savings in the right ways, they wind up with a wedding that doesn't meet their personal wishes or even one element of their dream wedding. One bride I spoke to said with a sigh, "My wedding had holes in it," meaning that she missed the elements she chose to do without. Throughout this book, I'll share stories of couples who cut too deeply, who now wish to help you avoid their mistakes. Shaving a little off the budget here and there is a wise action, but cutting entire wished-for elements out of the wedding with a resigned sigh and a smothered sense of deprivation is not the way to go. All "cuts" from the wedding plans should be fine with both of you.

7. Take no shortcuts. Large portions of this book will discuss how you can save money by not wasting it. Sounds a little elementary when written in black and white like that, but this is a big key in planning a beautiful wedding on a budget. Invest your time in researching your professionals, stay organized, know what you're agreeing to, protect your investments. Too many couples waste money by not hiring true professionals or by not handling their time and their available resources well. Their mistakes cost them extra dollars, and that's the true mark of a badly planned wedding. Nothing hurts more than having to throw away a much-needed portion of a $10,000 budget.

8. Speak up. I've saved this tip for last, since I find it to be the most important. You would be surprised at how many discounts and freebies you can get for yourself just by asking for them. Remember, the wedding industry is big business. The professionals in this industry depend upon *word of mouth referrals* from you to your sisters, friends, and cousins— from your praises alone they can get five more weddings. So, you may find that a reputable wedding professional will be willing to grant you some price breaks if you only ask for them. We'll discuss that in greater detail later. The same rule applies for family members and friends who offer to help out with the wedding. While I do warn you to consider the

realities of having Cousin Ernie man your video camera during the latter half of the reception, there are enormous benefits to allowing others to help out. The couples I spoke to said that the offers they accepted included the use of an aunt and uncle's summer home on the beach as the setting for the wedding and their ski house as a honeymoon site. In addition, family members may know someone in the floral or catering industry, and big discounts might come your way through those connections. Throughout this book, I'll encourage you to ask for discounts, to use your personal network and business connections to wrangle great deals, and to speak your mind when you feel an offer is unfair.

Now that you have the basics in mind, it's time to get started. From the very first foundational decisions for your wedding (size, style, and formality) to the relatively smallest of expenses (tips, taxes, and toss-its), you are well armed with this book to plan a beautiful wedding for less. You have at your disposal the advice of wedding experts, real life tips and warnings from actual brides and grooms from all over the country, and the means to get a realistic look at what $10,000 will buy you in your area, according to your wishes. You couldn't be better prepared to make the most of your wedding budget, and I welcome the opportunity to work with you, perhaps to inspire you, and to help you create a lovely wedding.

Wedding Day Reflections

When I first started out with my wedding plans, I was so disappointed that I just couldn't afford the enormous, ultra-chic wedding I'd always dreamed of. In fact, a wedding coordinator laughed in my face when I told her that I only had $10,000 to spend. I thought I'd be stuck with a cheapo little wedding that wasn't what I wanted, until I started putting good budgeting and prioritizing practices into effect. Over time, I found that a smaller, more intimate wedding meant that I could have the glamorous elements I wanted, just on a smaller scale. And my husband and I were thrilled at the day we planned because it was truly about "us" and not about the meal or the decorations or the entertainment. Our guests complimented us profusely, because we'd planned a beautiful little wedding that they enjoyed. Take it from me, money isn't everything.

—Erica

Your Wedding Planning Timetable

One Year Before the Wedding

❏ Announce your engagement

❏ Attend engagement parties

❏ Discuss as a couple what your shared wishes are for the wedding of your dreams

❏ Discuss your wedding plans with any family members who will participate in planning (or paying for) the wedding

❏ Begin looking through magazines and books for wedding-day ideas

❏ Hire a wedding coordinator (if you so choose)

❏ Choose the wedding date (and backup dates for booking purposes)

❏ Inform your family and friends of the wedding date

❏ Assess your wedding budget

❏ Decide who will pay for what

❏ Decide what part of your budget will get the most money (i.e., gown, reception, flowers, etc.)

❏ Begin online and phone research for dates, prices, and options

❏ Request brochures for destination weddings

❏ Create an organization system for all wedding plans (file folders, computer program, etc.)

❏ Decide on the level of formality

❏ Make up your own personal guest list

❏ Request guest lists from parents, fiancé's parents, and siblings

❏ Create your final guest list

❏ Select and book your ceremony location

❏ Select and book your ceremony officiant

- ❏ Discuss your ceremony plans with your officiant
- ❏ Select and book your reception site
- ❏ Research and book rental item agency, if necessary
- ❏ Create rental-item needs list
- ❏ Visit with rental agency planner to look at their supplies, choose linen colors, china patterns, etc.
- ❏ Choose the members of your bridal party and inform them of their roles
- ❏ Choose and order your wedding gown and veil
- ❏ Collect the bridesmaids' size cards and ordering information
- ❏ Choose and book your bridesmaids' gowns
- ❏ Choose a florist and meet with the floral consultant
- ❏ Choose and book a caterer
- ❏ Choose and book a cake baker
- ❏ Choose and book a photographer
- ❏ Choose and book a videographer
- ❏ Choose and book your reception entertainment, DJ, or band
- ❏ Choose and book a limousine or classic-car company
- ❏ Start looking at invitation samples and select your desired design
- ❏ Place engagement photo and announcement in local newspapers
- ❏ Notify your boss about your upcoming wedding and arrange for time off for the wedding week or weeks

Nine Months Before the Wedding

- ❏ Find out your local marriage license requirements
- ❏ Meet with your officiant about ceremony elements and premarital classes
- ❏ Meet with the caterer to discuss the menu, wedding setup, requirements, etc.

❑ Plan your beverage requirements and bar setup

❑ Select packages with the photographer and videographer

❑ Select packages with the entertainment

❑ Meet with your florist to design bouquets and floral décor

❑ Meet with your travel agent to plan the honeymoon

❑ Choose and book your honeymoon

❑ Apply for passports and travel visas, if necessary

❑ Notify out-of-town guests of the wedding date so that they may make travel plans

❑ Order your invitations

❑ Order your wedding programs

❑ Order your stationery

❑ Order your wedding rings

❑ Have your wedding rings engraved (if you so choose)

❑ Reserve all the rental equipment (tents, chairs, tables, linens, etc.)

❑ Choose and reserve a block of rooms for your guests at a nearby hotel

❑ Book your honeymoon suite for the wedding night

Six Months Before the Wedding

❑ Order preprinted napkins, matchbooks, etc.

❑ Create maps to the ceremony and reception locations to enclose in the invitations

❑ Begin to plan the rehearsal dinner

❑ Begin writing your vows

❑ Select the ceremony music

❑ Select the ceremony readings

❑ Audition ceremony music performers

- ❏ Book musical performers for the ceremony
- ❏ Register for your wedding gifts
- ❏ Send for name-change information, if necessary
- ❏ Book the hotel rooms for guests
- ❏ Book wedding-night accommodations for the bride and groom
- ❏ Arrange for transportation for guests
- ❏ Plan "wedding weekend" activities, such as brunches, sporting events, barbecues, and children's events, if necessary
- ❏ Begin pre-wedding beauty treatments: skin care, relaxation, massage, tanning, etc.
- ❏ If holding an at-home wedding, hire a landscaper to level your lawn, remove weeds, trim shrubs, add extra plants or flower beds, mulch, etc.

Three Months Before the Wedding

- ❏ Get your marriage license, following your state's requirements
- ❏ Go for blood tests, following your state's time requirements
- ❏ Attend premarital classes, as required by your faith
- ❏ Choose and rent the men's wedding wardrobes
- ❏ Begin gown fittings
- ❏ Choose shoes and accessories for the wedding day
- ❏ Schedule the bridesmaids' fittings
- ❏ Help the bride's and groom's parents choose their wedding day attire
- ❏ Choose the children's wedding day attire
- ❏ Consult with your wedding coordinator for updates and confirmations

❑ Consult with the caterer or banquet hall manager for updates

❑ Complete writing your vows

❑ Ask your favorite relatives and friends to perform readings at the ceremony

❑ Finalize the selections of ceremony readings and music

❑ Submit a song "wish list" to DJ or band you've hired

❑ Submit a picture "wish list" to the photographer

❑ Submit a video "wish list" to the videographer

❑ Arrange for baby-sitters to watch guests' kids on the wedding day

❑ Finalize and book plans for the rehearsal dinner

Two Months Before the Wedding

❑ Go for fittings of your wedding gown

❑ Choose and purchase your "going away" outfit and honeymoon clothes

❑ Address the invitations to guests

❑ Assemble the invitation packages

❑ Buy "Love" stamps at the post office

❑ Mail out invitations six to eight weeks prior to the wedding

❑ Order or make the wedding programs

❑ Order or make the wedding favors

❑ Meet with the ceremony musician about the song list

❑ Have the attendants' shoes dyed in one dye lot

❑ Formally ask friends to participate in the wedding, such as guest book attendant, wedding gift transporter, etc.

❑ Send for all of your name-change documents, such as passport, credit cards, driver's license, etc.

❏ Pose for the formal pre-wedding portrait

❏ Enlarge and frame a portrait of the two of you for the ceremony entrance

One Month Before the Wedding

❏ Pick up your marriage license

❏ Meet with your officiant to get final information on the ceremony elements, rules of the location, etc.

❏ Invite your officiant to the rehearsal dinner

❏ Plan the rehearsal

❏ Invite the bridal party and participating guests to the rehearsal and rehearsal dinner

❏ Confirm your honeymoon plans

❏ Confirm your wedding-night hotel reservations

❏ Get all incoming guests' arrival times at airports and train stations

❏ Arrange for transportation of guests to their hotel

❏ Arrange for transportation needs of guests throughout the wedding weekend

❏ Make a beauty appointment for the wedding day

❏ Visit your hairstylist to "practice" hairstyles for the big day

❏ Get a pre-wedding haircut

❏ Go for your gown fitting

❏ Pick up your wedding bands

❏ Attend showers

❏ Write thank-you notes for your shower gifts (by hand, no shortcuts!)

❏ Call the wedding guests who have not RSVP'd to get the final head count

❏ Make up a seating chart for the reception

❏ Write up your seating place cards and table numbers

❏ Pick up your honeymoon travel tickets and information books

❏ Make up the welcome gift baskets for guests

❏ Purchase gifts for each other, parents, bridal party, honored guests

❏ Wrap and label the gifts

❏ Arrange for wedding-day transportation for the bridal party if they will not be in limos

❏ Purchase a unity candle

❏ Purchase the garters (get two—one for keeping, one for tossing)

❏ Purchase the toasting flutes

❏ Purchase the cake knife

❏ Purchase the guest book

❏ Purchase the postwedding toss-its (birdseed, flower petals, bubbles, bells, etc.) and decorate or personalize small containers (if you so choose)

❏ Purchase the throwaway wedding cameras

One Week Before the Wedding

❏ Confirm all wedding plans with all wedding vendors, having them tell you what date, time, and place they have on record.

    ❏ Caterer (give final head count now!)

    ❏ Florist (give delivery instructions now!)

    ❏ Cake baker

    ❏ Photographer

    ❏ Videographer

- ❏ Ceremony musicians
- ❏ Reception entertainers
- ❏ Officiant
- ❏ Ceremony site manager
- ❏ Reception site manager
- ❏ Wedding coordinator
- ❏ Limousine company (give directions now!)
- ❏ Rental company agent

❏ Pay final deposits for all services

❏ Place tips and fees in marked envelopes for such participants as the officiant, ceremony musicians, coordinator, valets, etc.

❏ If supplying your own beverages, conduct a shopping trip (with plenty of assistants) to the local discount liquor and beverage supply house for a major spree

❏ Drop off guest welcome baskets at the hotel

❏ Pick up your wedding gown

❏ Groom picks up his tux

❏ Groom and ushers pick up the tux accessories, socks, shoes, etc.

❏ Pack for the honeymoon

❏ Break in your wedding-day shoes

❏ Remind the groom to get new shoes for the wedding day

❏ Remind the groom to get a haircut for the wedding day

❏ Arrange for house and pet sitters

❏ Notify the local police department of your upcoming absence, so that they can watch your property

❏ Get travelers' checks (if you so choose)

❏ Plan wedding-day brunch, and inform the bridal party about it

❑ Plan your special toasts

❑ Submit your address change notification to the post office (if you will be moving after the honeymoon)

❑ Attend the bachelor's/bachelorette's party (consider telling attendants and friends that this week would be good for you, as you do not want to be out the night before your wedding)

The Day Before the Wedding

❑ Supervise delivery of rental items to the wedding location

❑ Supervise setup of all items at the wedding location

❑ Finish packing your suitcases and carry-ons for the wedding night and honeymoon

❑ Stock your bag with your car keys, house keys, passports, ID cards, marriage license, wedding night and honeymoon hotel confirmations, medications, ATM card, etc.

❑ Arrange for someone to leave your car, with your suitcases in the trunk, securely in your wedding-night hotel's parking lot for use the next day

❑ Lay out all your wedding-day wardrobe and accessories

❑ Very important: Discuss with all residents in your home the shower/bath time schedule for the next day!

❑ Hand out printed directions to all family members and bridal party members

❑ Confirm times for all the attendants to show up on the wedding day and where to go

❑ Confirm with reliable friends/relatives that they will transport your wedding gifts to their home for safekeeping

❑ Arrange for an honor attendant or reliable relative to be in charge of handing out the payment envelopes

❏ Hit the ATM to get cash on hand for emergencies, tips, valet, etc.

❏ Assemble an emergency bag with extra stockings, lipstick, pressed powder, emery boards, cell phone, etc.

❏ Gas up the cars

❏ Go to the beauty salon to get waxed and tweezed

❏ Stock up on supplies for the wedding-morning breakfast

❏ Place the last call to the caterer or coordinator to answer last-minute questions

❏ Attend rehearsal

❏ Attend rehearsal dinner

❏ Get a good night's sleep!

On the Wedding Day

❏ Set out favors and place cards at the reception site, if the manager will not be doing it

❏ Set out postwedding toss-its where appropriate at the ceremony site

❏ Set out the guest book and pen

❏ Attend the bridal brunch

❏ Have your hair and nails done at the beauty salon and have a massage there as well

❏ Have your snapshot photos taken at home (if you so choose)

❏ Double-check that someone responsible has arranged for your suitcases to go to your hotel room or the car that will be taking you to the airport

❏ Double-check that the appropriate people have the wedding rings for transport to the ceremony

❏ Make sure the bag with your car keys, house keys, ID cards, passports, etc. travels with you to the wedding and thus to the wedding-night accommodations

❏ Relax and know that everything will be fine!

The Day After the Wedding (tasks for responsible family members or friends if bride and groom have left for their honeymoon)

❏ Have someone supervise the rental company's cleanup of the site, if necessary

❏ Get a signed receipt for the return of all rented items

❏ Have tuxes returned to the rental store

❏ Hold a day-after breakfast or brunch for guests and bridal party

❏ Graciously accept all compliments on the wedding

❏ Transport guests to airports, train stations, etc. for their rides home

The First Step

Size, Style, and Formality

SIZE. STYLE. Formality. These "Big Three" decide the depth and breadth of any wedding, not just a wedding on a budget. Size, style, and formality determine not just the financial aspect of your celebration but also the location, the décor, the menu, the type of entertainment, even the kinds of pictures you'll wind up with. So, as you start your wedding-planning journey, begin with these very crucial issues in order to set the parameters of the event you will create.

Before we begin discussing the various sizes and styles of your possible wedding scenario, I must remind you again to think about the types of wedding services that are available in your area. In some regions of the country, you can plan two weddings for $10,000. In others, you might not be able to get the gown you want for that amount. Since I am writing for all of you, for brides in every corner of the country, I am bound by practicality to deal with the national averages spent on each aspect of a wedding. I must generalize on amounts, but I encourage you to apply the practices I mention to your own specific regional offerings.

Size Does Matter

IT'S a matter of simple math. Having 200 wedding guests at a reception hall where the price per head is $75 means you will spend $15,000. No gown, no cake, no photographer. Take those 200 guests and put them at a much more informal reception where the price per head is $30, and you're at $6,000. If you invite 100 people to the same two weddings, you'll pay $7,500 for the formal reception and $3,000 for the informal one. Obviously, the bottom line is: "If you want a formal wedding, invite fewer people." I wish it weren't so, but those are the cold, hard facts.

So, how large a wedding do you want? Are you set on a big event with your enormous extended family, your groom's enormous extended family, all of your clients and colleagues, college roommates, high school friends, and everyone's kids? Would you be sorely disappointed if you couldn't have a wedding that includes all of your loved ones? Or would you be happy—perhaps even relieved—if your wedding was a more intimate affair shared with just your immediate family and closest friends? For some brides, this may mean only fifty, thirty, or twenty guests, and they're perfectly fine without the huge guest list.

How many guests do you want at your wedding? Would it break your heart to limit your list to only fifty people, if that number were all you could afford for the more formal wedding you've dreamed of? It's crucially important at this early stage for you to be honest about who you wish to include in your wedding. Sit down with your fiancé and talk guest list in terms of "How big do we want this wedding to be?" If your parents are involved in the planning, they too will need a serious sit-down discussion, best done with price lists from area wedding vendors to show them the true expenses in black and white, bringing into perspective their own visions of that huge wedding. Many parents get carried away when it comes time to create the guest list, wanting all of their friends and colleagues to attend. It's very im-

Don't Panic!

Right now, you might be tempted to throw up your hands and shout, "Forget it! I'm doomed to a tiny, nothing wedding!" I urge you not to panic. You haven't yet seen the many ways in which you'll be able to stretch your budget to have the wedding you want. Since I always encourage brides and grooms to create the weddings of their dreams, I am not going to encourage you to "settle" for wedding plans that may fit your budget but don't even come close to your true wedding vision. Yes, it will be a challenge to create your much-wished-for wedding on a budget, but it is possible. By making adjustments to size, style, and formality—changes you can live with—your wedding will come together to your satisfaction.

portant, right now, to lay down the law about having a limited guest list. Consider it a preemptive strike that will avoid later battles.

Use the Tier System for Your Guest List

When couples are just starting to look at the size of the guest list as a major factor in their budget, I always advise them to write out a sample guest list. This isn't going to be the final list, but it does put some actual numbers into perspective. Here's your first task: On your computer, or on a few sheets of paper, write down your proposed guests according to a ranking system. The best method for this is to assign "tiers" to your guests. By this, I don't mean that people in Tier 1 are the people who give you the best birthday gifts. Your list might follow this example:

- Tier 1: Parents, sisters, brothers, in-laws, your own children, grandparents, godparents
- Tier 2: Aunts, uncles, first cousins, great-aunts, great-uncles
- Tier 3: Second cousins and extended cousins you're close to

- Tier 4: Closest friends
- Tier 5: Clients and colleagues with whom you are very close
- Tier 5: Close friends whom you haven't seen in a while
- Tier 6: Extended family whom you haven't seen in a while
- Tier 7: Clients and colleagues with whom you are merely just friendly, as well as parents' clients and colleagues
- Tier 8: Neighbors, children's friends
- And so on

You get the picture. By creating this ranking list, you'll see just how many people are must-haves at your wedding and how many others you can invite if the budget allows. I know it seems a bit odd to "rank" your loved ones, but I've found it's the best way to determine the true size of your wedding, according to the most important factor: who you want to share your day with.

DON'T FORGET THE LITTLE ONES

What do you do about the children? Perhaps many of your guests have kids. Perhaps you haven't even seen your college roommate's baby yet, and this wedding would be a great chance to do that. Whether or not to invite children is often a major sticking point in wedding guest list plans. As a wedding consultant at AllExperts.com, I receive letters from hundreds of brides and grooms who ask how they should handle the issue of guests wanting to bring their children to the wedding. As always, I must answer that it's a purely individual decision. At most formal weddings, children other than the couple's own kids and the children in the bridal party are not invited. Guests are informed of that rule through the wording of the invitation and perhaps by your diplomatic reminder of space and budget constraints when parents call for permission to bring their kids. At less formal and outdoor weddings, however, children are often invited as part of an extended family event.

If you're undecided about whether or not to invite children, remember that many caterers charge full price for even the smallest child. So, you might be paying $50 per head for a six-year-old who just picks from the cheese platter all night. Although some kindly caterers offer lower rates for children, you do have to think of your budget when deciding if children are a must for you.

If you leave children off the guest list, it's a good idea to provide some sort of baby-sitting services for the parents who will be dancing the night away at your reception. Some couples with larger budgets do pick up the expense of hiring on-site, well-trained, and certified baby-sitters to watch the kids in one place, either at a side room near the wedding or in the parents' hotel rooms. On a tighter budget, you might choose to prescreen qualified baby-sitters in your area and then send your invited guests a printed phone list of their names so they can do the hiring. As an added bonus: The arrival of this baby-sitter slip in the mail or e-mail makes it clear to your guests that the children are not invited to the reception (in case the etiquette of the invitation wording isn't clear to them).

Now that you have a general idea of how many guests you'd like to invite, you can start thinking about the style and formality of your wedding.

A Matter of Style

No question, the most common wedding style that comes to mind is the formal one. The couple is usually married in a house of worship, and then everyone goes to the reception hall where they enter a lavish cocktail-hour buffet and then proceed to the ballroom for the sit-down or buffet meal, entertainment and dancing, the throwing of the bouquet, and the cutting of the cake. That's the standard wedding style. According to the Association of Bridal Consultants, 89% of brides and grooms have such weddings. (While we're on the subject of national averages as reported by associations like this one, the average number of wedding guests is 192, and the average amount spent on a reception is $4,217.)

Cutting the Guest List . . . Diplomatically

Since keeping the guest list on a smaller scale is key to planning a wedding on a budget, here are some ways to limit your guest head count:

• Don't give an "And Guest" invitation to any guests who aren't in a serious relationship. I know, the etiquette books say that it's only proper to give adult guests the chance to bring a date, but you're on a budget. You'd rather have a friend from college at your big day than someone's Rent-a-Date. So, explain to your single guests that space and budget prevent you from allowing them an "And Guest," as much as you wish you could. Then point out that weddings are great places to meet other unaccompanied singles.

• Hire a DJ, not a band. It is a matter of courtesy to feed the entertainers. That means including them in the headcount for the caterer. Think, would you rather spend $60 for one DJ to eat, or $480 for an eight-person band to eat?

• Sometimes a relative might call to ask if their teenager can "bring a friend" for his or her comfort level at a party full of strangers. Unfortunately, you'll have to take a stand against this kind of guest list add-on. Explain that you wish you could, but there's just no room.

• Avoid the "If/Then" thing, such as, "If I invite one of my sorority sisters to the wedding, then I have to invite all twelve." Don't put that kind of political pressure on yourself. Either just invite the ones you're closest to or don't invite any if they're not dear, close friends.

• Avoid outside pressures. Parents can be sneaky little devils sometimes. So, if you find a name or two scribbled onto the guest list in Mom's handwriting, stand up and say no. You might think it's better to include the person in order to avoid a parental argument, but this kind of intrusive takeover of your decisions is a little bad habit that can grow and increase throughout the planning if you let it go.

• Choose a smaller bridal party. Having fewer bridesmaids or ushers not only translates into fewer "And Guests," it also means fewer gifts to your bridal party.

The tradition of the formal wedding is a long-standing one, and you'll be happy to know that this option is not out of your realm of possibilities. As you'll see later, you can have a formal wedding if you take the right steps with regard to the timing and details in your planning process. At this time, however, I'd like to place some alternative ideas before you, just to get you thinking about other styles that might fit your budget and your preferences.

OUTDOOR WEDDINGS

Take the outdoor wedding, whether it be a beach wedding, a backyard wedding, or even a wedding held on a yacht. These alternatives are part of a growing trend and represent a departure from the usual, traditional, indoor wedding described above. An outdoor wedding adds a unique quality to a marriage ceremony, as the bride and groom take their vows with nature as their backdrop, perhaps with the sound of rolling surf as the ceremony's accompaniment. In my book, *The Complete Outdoor Wedding Planner,* I discuss the ins and outs of planning this popular style of wedding, including the built-in budget-busting aspects of some types of outdoor af-

Wedding Day Reflections

*W*e never really thought about a backyard wedding until we ran out of sites that fit our budget. Once it was suggested to us, once we saw that a really beautiful tent in my parents' big backyard would make a great setting for our day, we began to plan a more gorgeous wedding than we ever could have created if we followed the traditional model.
—Wendy and Alan

fairs. Is an outdoor wedding always less expensive than a traditional indoor wedding? No, I can't promise that. The cost is in the details, and an outdoor wedding can be every bit as expensive as a wedding held at the ritziest five-star hotel. It's the style of the outdoor wedding, the more informal setup and offerings of a backyard bash or the more laid-back appeal of a small yacht wedding, that might open up new vistas for your wedding vision on a budget.

An outdoor ceremony can be any style, from the sit-down formal wedding to the more informal. I've heard stories from brides who planned on-the-beach clambakes with their guests sporting informal outfits or backyard barbecues with scrumptious Hawaiian-themed menus and tiki torches lighting the grounds. I've also heard raves about smaller, more intimate, but ultraformal parties aboard a friend's yacht in New York harbor, complete with a champagne toast to the Statue of Liberty and a menu featuring lobster tails and caviar. Clearly, these brides opened up their creativity more so than their wallets and planned weddings that were uniquely "them."

Brunch Weddings

Another hot trend in wedding styles does away with the big dinner. As you'll see in chapter 4, the time of day greatly affects the entire price tag for the wedding. So, what about a lavish brunch instead of that cocktail party buffet and the five-course meal and the full dessert table? I don't know if you've been to a really good brunch lately, but it's not all bagels and scrambled eggs anymore. At high-quality brunches, you'll find carving stations with juicy hams and prime rib, omelet stations, blintzes, smoked salmon and caviar trays, international breads, salads, and a lineup of desserts that is the sweets-lover's equivalent to a small child let loose in a toy store. I must admit, I actually measured one dessert table at thirty feet long, and there was very little clear space between the various pies, cakes, tarts, and chocolate mousses. The best part of a brunch wedding may be the lower per-guest price (particularly when you factor in the lower consumption of alcohol at a brunch) at $20 to $25 per person rather than $65 to $100 a person for a standard reception, but also high up on the list of advantages is the fact that so many guests appreciate attending unique wedding events such as this one.

Wedding styles can vary from a formal brunch to an afternoon tea in the garden of an estate home, a very chic cocktail party in a museum to a cozy champagne and dessert-only reception at your own

Get Out of Here!

Wedding planning is a big ordeal, often taking a lot of effort to find the right vendors and services to suit the couple's tastes and budgets. Sometimes, the couple doesn't have the time or even the desire to put so much legwork into planning their day. In that case they might opt to plan a getaway wedding just for the two of them. Sarah Stitham of Real Simple Weddings (www.realsimpleweddings.com), a getaway wedding planning company in Olivebridge, New York, plans these kinds of weddings for harried and budget-pressed brides and grooms.

Sarah explains: "The couples who come to me are busy professionals who don't have time to 'micromanage' their special day. Instead, they may love the idea of taking and celebrating their vows at a small luxury inn for just a fraction of what they would have spent on a full-blown wedding. Plus, many of my brides and grooms have family and friends scattered all over the world, and asking them to travel so far and at such great expense is just beyond what they'd like to request. A 'Real Simple' wedding is just that . . . simple, affordable according to the couple's wishes, and very personalized to the couple's styles and personalities. So, with this kind of planning, that $10,000 you might have spent on your wedding flowers alone can be better spent on a full-blown trip to Bali for two."

Clearly, Sarah's company has tapped into the trend toward simplifying things. It also appeals to the couple who might just want to be married without a lot of fuss and input from their loved ones. Another great source for this kind of escape is Get-awayWeddings.com, which offers a full library of destination wedding locations and packages. In my eyes, planning a getaway wedding is one way to make that $10,000 create a once-in-a-lifetime wedding that might be beyond your wildest dreams. It all depends upon your personal wedding style.

home. Another option you might consider is omitting your 120 guests and spending your entire budget on an exotic trip for two (or five, if you'd like to take a few guests along). At this budget you can get a dreamlike destination wedding on a black-sand beach in Hawaii, by a secluded waterfall in Nevis, or a too-cute-for-words ceremony at a bed and breakfast in New England during the fall foliage season.

Always keeping the realities of your budget in mind, you can see how $10,000 will buy you different styles of celebrations in different areas of the country, depending upon the details you include in your day and regardless of the dreamy stylistic elements you may compose. As much as personalities and beliefs differ in this world, so too do wedding styles.

It's Just a Formality

With any wedding, the formality of the event will determine many of its aspects, from the gown to the catering to the décor. You're already well aware that a formal wedding brings to mind a graceful ball gown for the bride and tuxedoes for the men, a lavish reception, and fine décor. An informal wedding might find the bride in a simple slipdress and the groom in a crisp, white button-down shirt and khaki pants, with the menu scaled down and the décor at an appropriately laid-back level.

As a rule, ultraformal and formal weddings cost more per person than informal ones. You'll see why when we talk about menus for formal and informal receptions, floral budgets for elaborate vs. simple affairs, limousine charges, and the huge differences in guests' liquor consumption at an evening formal event vs. an afternoon affair. Simply put, every part of your wedding is affected by the formality of the event, and price tags adhere to the same rules.

It all works together. Your budget is determined by the fluidity of the Big Three working with several other important planning factors. In chapter 2, when we really start talking about your money, you'll see a few sample budgets that reflect the differences between formal and informal weddings of the same size and style. For now, before we get into dollar signs, your next assignment is to brainstorm what you want your wedding to look like and feel like. Ask yourself the following questions so you can put your affordable wedding vision into words for those all-important planning meetings with the professionals who will help you shape your day.

Worksheet: What Will Our Wedding Look and Feel Like?

What wedding style do we prefer? Formal and traditional? A more informal outdoor wedding? Just the two of us in the Italian countryside?

What kind of gown do I favor? A full ball gown? Something sleek and sexy? A more casual look?

What kind of party will our guests enjoy? The standard evening blast, or something more laid-back and casual?

What kinds of foods do we want at our wedding?

(continues)

What kind of entertainment do we want? A band or DJ playing a wide range of music we can dance to for hours, or more easy-listening background music?

How big do we want this wedding to be? Is it possible to cut down to a small guest list?

What details are our "Must Haves"?

What can we really do without?

What is our personal style? What kind of celebration is more "us?"

Everything Has Its Price

Setting Your Budget

It's never fun planning a wedding limited by a budget, but it has to be done. In this chapter, we'll discuss the ins and outs of creating and maintaining a realistic budget, divvying up the expenses in a fair manner, and keeping the budget issue in perspective with the planning process.

Remember, planning a wedding is supposed to be enjoyable, and even on a budget, it can be! In fact, some couples see their budget not as a black-cloaked enemy but as a challenge. They make it into a game to see if they can "beat the budget" and wrangle deals for less than they'd expected. That's the healthy approach. The unhealthy approach, and I see this all too often, is letting the budget weigh you down and control you so that you feel constricted. Having too-high expectations for the available financial supply is the big one. *If you're not realistic about what you can plan on your budget, you're going to be very, very unhappy.*

It always makes me sad to hear about brides who never got the wedding they truly wanted. Looking back on their big day, they wish they hadn't agreed to carry the super-cheap and poorly made bouquet, and they wish they had hired a real videographer instead of asking a relative to do the filming. I look back on my own wedding and cringe at the places where I cut too deeply and made choices that saved my father money but didn't come close to what I really wanted (and, sadly, could have arranged) for my own wedding. Regrets are not what I hope you'll take from this process, so don't rip yourself off and compromise your wedding's outcome all for the sake of money. The key is to be realistic, creative, and assertive—do not surrender to the inevitability of a cheap wedding. There is a difference between an inexpensive wedding and a cheap wedding, and there is a big difference between using your budget well and allowing your budget to overshadow every step of the plans.

Where to Begin

As I've already mentioned, prices and styles vary all over the country. The best way to see what your budget will buy in your neighborhood, state, and region of the country is to do some research. Very often, that's as simple as logging onto an official bridal Web site for your state. As a native of New Jersey, I logged onto www.njwedding.com and found links to wedding professionals in every area of the bridal industry. Some of these vendors' Web sites included prices, full package explanations, and letters of referral. Others didn't. Still, it was good to get a general look at the average prices as quoted by experts in my area. Next, I looked at regional bridal magazines for my area and found prices and Web site links for further research. The same goes for special bride and groom inserts in newspapers, where I found even more local experts. Having taken a good look at who was advertising in my area, I went to the big source, the Association of Bridal Consultants. I checked their Web site (www.bridalassn.com) to find referrals to experts in my area who are members of that prestigious national organization. At this point, it was simply an exploratory mission to get a look at the numbers I'd be facing when it was time to do the actual interviews, booking, and buying. Even though prices varied among all these different professionals and packages, I now had an idea of price ranges and could make a smart and solid preliminary budget.

Similarly, your first steps might be to collect data on average wedding expenses near you. When you have these numbers, plug them into a photocopy you'll make of the sample budget worksheet found in appendix A. Label it, "Exploratory Budget Search," so that you don't confuse it with later, more precise versions. Once done, congratulate yourself . . . you've taken Step One to creating a realistic, workable budget. Please fully expect that the numbers you write down are going to top $10,000 by a wide margin at this early stage, but don't be discouraged. As we continue through this book, you'll shave those numbers down.

This numbers search can take a good chunk of time, perhaps an afternoon, perhaps a few days. But it is worth the effort. If you don't have the time to devote to this task, then I wholeheartedly suggest you hire a wedding coordinator who will do the research for you. We'll talk more about the benefits of professional wedding coordinators, as well as tips for hiring and working with them in chapter 3, but I can assure you now that a *good* wedding planner can save you time and money by scouting out the best buys from the best wedding professionals in your area. A *good* wedding coordinator can help you create a manageable, realistic budget and make sure you stick to it.

Wedding Day Reflections

I almost passed out when I saw that our exploratory look at prices totaled three times what we wanted to pay for the wedding. But then I remembered that I hadn't even started looking or working to find bargains, nor did I have time to use my charming negotiations skills yet! These prices didn't have anything to do with the size, style, formality, date, time, or location of my wedding. Then, when the time came for us to write down actual numbers, we were happy to see that we were beating the early big numbers by a mile.

—Joanne and Eddie

You might think that hiring a wedding coordinator is an indulgence you can't really afford on your budget and is just an extra expense you can devote to another area of the wedding. I encourage you to think again on that. A *good* wedding coordinator can save you a bundle and more than make up for the flat fee or cost of her services. She will also remove a large portion of your wedding stress—an absolutely priceless benefit.

What's Going on Out There?

Yes, I know I've mentioned that wedding prices do vary throughout the country and that there's really no way to publish hard numbers on exactly what you should spend. But the Association of Bridal Consultants has used its vast network of members nationwide to compile the average amounts spent in each category of wedding spending. So, use the percentages in table 2.1 to see just what's going on out there and the areas in which other couples are devoting the majority of their wedding budgets. Then we'll work on how you want to break down your own expenses.

Remember, this is just the average wedding budget breakdown by percentage and should *not* be used as some sort of restricted budget guideline for you. I just wanted you to get a look at where other couples were devoting the larger chunks of their budgets.

Of course, you may not prefer to spend more money on the bachelor party than on your veil or more for the wedding music than your cake. Here is where you take the next step: *prioritizing* where you want the larger portions of your budget to go. Perhaps your dream wedding wouldn't be complete without that gorgeous designer wedding gown. Or perhaps you couldn't care less about the flowers or the limousine, but you strongly desire a top-notch reception menu filled with pricier entrees and a full dessert table. As you identify the items on which you and your fiancé don't want to cut corners, you can shuffle percentages between your categories and watch your budget come together more clearly.

Use table 2.2 on page 18 to fill out your own budgeting priority chart. (If you need to follow an example, see the sidebar on page 19.) Next to each category name, rank your choices from $ to $$$$$, or even FREE to denote your priority level for each section of your budget. Then use this priority list so that you know where to shift more of your dollars when the time to shop comes around.

Item	Percentage
Reception	22.6%
Wedding consultant	15.0%
Wedding rings	9.2%
Flowers	5.4%
Photographer and videographer	5.3%
Wedding gown	4.9%
Music	4.2%
Bridal party apparel	3.6%
Rehearsal dinner	3.4%
Tuxedoes	2.6%
Invitations	2.2%
Gifts to each other	2.2%
Cake	2.0%
Accessories	2.0%
Bachelor party	1.8%
Attendants' gifts	1.7%
Veil	1.3%
Church/Clergy	1.0%
Limousine	0.7%
Groom's apparel	0.6%
Other	8.3%

Table 2.1   Wedding Budgeting by Percent

Category	Priority Rank	Comments
Engagement announcements		
Engagement party		
Ceremony site		
Officiant's fee		
Ceremony musicians		
Reception site		
Rental items		
Wedding gown		
Veil or headpiece		
Accessories and shoes		
Wedding day and pre-wedding beauty treatments		
Groom's clothing		
Bridal party wardrobe (if picking up the tab)		
Wedding coordinator		
Invitations		
Programs		
Caterer's menu		
Liquor		
Cake and dessert		
Flowers		
Reception entertainment		
Photography		
Videography		
Limousines/transportation		
Lodging for guests		
Favors		
Gifts		
Rehearsal and rehearsal dinner		
Extras: Taxes, tips, etc.		

Table 2.2 Where Does the Money Go? Your Priority List

Sample Budget Priority List for Rita and Sam

In this sample worksheet, you'll see that the couple wrote more than one dollar sign to signify things they'll spend the most money on that are nonnegotiable, and one dollar sign for things that are not a high priority.

Category	Priority Rank	Comments
Engagement announcements	$$	We'll get ones that match our invitations
Engagement party	FREE	R's parents want to host the big bash; maybe it'll get the Extravagant Bug out of their systems
Ceremony site	$	Only $25, since we belong to the church
Officiant's fee	$$	The reverend requires $100 for his work
Ceremony musicians	FREE	We'll use the church choir and church organist (with a small tip, of course)
Reception site	$$$$	We want our reception to be extra special, complete with cocktail hour and open bar. Perhaps a time earlier in the day at the hotel ballroom, so it's less money?
Rental items	FREE	We're not renting anything—it all comes with the site.
Wedding gown	$$	R's going to hit the trunk sales, and she's going with a less elaborate gown
Veil or headpiece	$$	R will get at trunk sale
Accessories and shoes	$	R's getting shoes on sale, and accessories will be S's gift
Wedding day and pre-wedding beauty treatment	$$	R wants the salon visit, but she's not paying for the bridesmaids' treatments
Groom's clothing	$$ or FREE	S will negotiate to get his tux gratis with his five ushers' order
Bridal party wardrobe (if picking up the tab)	FREE	The women will pay for their own

(continues)

Category	Priority Rank	Comments
Wedding coordinator	$$	Hiring a coordinator for wedding day only
Invitations	$$	We'll use a great discount invitations company and order simpler style
Programs	$	S will design and make these on the computer for the cost of nice paper and ink
Caterer's menu	$$$$	See Reception Site—we're going all-out
Liquor	$$	Will have open bar, but limited choices for guests; plus, if we have a wedding earlier in the day, we'll need less alcohol
Cake and dessert	$$	Will get beautiful cake through reception site, plus limited dessert menu
Flowers	$$$	R wants gardenias in honor of her grandmother, but centerpieces will be smaller
Reception entertainment	$$$	We want a great show for our guests, but we're going with a DJ
Photography	$$$	We want good pictures, so we're going to find a pro
Videography	$$	We want a good video, not a shaky handheld version
Limousines/transportation	FREE	We'll use S's convertible and Dad's convertible for the bridal party
Lodging for guests	FREE	We're not even offering to put them up. Will find quality, inexpensive rooms for out-of-towners
Favors	$	R can find great favors at the craft store
Gifts	$$	R knows a great Web site where she'll get the gifts for everyone. (S's gift to R is more like $$$)
Rehearsal and rehearsal dinner	$$	S's family plans to host a casual dinner for everyone
Extras (taxes, tips, etc.)	$$$	We're good tippers

Extra Expenses

Even while you're concentrating on the major categories of the wedding, don't forget about the annoying but necessary extra expenses: taxes and tips. I bring this up now, because I've seen too many surprised couples at the end of their wedding planning process who overshoot their budgets in order to meet these necessary expenses. This is a "live and learn" lesson passed down to you by brides and grooms who have traveled the budget road before and wish to warn you to take the little extras into account now as part of your general planning. Here are some "extras" to keep in mind:

TIPPING

Gratuities are a must! Here are the average amounts tipped to the various wedding professionals you'll encounter. But be warned! Tips are sometimes included in the wedding package you purchase or the contract you sign. Triple-check to be sure the tip isn't already coming out of your pocket before you slip them an extra few bills.

- Site manager: 15% to 20% of entire bill for the reception
- Valets: $1 per car
- Waiters: $20 to $30 each, depending upon quality of service
- Bartenders: 15% of liquor bill
- Coat check: $1 per coat
- Limousine drivers: 15% to 20% of transportation bill
- Delivery workers: $10 each if just dropping items off, $20 each if dropping off and setting up to great extent
- Tent assemblers and rental agency assemblers: $20 each
- Entertainers: $25 to $30 each
- Beauticians: 15% to 20% of beauty salon bill
- Cleanup crew: $20 each
- Baby-sitter: $20 or a gift

Permission Fees

- You may need to pay for permits, for example, to use a local landmark estate home or a private beach for ceremony and reception.
- Depending upon the location of your wedding, you may need permits for parking large numbers of cars on a residential street, permits to hold a large gathering, and other permits as explained in chapter 3.

Delivery Fees

- If your flowers, cake, or rental items require delivery, always see if you can negotiate free delivery. If you can't, or if the company you hire doesn't offer free delivery and pickup as a courtesy, then remember to budget for delivery fees as stated in your contracts.

Unexpected Extras

- It's a good idea to have extra cash on hand for the wedding weekend, to cover unexpected expenses that will arise. At one recent wedding, the bridesmaids had to run to the store to buy more champagne, and at another the bride's father had to go to the liquor store for extra bags of ice when the hot weather melted the supply at a backyard wedding.
- You might have to shell out for cabfare to transport tipsy guests home safely at the end of the night.

Since you can't predict the unpredictable, it's best to have a little extra money on you to deal with whatever comes up.

Now that you know where you're going to devote significant portions of your budget and which section gets the big bucks and which sections are free, it's time to ask the question: "Who gets to pay for this?"

Assigning Family Contributions

Unless you're paying for the wedding yourselves, you'll need to sit down with your parents and discuss who will pay for which parts of the wedding. Here's where the fun family interaction comes into play, and I say this with a smile because the scenarios do vary wildly between two extremes: Some couples find that both sets of parents communicate well and divide up the financial responsibilities with little hassle and great ease. Others create a dramatic fiasco filled with unspoken (or, worse, spoken) resentment about one family's higher financial bracket and various stepped-on toes when the groom's family offers to assume part or all of the wedding expenses. I've also heard stories of families that picked wedding expenses randomly from assignment cards in a spaghetti bowl. I kid you not.

It's no secret that two families working together on a wedding face many potential hazards, and some families handle them more diplomatically than others. According to the Association of Bridal Consultants, 53% of weddings are funded by *both* sets of parents, 19% are paid for by the bride's family alone, 27% are paid for by the couples themselves, and 1% are paid for by other sources (guardians, grandparents, etc.). If you fit into the majority of couples that have financial—and more important, nonfinancial—input from parents, it's best to start this group process off on the right foot.

Gather the major players together for a casual dinner or drinks, and discuss your wedding plans and prioritized budget list. Then,

Penny-Wise

Decide now what you don't have to pay for. For instance, you won't have to pay anything for your ceremony site fee if you're having the wedding at home. Perhaps you won't need anything in your limousine budget because your sister's lending you her gorgeous new convertible on the big day. Getting to write in a big "$0!" or "Free!" or "Nada!" is a big thrill when you're piecing together your budget, so take the time to identify where you won't need to spend any money. Again, don't cut too deep. Discuss and decide what you truly can do without.

very clearly and inviting healthy discussion, ask the parents what they'd like to contribute to the financial pool.

I can't warn you enough that when you mix money, status, an important emotional and social event like a wedding, and your par-

Wedding Day Reflections

*W*e made a major gaffe right at the beginning by *telling* my parents what they'd be paying for. My dad's very Old World, and he resented that I told him, instead of asked him, what he wanted to do. Dad can be a pain some-times, and I think he may have enjoyed seeing me squirm when I had to back off and ask him again, nicely. I really hated that.

—Amy

ents' individual parenting styles, you'll need to practice skilled diplomacy. You know your family, and you know your family's attitude about money. So bring up the subject in a way that works best for all of you. Many brides report that they started off this tense conversation with a breezy introduction, such as, "We are so excited about planning our wedding, and we're also excited about having you be part of the planning process. We'd like to ask you what you wish to con-tribute and *how* you wish to contribute, so that we can have our dream wedding." What-ever you say, be sure you express your appre-ciation for their offer to help. Some couples are not so lucky.

The aforementioned statistics show that payment for the average wedding today does not follow the old etiquette dictates of "the bride's family pays for . . ." and "the grooms family pays for. . . ." The statistics personalize who assumes each ex-pense, but I thought I'd include the traditional list here in case any of you feel strongly about going "by the rules." You can either follow this model, individualize your expense assignments, or get out that spaghetti bowl for the big drawing.

CREATE A BUDGET POOL

Sounds good, but what happens if it becomes an "Us vs. Them" thing, with one side resenting the greater financial freedom of the other?

The Traditional Bride's-Family and Groom's-Family Expense Assignments

The Bride's Family Pays For

Wedding announcements	Catering
Engagement party	Flowers
Bridal consultant	Photographer
Invitations	Videographer
Wedding gown and veil	Reception entertainment
Bride's accessories and shoes	Limousines
Reception site	Tips

The Groom's Family Pays For

Officiant	Boutonnieres
Marriage license	Rehearsal dinner
Bride's bouquet	Honeymoon

What happens if the groom's father can give more than the bride's father? What if the groom has two sets of parents of his own, and everyone wants to kick in? My best advice to you to prevent any ego-destroying comparisons between families or individuals is to avoid the itemized category payments altogether. Instead, create a budget pool. If the parents wish to contribute to the expenses of the wedding, let them put their donation into a general collection or bank account for the wedding as a whole.

This practice may help you avoid the measuring sticks that some families can whip out between themselves, and it also removes what can be a bigger problem for some couples whose parents hold the checkbook and thus, the reins. I still hear about wedding scenarios in which parents feel that their financial control of the wedding gives them creative control as well. It's a slow boil, but eventually the couple and the parents are fighting over which band to hire or which music will be played before the bride's approach down the aisle, and some last straw is dropped on a parent's back. Veins start throbbing, faces turn red, palms grip tightly, and all of a sudden your mother gets that look in her eyes like Gloria Swanson in *Sunset Boulevard,* with that freakishly twisted face ready for her closeup. Your future father-in-law turns into a dangerously simmering Tony Soprano on a bad day. That's when the parent yells, "I'm paying for this, so we're doing it my way!" It sounds like a scene from a bad TV movie, but that kind of blowup and power play takes place incredibly often during wedding planning. Laying out the money gives some people a sense of overall entitlement, especially when perspective has been lost and the parent is more concerned about how the wedding will make him or her look personally. It happens all the time, especially when money becomes a larger issue than it has to be. I can't promise you that this

Watch Out!

I see a lot of couples who stick to their budgets and stay within their means throughout the early stages of the planning process. However, as the wedding approaches, they increase their spending and go a bit beyond their budgets. Others completely *blow* their budgets and spend money like water. Why does this happen? For some, it's sheer nerves. When they're nervous, they spend more because it makes them feel better. Others feel more pressure to make the wedding beautiful and start adding features they've avoided along the way. Still others see that their budget wedding won't compare with the one the bride's wealthy cousin just started planning, so competition starts brewing. Whatever the reason, it's very important to maintain the budget *throughout the process.* Keep in mind that throwing the budget out the window is only going to hurt more, especially after the wedding.

kind of entitlement scene won't take place for you, but I can suggest removing the seeds for it by creating a bridal budget pool. Then, no one can compare what they're giving compared to what others are giving.

Time to Draw up the Budget

This is it, the moment you've been waiting for. This is your first realistic pass at drawing up your budget and showing where you want to focus your expenses. Go to appendix A and make a photocopy of the Sample Budget Worksheet. As you fill this budget sheet out, keep in mind that this is only your first pass-through. Allow yourself a little bit of flexibility, and always keep the bigger picture in mind. Money is a factor in the wedding, but *you can't let your wedding become only about the money.* Budgeting is a difficult job, especially with so much emotion and importance attached to each aspect of your wedding. As hard as it is to stay in the neighborhood of your budgeted amount for each purchase or contract, it will be harder to make up the difference in another area if you lose your head and spend way more than you've estimated for that category. Use your budget as a general guide, not rigid law, and refer to it to help you keep your spending under control. Allow yourself the grace of playing with the numbers as you go along.

> ### Simplify It
>
> *D*on't even write down or keep track of how much each set of parents gave, and certainly don't talk about it with anyone else. Make it a vow of silence to protect your parents' feelings and the peace, sanity, and integrity of your own wedding plans.

Sample Wedding Budget Worksheet for Rita and Sam

Informal Wedding, 70 Guests,
at a Hotel, Saturday Afternoon

Item/Service	Budgeted	Actual
Engagement announcements	$100.00	S making them $10
Engagement party	$0	$0
Ceremony site	$25	$25
Ceremony décor	$250	included in florist fee
Officiant's fee	$100	$100
Marriage license	$60	$45
Pre-wedding counseling/classes	$75	$75
Reception site	No site fee	$0
Rentals for reception site	No rentals	$0
Preparation of reception site (landscaping, cleaning, etc.)	$0	$0
Additional permits for parking, etc.	$0	$0
Wedding gown	$250	$200
Wedding gown fittings	$100	FREE
Accessories and shoes	$100	$30
Bride's manicure, pedicure, and hair	$150	$70
Groom's clothing	$150	FREE
Groom's accessories	$50	FREE
Wedding coordinator	$1,000	$400
Invitations	$500	$300
Postage	$70	$50
Programs	$20	$15
Thank-you notes	$50	$50
Caterer's menu	$3,500	$3,500
Liquor	$400	$300

Cake	$250	$100
Flowers	$1,500	$1,000
Reception décor	included above	
Reception entertainment	$1,000	$790
Photography	$1,000	$850
Videography	$800	$800
Wedding cameras	none	$0
Limousines or classic cars	none	$0
Other guest transportation	none	$0
Favors	$300	$300
Gifts	$400	$300
Toss-its	none	$0
Tips	$200	$200
Totals	**$12,300**	**$9,965**

In appendix A, you'll find a blank budget worksheet for your use. Make several photocopies of this worksheet so you can create your own preliminary and working budget forms.

Smart Money Matters

Save Money by Not Throwing It Away!

SMART SHOPPING skills will save you more money than any great discount Web site, cousin in the floral business, or secret handshake. You will be sorting through many different vendors' deals and contracts, making important business agreements, and signing on the dotted line often in the coming months. The wedding industry is an *enormous* one, filled with both highly professional and unscrupulous vendors, and some deals are better than others. You might see on your local news a story about a shady, fly-by-night bridal shop that disappeared with several brides' gown deposits and the heroic watchdog reporter who tracked the shop owners down for payment. While it's wonderful that these brides got their money back, the issue of "How smart was that hiring decision?" has to be addressed. You won't always have a watchdog reporter come to your rescue. The key is to make smart shopping decisions so you're not a victim of fraud or ignorance.

Yes, there are bad deals out there, and those too-good-to-be-true prices are sometimes portents for disaster. Smart shopping rules are as important in planning a wedding as for buying a house or car, or choosing a college for your child. You'll be spending a *lot* of money on your wedding, so be sure you're putting it in the right place. The success of your wedding day depends upon the consumer actions you take from here on out. So keep the following rules for smart wedding shopping in mind with each step you take.

1. Do your homework.

The key to good wedding planning is having a broad knowledge of what's out there for you. So spend some time researching wedding packages, comparing price lists, asking questions, and inspecting examples of vendors' work. Yes, this step is time-consuming, especially when your life is filled with important obligations such as your job, your family, and your active daily life. But this is a step you cannot skip. You simply cannot make informed decisions without some insight into what the industry offers.

2. Run some checks.

You're going to be forking over a lot of money and responsibility to the professionals you hire, so it's crucial to contract with only reputable vendors with great reputations in their fields. The best professionals belong to industry associations that require high codes of conduct, integrity, years of experience, even updated training at regular intervals. These associations often list their members on their Web sites. You can usually receive detailed descriptions of vendors' offerings right from the association that proudly counts them among its members. In the planning chapters of this book and in the resources section in the back, you'll find the contact information for many wedding industry associations that you can consult to check on your wedding professionals. Keep in mind that a listing with a professional organization doesn't mean you'll have no problems with your vendor. Some associations have better screening processes than others. Just take it as a good sign that your vendor belongs, and use that organization as a tool to find out how long the vendor's been in business, what kind of awards they've won, and other indications of a long and healthy track record.

3. Allow plenty of time for planning.

Good deals can be found if you're planning way in advance of your wedding. Rush jobs mean rush fees, and you certainly will not have enough time to scout out great deals, think through important decisions, and find the best offerings out there. So don't sit around admiring your engagement ring for the first four months, thinking, "There's plenty of time to do all this." Get out there and start researching your investment potentials.

4. Ask for referrals.

Sure, that full-page ad in the Yellow Pages looks great, but how's the service? Firsthand experience is really the only way to tell how good a wedding professional really is. And by this I don't mean asking the wedding vendor to provide you with referrals. Sure, they have glowing letters from happy brides and grooms, and I'm sure the vast majority of them are legitimate. But my friends could easily write a letter saying that I'm a great house painter, and I certainly am not. Plus, no wedding vendor is going to hand you a letter written by a disgruntled customer with an arm's length list of complaints. The referral I'm talking about comes from your recently married friend or relative. Find out who they hired, and whether or not they were happy with the outcome. In the wedding industry, word-of-mouth referrals bring in a lot of new business for the best professionals, so ask around and take some notes. Your friend with flawless taste and a budget similar to your own may know of the perfect seamstress, cake baker, or floral designer for you.

> ## Simplify It
>
> You might also opt to check the vendors out further through your state consumer affairs department or the Better Business Bureau. For online companies, check with www.bbbonline.org, the Better Business Bureau's Web site complaint department. Again, a listing on these sites is not an automatic thumbs-up. Just use them as a reference tool in your complete planning process.

Beware of the Handshake Deal

We thought we'd found the best caterer ever, but she said she didn't offer a contract. She just completed an order form. And she said that was standard for her industry. Is that true?

No, it's not true. Any professional who doesn't offer a standard written contract should not even be considered. Some professionals might offer a combination of an order form and contract, so look carefully at the contract statements and terminology. I spoke to a consumer attorney on this, and she assured me that it's often a sign of past legal troubles when a professional tries to avoid offering or signing a contract with you. So, ask for a contract in all cases. A quality professional will be only too happy to present you with one, explain it, and make any reasonable changes that you request.

5. Read your contracts.

Read every word. Ask questions if you don't know what something means. For instance, what is a "price escalation clause?" That little paragraph hidden on the bottom of page 3A of your contract means that the company has a right to raise their fees between the time you sign and the time of your wedding, and you'll have to pay the new higher amount, regardless of what you sign for now. Sounds ridiculous? Most slippery contract clauses are. Not every vendor offers a contract filled with sand traps like this one, but you should be aware that some shady contract wording might be in those tiny little lines of print. So always read your contracts thoroughly. Take them home and have a friend with legal knowledge do a pass-through. A good vendor will allow you plenty of time to read, review, and question your contracts. If the vendor seems to be rushing you through your reading, answering your questions vaguely, or handing you the old, "Oh, that's just a standard part of your contract and it doesn't mean anything," run far away. This is your contract we're talking about, a legally binding document that spells out what you're going to pay and what you're going to get for your money. Always, always, always be sure that every little detail of your agreement is spelled out, right down to the number of roses in your bouquet and the exact time the bouquets will be delivered to your door. Everything. The dates and amounts of your deposits. The names of the people in the band you hire. Everything. Secure a solid, complete contract, and keep a copy with all changes initialed for your own records. This one step can save you a fortune and protect your investments in court for a full or partial refund if something goes wrong.

6. Use your credit card.

While I would never encourage you to run up or max out your credit cards, as that's a mark of financial irresponsibility, I do urge you to use your credit card for all of your wedding purchases. A credit card payment can be registered, tracked, and protected through various credit agreements, whereas a cash payment cannot be proven in court, should it come to that. So when it comes time to make purchases, whip out that plastic. Especially if you have a credit card that offers points, frequent flier miles, or a cashback bonus. Just use your card responsibly and make timely payments so that your $500 purchase doesn't rise to $1,000 with a carried balance and interest rates.

7. Don't shop when you're wiped out.

If you're exhausted, you won't have the mind-set to make smart decisions, and you might make impulse buys just to get the hell out of the store. Simply put, don't try to shop, decide, or plan any aspect of your wedding when you're not at your best. Shop early in the day, if you have to, or take a day off work to make some visits or conduct interviews with vendors.

8. Stay organized.

I can't tell you how many times I've heard stories of unorganized couples spending more on their weddings than they had to. Perhaps they lost a receipt and had no record of their deposit to a vendor, or perhaps they simply missed an appointment and lost a great deal because they weren't there. To stay organized, create a record-keeping system, whether it's a collection of file folders or a computer software program. Staying on top of your plans means you have a better handle on all the costly details, and you will avoid late fees, extra charges, or even paying twice for the same service. At the same time, keep your bridal party and family members organized and well-informed, so they don't add to their own stress and expenses—or yours!—due to a misplaced receipt, a forgotten fitting, or a lost phone number.

9. Speak up!

You'd be surprised at the discounts you can get if you simply ask for them. While I wouldn't advise walking into a dress shop and attempting to bully your way into a 20% discount because of a stain on a gown's hem, I do encourage you to ask for a break on first-offered prices. Ask for a percentage off for special circumstances. If you have a large order, such as at the tux rental shop, ask for the groom's tux for free. It never hurts to ask. Again, remember that these shops want you to recommend them to your friends . . . so giving you that 15% off might be worth it to them.

The same goes for standing up for your professional agreements. If the contract you signed states that you get five hours of service from the band, make sure you speak up about getting your five hours' worth, excluding breaks. Be firm but diplomatic, and remember that the hard sell, the tough act—okay, being bitchy—will not get you as far as being assertive but fair.

10. Assess offers of free help.

Perhaps your aunts offered to make the wedding cake, or your cousin offered to act as your chauffeur on the wedding day. Very often, family members and friends chime in with their offers to help out with everything from the menu to the photography to the entertainment (as in "Cousin Melissa is applying to Juilliard in the fall, and she'd *love* to sing at your ceremony!"). With a budget wedding, these offers can be a blessing. Just be sure to check that the generous family member can actually *deliver* well on the wedding day. All of the good intentions in the world won't matter if the aunts have never cooked for 100 guests before or if Cousin Melissa can't sing "Happy Birthday" on key. So try them out, sample their services, and then judge if the free offer is worth it. Same goes for helpful friends and family that you ask for assistance. They still need to be put to the test, for the sake of your wedding's success. In the end, tell them that their contribution stands as their wedding gift to you . . . no other presents needed.

11. Don't go for rock bottom.

Sure, you might find a videographer who charges one-tenth what others do, but I wouldn't whip out the Visa card just yet. Often, those too-good-to-be-true finds are danger signs, meaning you should investigate a bit further. There's often a good reason why the service is so cheap.

12. Stick with the budget.

It may not be fun, but a solid budget keeps you within your boundaries. Even if you're a bit flexible with your numbers, keep your budget with you as you make your plans, and adhere to it as best you can.

13. Get creative.

Certain elements of your wedding plans may fit your creative nature, and you might choose to take on a do-it-yourself role. If you have the time and talent, you can make some of those costly accents, such as favors, décor, and some desserts. Consider your own skills and available time for the things that you can do at little expense.

14. Don't cut too deep.

I've said it before, but it's worth repeating: Don't go overboard with the cost-saving campaign, and don't cut much-wanted items out of your day for the sake of money. There's more than a fine line between striking great bargains to shave money off the budget and ripping yourself off. Don't sacrifice too much or you will regret it. Just practice smart shopping, make an effort to find great deals, and plan the best wedding possible.

Who Has Time for All This Checking?

Yes, the key to smart wedding shopping is spending time doing a lot of research and checking. Being "in the know" is a huge benefit in dealing with the wedding industry, and who's more in the know than a good wedding coordinator? You might think, "On a tight budget, who has room to spend even *more* money on a wedding coordinator?" I can assure you, if you hire the right person, the investment will be well worth it.

A quality wedding coordinator is more than just a researcher. This person may have connections with top-notch vendors who will grant you big discounts. He or she knows which professionals are worth their prices and offer fair packages, and which are not. A wedding coordinator can help you create a realistic budget, and she can keep you within that budget. As your right-hand man or woman, the wedding coordinator can be a great asset in your entire planning process.

What Will You Do?

According to the Association of Bridal Consultants, brides over age thirty are much more likely to hire a wedding coordinator than to accept help from a relative or friend. Of those who do hire wedding coordinators, the average couple devotes 15% of their wedding budget to paying for the expert help.

I've spoken to many wedding coordinators over the years, and I can assure you that it's not just the rich and famous who hire professional planners. Busy couples, couples with children, couples planning a wedding in less than a year, couples on a budget . . . all might hire a knowledgeable wedding planner to help bring together their big day and keep things running smoothly at the wedding itself.

What Does a Wedding Coordinator Do?

So just what can a wedding coordinator do for you? Besides letting you know which cake bakers offer the best, most affordable chocolate ganache cake, a quality wedding coordinator can:

- Give you a realistic view of what your budget will buy in your geographic area
- Show you price lists and brochures from wedding vendors you might hire
- Help you decide which professionals to hire
- Help you create your wedding packages with each professional
- Create a personalized timeline to keep you organized
- Introduce you to great locations for your wedding, pointing out little-known sites
- Organize your contracts and order forms
- Review your contracts
- Complete the entire invitations task, from ordering to wording to mailing
- Confirm with all of your wedding vendors before the wedding
- Help plan your honeymoon
- Attend the rehearsal to organize the processional and recessional, direct all ceremony participants in their roles, answer questions, and keep the process flowing
- Act as ringleader on the wedding day to handle all of the little issues that may come up, direct vendors so that they're in the right place at the right time, save the day by running to pick up a replacement item

- Act as your diplomacy expert, smoothing over scuffles with family members and vendors alike
- Take away the burden of worrying about every little thing

How Much Help Do You Need?

If you do decide to hire a wedding coordinator, take some time to figure out just how much help you're going to need. Do you want someone to take over the entire vendor research process and work every detail with you right through the big day, or do you just want someone to do all the initial vendor research? Or, perhaps you've already started your research and interviewing but are finding that you just can't handle all of this planning *and* your nine-to-five job, so you want someone to step in. The wedding-coordinating industry knows what it's like out there for you brides and grooms, so many professionals offer a personalized range of wedding planning services designed to fit individual needs. Here, then, are the types of wedding packages you might consider:

Professionally Speaking

The most important way a wedding coordinator can save money for the couple is by saving time. A good coordinator can save valuable time right from the start by helping the couple create a realistic vision. For instance, I might be able to save a lot of time and money by showing the bride that some item is not readily available, or something cannot possibly fit into the hall. When the coordinator takes on the role of finding and talking with vendors, she is saving the couple valuable time off from work, free time, even mileage. In addition, established coordinators may be able to pass along discounts from vendors to the couple and locate wonderful wholesale deals on items such as linens, decorations, favors, and the like.

— Deborah Carpenter, wedding coordinator and owner of
Opulent Affairs in Hamden, Connecticut

• The All-Inclusive Package. The wedding coordinator is involved with nearly every step of the planning process from early discussion of your styles and tastes for the wedding, drawing up a budget, helping to research vendors, assisting you with contracting the vendors, and so on all the way through to micromanaging every detail of the wedding day . . . and then returning the tuxes to the rental shop the day afterward.

• The Partial Wedding Package. The coordinator does only a portion of the work, such as interviewing vendors only. Or, she might perform every function after the bride and groom have already found and hired their vendors.

• The Wedding-Day-Only Package. The coordinator steps in one month prior to the wedding and checks in with all of the vendors, reviews contracts to be sure all services are on schedule, creates a schedule for the wedding-day venue, attends the rehearsal and provides directions for the entire wedding party and ceremony participants, and finally, attends the events of the wedding day for a specified number of hours to direct all vendor activity and keep everything running smoothly.

Certainly, the coordinator you choose should be willing to create a personalized package for you, taking into account your needs. There's no question that on a day as important as your wedding, the value of a point person is incredibly high. So I encourage you to assess your own needs, and if you so desire, create room in your budget for a wedding coordinator, especially if you're doing long-distance planning from a town or state other than where you will marry, or if you're planning a destination wedding.

WHAT WILL ALL THIS COST?

Quality wedding coordinators have different pricing methods. Most offer a flat fee pricing system, depending upon the type of package and amount of help you request. That is the ideal setup: so much money for so much effort, or for so many hours of work. Other planners still adhere to a pricing plan set up as 10% to 15% of the total cost of the wedding. The percentage plan isn't the most optimal arrangement, because a coordinator may benefit from a budget that extends beyond the original estimate. I wouldn't go so far as to say a coordinator may encourage you to extend beyond your means, but I'm sure you recognize the danger of this happening with a less reputable planner. I'd also steer clear of coordinators who offer their services *at no cost to the couple*. They take their commissions from the professionals they hire for your wedding, and that also opens up the possibility of overreaching your budget.

As you create your individualized package with the coordinator, discuss the price system as particular to your event. Find out what the coordinator includes in her basic flat fee, if rehearsal attendance is included, what's considered "extra," how much she charges for overtime, and what her additional fees may be. Then be sure they're all spelled out clearly in your contract.

Questions to Ask the Wedding Coordinator

Okay, you've found a few contenders, you've assessed their office space and their samples, and they have a friendly demeanor. All's clear up to this point. Now it's time to get into detail and ask some very important questions about their experience, what they offer, and what's expected from you.

- How long have you been in business?
- Which professional associations do you belong to?
- How many weddings have you planned?
- How many weddings *like mine* have you planned? (Useful information if you're planning an at-home or outdoor wedding)
- Have you planned any weddings at our chosen location?
- Do you plan weddings for budgets like ours? (Some coordinators do not, unfortunately)

FINDING A WEDDING COORDINATOR

You can start with the Yellow Pages or an Internet search or consult with recently married friends. Above all else, be sure your wedding coordinator is affiliated with one of these professional event-planning national associations:

The Association of Bridal Consultants: 860-355-0464,
   www.bridalassn.com
Association of Certified Wedding Professionals: 408-528-9000,
   www.acpwc.com

Membership in an association is a mark of trusted service, an established history in the business, an adherence to codes of ethics and conduct, rave reviews, and perhaps even high-profile accounts. As always, be sure to research the coordinator on more than just the fact

- Can I get references for you and your business?
- Can you personalize your wedding package to suit our needs?
- May I take a look at your contract?
- What are your fees? Your overtime fees?
- What's not included in your package?
- What can I expect throughout the process with you?
- Will I be able to call you outside of business hours? (Many coordinators allow business-hour access in the beginning of the process, and then all-hours access closer to the wedding.)
- Will you give me your cell phone number for easy access during the planning process?
- What will you expect from us?
- Tell me about some of the most memorable weddings you've planned …

that his or her name comes up on a search through an association's Web site. These sites can save you time by allowing you to plug in your preferences and then delivering a list of suitable candidates' names and phone numbers, but it's up to you to take the next step.

When hiring a wedding coordinator, you're doing more than hiring a standard vendor. Since you'll be working in close contact with this person, she is in essence becoming your partner and you'll need to make sure you have great rapport and a comfortable partnership. So, you're also hiring on the basis of personality and how the two of you "fit" together. You might prefer to hire someone who's all business, super-efficient, highly organized, and has a Type-A personality. Or, you might want to hire someone who gets the job done but is more laid back and easygoing. In all interviews, see if your candidate listens to you, asks you what you have in mind, stays attentive, and answers your questions completely. Be sure she offers a written agreement, an organized presentation of her price packages, and perhaps shining examples of her work. See if her office is organized and seems to be running efficiently. Beware of stacks of little pink phone messages from last week sitting next to her phone. Are towers of overflowing files stacked up by the window? Is the phone ringing off the hook with no one to answer it? Keep these little things in mind, because it might be *your* call that doesn't get returned in a few months.

Yes, the coordinator works *for you!* Don't be afraid to speak up if you feel your coordinator is taking the wedding in a different direction, and don't be afraid to voice your opinions. These professionals are there to help you create *your* day, and they want you to say what you like and don't like about what they present to you. Your coordinator is a sounding board; she's been through it all many times before, and her experience can certainly save you big money when she prevents you from making an expensive mistake. She has the foresight to predict what steps need to be taken in many situations, and she has the hindsight of knowing what doesn't work in a situation like yours.

According to some brides, she will also tell your parents or that bitter bridesmaid (sweetly, and with a smile) to just back off and let you plan your wedding. How priceless is that?

Handling the Legalities of Your Wedding

Get your mind off the money for a minute. We need to make sure that all of your plans are going to celebrate a marriage that's *legal.* Plus, beyond the beauty and the niceties of everything from your reception to your gown to the sleek limousine that may whisk you away to your hotel, there are *legalities* for every purchase and contract you sign.

YOUR MARRIAGE LICENSE

Securing your marriage license is perhaps the most important step of all. Since every state has its own rules on the various steps, required tests, and valid time periods, it's crucial that you check on *your* state's official rules for the state in which you will be married, especially if you're not marrying in your home state. Go to your town hall and ask to speak to the Marriage Registrar or the clerk who handles wedding licenses. They should be able to hand you a brochure describing all the state prerequisites. Most of these brochures outline the following topics:

- Who is licensed to perform valid wedding ceremonies: a religious official, the mayor, superior court judges, municipal court judges, members of the town council, etc.
- The duration of the license's validity. In some cases, you *must* get married within six months of completing your license application
- License fees and extra charges
- Identification and paperwork needed, such as birth certificates, divorce decrees, death certificates for widows or widowers, and whether these documents must be notarized

- Blood test requirements
- Parental permission for brides or grooms under a certain age
- Witness requirements
- A phone number to call for any questions or verifications

I strongly advise that you talk to your town hall or the town hall of the location where you will be married for this information, because state laws change all the time, and recent changes might not be reflected on the wedding Web site you might go to for this data. When you do call for this information, ask them to send their brochure to you, via fax, e-mail, or the mail, so you have a record of what you need to do. When you speak to the clerk, write down that person's name and the date you spoke, keeping careful track of all the information.

When it comes to licenses, leave no question unanswered. Be sure you cover all details, and time your application so your license is valid at the time of your ceremony. It would be a shame to stand before the officiant at the rehearsal and see him shake his head because your license isn't valid anymore.

Simplify It

Start researching marriage license and medical test requirements right away. Some states in the U.S. have extensive waiting periods, and in faraway resorts in other countries or islands, the legal process can take months. So don't leave the legalities until the last minute. Check into them now, add them to your calendar, keep track of valid time periods, and start any international application process as soon as possible.

YOUR BLOOD TESTS

Blood test requirements also vary from state to state. Some states require a battery of tests from HIV to hepatitis, and others do not require blood tests at all. Be sure to find out not only which tests you need, but—and this is very important if you'll marry at a site other than where you live—whether or not test results from your local hospital or doctor's office are valid in the area where you will marry.

A Matter of Insurance

Some couples feel more comfortable with their wedding plans if they take out insurance, especially if they're dealing with the weather at an outdoor wedding. While you will certainly ask all of your wedding vendors if *they* are insured, you might consider checking into insurance for events that take place at your home or at an uninsured location. Talk to your family insurance agent for more details and to locate the wedding insurance provider that suits your needs.

Why am I talking about all of this blood test and license stuff in a book about saving money? Because licenses and medical tests cost money. In the grand scheme of things, these amounts may not add up to a lot, but the rest of the wedding hinges on their completion. Plus, I'd hate to see you throw away another $100 when you have to reapply for a marriage license, add on a rush fee, retake blood and medical tests at large cost, and then pay for another officiant to formalize your vows. This little step done well will save you money and great stress in the long run.

DO YOU HAVE PERMISSION TO PARK ALL THOSE CARS HERE, MA'AM?

A marriage license may not be the only legal document you need on your wedding day. Let's say you've decided on a formal backyard wedding at home, avoiding costly site fees and outrageous per-person charges at the more expensive banquet halls. You've saved a bundle of cash, and you're confident that the tent will be lovely and the caterer will serve up delectable meals for your guests. You have every detail planned to perfection, right? Not quite. Have you thought about the fact that you might need a permit to park seventy-five cars in your residential area? If your gorgeous wedding will be on the beach, you might need permits for gathering on a public beach, as well as permits for drinking alcohol.

These are the little details that can slip through the cracks and cause big headaches. So, to keep the cops from shutting down your party just because it's after 9:00 P.M. and people down the street are trying to sleep, be sure to check on the need for *any* additional permits in your area. Again, call the town hall to research the need and permit application process for:

- Daytime parking on a residential street
- Overnight parking on a residential street (in case some of your guests responsibly choose to take a cab home after drinking too much. An overnight parking permit is often different from a daytime parking permit)
- Public gathering of a large number of guests
- Cooking outdoors or use of open flame outdoors
- Liquor consumption
- Bringing in extra electricity
- Construction of tents or structures
- Exemption from neighborhood noise restrictions
- Other permits your location may require

Permit needs vary with location. Some neighborhood associations have the right to refuse you permission to hold your wedding at home or on their nearby public beach. Some towns have rather odd laws and restrictive gathering rules, so it's best to check with local authorities. Again, these permits may not be very expensive, so handing over $20 for a gathering permit is worth the money if it keeps your $3,000 reception from being moved or cancelled due to some violation.

Religious Permissions

If you're planning to marry in a house of worship, you will undoubtedly face a long list of rules set by the religious institution. I include this subject matter here, because I have heard of too many couples who spent a fortune on their weddings, set their plans in stone, but then ran into a screeching halt and a migraine when the house of worship slammed the door on them due to the couple's "ineligibility" according to the church's standards. I'd like to help you avoid this kind of nightmare and its resulting emotional and financial impact.

Many religious officiants require the submission of an official application (with a small filing fee, of course), perhaps an essay, an in-person interview, proof of your divorce or annulment, or a death certificate if one or both of you has been widowed. Without these steps, some officiants may refuse to marry you. I've even heard about clergymen refusing to marry couples who are not registered members of the parish, or who are judged as not attending enough services!

Unfortunately, securing religious permission to marry isn't always a smooth process. Some couples confided that their religious arrangements were more difficult to secure than the legal requirements. Yes, as with any other industry, you might run into a few difficult personalities or subjective decisions that don't seem fair. Just continue on and seek out the right religious officiant for you. Again, start this process right away—a good religious officiant is key to the quality of your ceremony.

Pre-Wedding Counseling

Aside from the kindness and quality of the religious leader, you may also have to deal with the house of worship's additional requirements. Some make it mandatory for couples to attend pre-wedding counseling sessions or lengthy courses designed to get couples communicating about their partnership, their issues on having and raising children, their personal and family values, and their faith. In some cases, you might find yourself signed up for an evening session or several weeks of intensive courses with homework. You might even have to attend a weekend retreat in order to complete the required course.

If you and your fiancé live in different cities, or if you don't live in the town in which you will marry, you might have to take the time and the expense to find out if the house of worship will accept a course "diploma" from a church near you. In some cases, couples could not marry in the church they attended for years, simply because the fiancé could not come into town to attend pre-wedding classes. I cannot say that exemptions will not be made if you ask for them; I certainly hope they will, for your sake. But I encourage you to investigate and plan for every requirement imposed by your house of worship, so that you can proceed to the planning stage with a minimum of hassle and expense.

Wedding Day Reflections

We couldn't believe it when the priest from our town church said he wouldn't marry us because he felt my fiancé and I hadn't known each other long enough, and, I quote, "It just didn't seem like there's enough love there." What is that all about? With an attitude like that, we didn't want him marrying us anyway!

—Lisa and Reginald

What's the Date?

How the Day You Choose Affects Your Expenses

So, WILL you have a romantic Valentine's Day wedding, a summery June wedding, or a colorful autumn wedding? The date you choose will not only determine the weather for your Big Day, but also the expense. As you'll see in this chapter, some busy months are classified as "high wedding season," and the bridal industry naturally charges more for services during those times. Since you wish to save money on your wedding, you can save a bundle right at the outset just by choosing a less popular month. Yes, it's all in the timing, and that extends even further to day of week and time of day. You'll be surprised at the price differences when you start looking at times that are less in-demand, and you will certainly get more wedding for your money by opening up your options and figuring a better time for your event. Now, let's find the right date and time for you.

See You in September

Throughout the wedding industry, you'll find that May through October is considered "high wedding season," highly booked and more expensive all around. These fair-weather months bring a large majority of business to industry professionals, and in turn their prices hit the ceiling. It's that old supply and demand thing. To find better rates, and also better availability for your sites and professionals, I highly suggest you consider the off-months of November through April for your wedding. You'll be surprised at the difference in rates on everything from your catering costs to your limousines to your flowers. In fact, one of the smartest things you can do on a limited budget is to choose one of these less-in-demand months.

June and August rank as the top hot wedding months, and the concept of being a "June bride" still resonates with today's engaged women. June has been the perennial favorite wedding month for a *long* time. Its designation as *the* wedding month dates back to the old agrarian days when June fit right into the village's schedule between planting of the crops and the harvest. Some historians believe that June was also the most-favored month because of its connection to Juno, goddess of marriage. As time progressed, June became the top wedding month because couples got married right after school let out for the year. Now, while June is more of a sentimental favorite than a practical one, couples are still choosing those fair June days for their wedding plans. And wedding professionals are right there waiting for them.

Wedding Day Reflections

*W*e planned our wedding for January. The weather isn't a big factor, since the entire wedding will be indoors, so even if it snows we'll be fine. Plus, I've heard an old marriage superstition that if it snows on your wedding day, you'll have a lot of wealth. We're hoping that's true!
—Elizabeth and Todd

Weather

Yes, the weather is a big factor when looking at those less-expensive off-months. In some areas of the country, the weather is so miserable in January or in April that people don't even want to leave their houses, much less attend a wedding. So, when considering an off-month in your area, look not just at the financial break but at the reality of planning an important event during the snowy or rainy season. Spend some time doing research on the average temperatures and precipitation levels in the area in which you will marry. Check www.worldclimate.com for month-by-month charts on average rainfall and heat-wave conditions in your chosen spot. Mother Nature has been known to make a crash entrance at some weddings, and her unpredictability is often the reason there are so many available and inexpensive reception slots during tornado season. So keep a thought on the skies when you're choosing your Big Day.

Holidays

Another topic to consider when choosing your wedding date is that some holidays offer their own advantages and disadvantages when it comes to expenses. Valentine's Day and Mother's Day weddings almost certainly mean floral expenses will be elevated, since flowers are in white-hot demand at those times. On the flip side, holding your wedding during the Christmas holiday season might mean that your ceremony site will already be filled with wonderful decorations like vibrant red poinsettias and white candles. Your ceremony décor budget becomes a big $0, in that case.

Aside from the traditional holiday schedule, consider the month at your chosen location in terms of tourism. Think ahead and ask when you have an eye on a particular month in your area. Is there a big event

Check Out Holidays

Certain holidays offer their own attractions for wedding planning, such as the romance of Valentine's Day (just beware of elevated flower prices), the celebratory nature of New Year's Eve, and the free-fireworks-provided excitement of the 4th of July. Holiday weekends such as Memorial Day or Labor Day can allow your guests more travel time, and you can save money by planning your wedding on the Sunday night of a holiday weekend—since you all have Monday off. So, consider those holiday boxes on your calendar to find a wedding time that offers something extra special.

coming into town that weekend? A major league championship game, a NASCAR race, a big-time professional conference that will fill up the hotels and jack up the price of everything from limousines to meals? Will it be top tourist season in your chosen destination? Upcoming events and their implicated demands *do* affect the prices for any purchases, plans, or professional agreements in the area, so do some checking first and steer clear of the months when prices are higher.

Steer Clear of Saturday

Since many brides traditionally choose Saturday weddings, you can save 10% to 40% on some of your expenses just by holding your wedding on a Friday or Sunday night instead. Saturday weddings will never go out of style, but a growing trend for the formal Friday night wedding is finding couples spending far less for the same gorgeous, formal wedding on Friday night than they would have on Saturday. I spoke with several couples who held their weddings on Friday night, and they raved about the savings. Their guests did have to scramble a bit to make it to the church on time after work, and some guests did need to take the day off, but the Friday night wedding was a winner on the budget front. Several of the brides I spoke to said that their $10,000 budget made the Friday night option their only possibility; if they'd held out for Saturday night, they would have had to limit their plans and invite fewer guests.

It's safe to say that you're not just limited to Saturday anymore. The professionals of the wedding industry now make it enticing to choose that Friday night or Sunday wedding. Several reception hall managers and caterers confided that they also like doing Saturday *afternoon* weddings, with receptions starting at 1 P.M. and ending at 5 P.M. This setup allows them to sell their establishment for two weddings in the same day, with the next event starting at 7 P.M. or 8 P.M. The earlier couple gets a break on the price—even though they may be eating the exact same scrumptious fare as the couple celebrating later that night in the same room—saving as much as 15%. It's something to think about.

> ### Simplify It
>
> Check www.Festivals.com to see if your intended wedding location will play host to a major festival or tourism event on your wedding weekend. Sometimes, these big spectacles can mean higher prices in town.

Morning, Noon, and Night

You've already seen that an afternoon wedding can be less expensive than an evening wedding at the same location. That rule holds true in most cases. After all, weddings held earlier in the day are usually less formal than evening celebrations. As such, the menu will be less lofty, perhaps full sit-down meals will not even be offered, and alcohol consumption is usually much lower—at least one would hope so for an 11 A.M. reception.

The Other Weekend Option

We'd like to plan our wedding for a non-Saturday, but we couldn't ask our guests to skip work to travel and arrive in time on Friday. That's putting a lot of people out. What about Sunday?

Sunday too is a fine choice for weddings, and you avoid that Saturday night prime time with its prime rates. You would, however, have to plan your ceremony for a time that works with your ceremony site. If you're marrying in a church, you'll have to ask about available times after Masses and post-Mass catechism classes or youth group Masses. For this reason, Sunday weddings—estimated at 10% of all weddings by the Association of Bridal Consultants—are highly favored by couples who take their vows at an outdoor or home wedding, not in a church or synagogue. Many Sunday weddings do take place in the afternoon, either as brunches, teas, or afternoon affairs, to allow the guests time to get home and ready themselves for the upcoming week.

Think about an early afternoon wedding. It might be a carbon copy of a formal affair that takes place at 4 P.M., or it might be a cocktail party, a luncheon, a brunch, or a tea. The menu, which should be as appropriate to the style of wedding as the wedding is to the time of day, determines the cost of the reception. That formal reception with the five stations at the cocktail hour, the five-course sit-down dinner, and the full dessert spread and open bar might run you $150 per person, depending upon where you live in the country. If you plan an elegant cocktail hour appropriate for a 2 P.M. time slot—when none of your guests will expect a lunch or a full dinner—your menu might include a dozen or so appetizers and a sampling of desserts. Your cost:

$25 to $65 per person. That's a mighty difference in price, and it's all determined by the time of day.

While looking for savings on receptions, I canvassed a major chain with hotels in several cities and asked for their per-person charges for appropriate receptions at certain times of the day. Knowing that prices vary by region, I wanted to discover the price *differentials* for an afternoon wedding versus an evening wedding. Here's what I found in just a few cities:

In the northern New Jersey/New York area, a lovely afternoon wedding with a three-hour cocktail party costs $95 per person, while a more formal evening affair with a cocktail hour in one room, full

Not All Weddings Are Super Formal

We'd like to do a simple afternoon cocktail hour, but my mother is squawking that the guests will be insulted that there is no full meal offered. She's concerned, because my cousin just had a reception where there were more food choices and courses than guests in attendance. We're trying to save money, but we don't want to insult anyone or look bad in comparison. What can we do?

First of all, never compare your wedding to anyone else's. Trying to outdo others is a budget disaster in the making. Your wedding is your wedding, and your budget is your budget. Your cousin may have had an impressive full dinner for her guests, with enough food left over to feed several small European countries. That was her choice. Your appetizer menu at your afternoon wedding can impress your guests just as much. I've been to plenty of weddings, and I've never heard guests complain that a sit-down meal wasn't served. It's all in the presentation.

dinner served in a larger ballroom, and Viennese table of desserts plus the wedding cake topped the expense scale at $135 per person.

In the Atlanta area, I discovered afternoon-wedding cocktail-hour packages at about $80 per person, as compared to the full-blown evening formal reception with cocktail hour, extensive sit-down-dinner menu, and more desserts than you could handle at about $100 to $120 per person. In both cases, same lavish place, same high quality of gourmet food, just $20 to $40 more *per guest* if you chose the lavish evening formals over the pleasing but less indulgent afternoon packages.

As great as those $40 per-person savings are, as wonderful as it is to put $4,000 back in your budget to use towards your gown, your flowers, or even your honeymoon, you can save even more by timing your wedding just a little differently. Another popular option is the late evening dessert and champagne reception. No big meal, no cocktail hour, no $150 per-person charges. This type of reception features champagne, a wide selection of cake and desserts, and a variety of exotic coffees and after-dinner drinks. Guests love the simplicity and elegance of a dessert-and-champagne reception, if only because it is such a departure from other weddings. Remember that offering "something different" pleases guests tremendously, and you'll find that the price tag for this late-night dessert-fest will please *you* tremendously.

We'll talk more about reception style and menu options later in the book. In this chapter, I just wanted you to think about time of day as it relates to your reception style, not just convenience for booking a site.

Wedding Day Reflections

Since we were planning a smaller, more intimate wedding and since our guests all live in or near our town, we booked our event for a Thursday night in a smaller party room at a restaurant. We couldn't believe that we were only paying about a third of what we would have paid on a Saturday!

—Lisa and Jeremy

It's About Time!

Type of Reception	Time of Day (Start Time)
Brunch	11 A.M. to 1 P.M.
Luncheon	12 noon to 2 P.M.
Tea	3 P.M. to 4 P.M.
Cocktail Party	4 P.M. to 7 P.M.
Dinner	5 P.M. to 8 P.M.
Champagne and Dessert	8 P.M. to 10 P.M.
Late Night	9 P.M. to 12 midnight

Just remember that the date, day, and time all work together to set the stage for your overall wedding look and style. This choice determines your every expense and your every opportunity to save money while planning the beautiful wedding you desire. You could do yourself no greater service than to look at your options, be flexible with your plans, and seek out the perfect time for your Big Day.

The Palace Ballroom or Your Own Backyard

Choosing a Great Location for Less

We've got the Who, What, and When all mapped out with an eye toward saving you money. Now all that's left to do to form your wedding's foundation is figure out the Where. This is an important factor, since the locations you choose will also determine your expenses. As you start your search, you'll discover the fun world of site fees, which is a chunk of change you have to put down just to reserve the space for the day. The fee may be $100 to book a historical estate home, or it may be $1,000 to book an arboretum for the day. In the upper stratosphere of site fees, retainers go for $10,000—your entire budget. Obviously, your best deal is a site that's totally free. It might be a wharfside restaurant with a great view of the ocean, or it might be your own backyard. In this section, we'll figure out the best locations for your ceremony and reception, keeping both practical and economical considerations in mind. I'm going to ask you to expand your search beyond the traditional ballrooms, to see if you can find a better deal in your area.

What to Look for in a Wedding Location

Before you start looking at ceremony or reception sites, be sure you've thought about the crucial factors that will determine the right spot for you:

• The size of your guest list. You'll need to know how many people are on your roster, so you can book a location that will fit them comfortably and within that site's safety code. A smaller guest list opens up some unique and inexpensive possibilities for wedding locations (such as a winery's tasting room or your own home), while a larger list will deliver you to grander options such as a beautifully decorated barn, a beachside spread, or the big room of a traditional banquet hall.

• The style of your wedding. Certain locations are just a better fit for a smaller, more intimate informal wedding. If you know you're looking for a laid-back spot for your thirty guests, your options are different than if you're looking for a formal setting for 100 guests. Just the same, if you have your heart set on an outdoor wedding, that wish determines the scope of your search.

• Your budget. On a scaled-down budget, you're probably not going to be look-ing at that five-star hotel's main ballroom. Your budget determines nearly every choice you make for your wedding, and location adheres to the same rules. Some sites do require a minimum expenditure of $8,000 to $15,000 to even let you in the door. So knowing your budget ahead of time will eliminate these costly options and open doors to more reasonable ones.

• Your personal preferences. Even on a budget, you can have elements of your dream wedding. Some couples I spoke to said they wanted to see the sunset over the ocean. No negotiation. That's what they wanted, and they searched out a spot that gave them their one "must-have" in their wedding vision. Other couples know that they want an outdoor celebration or they want a spot that's sentimental to them. Even though we're talking about saving money, it's vitally important that you not sacrifice what you really want for the sake of your checkbook. So if there are elements of your perfect wedding location that really matter to you, if your wedding just wouldn't be right with-out them, then spell them out to your wedding coordinator or keep them paramount as you and your fiancé search for that right spot. You'll know it when you see it.

We're not just talking about site fees here. We're also talking about inherent fees, like a banquet hall's requirements that you hire their caterer and baker, or the significant costs of renting items for an outdoor, backyard wedding. As you've probably figured out by now, there's a lot to consider when booking your location beyond its size and its sparkly chandeliers. So I'll lead you through the questions to ask, the savings to be found, and smart booking strategies that will save you money as you select the backdrop for your Big Day.

Your Site-Search Rules

Before we start with the nitty-gritty details of your location scouting; before you hop into your car to check out that botanical garden, state park, or hotel ballroom, keep the following rules in mind to maximize your budget:

1. Stay local! If you plan a wedding close to home, you'll avoid added expenses for travel, hotel, and even long-distance phone calls. Staying close to home also means that you can hire wedding vendors with whom you may have a long-standing history, such as the town florist who knows you by name, the town baker who does the cakes for all of your family's big events, and the restaurant owner who always buys you a drink at his bar. The hometown advantage can add up to significant savings.

2. Use your connections. One bride and groom booked their reception at a restaurant owned by the groom's parents' friend from high school. That longtime connection earned the bride and groom a 40% discount on the catering fees. Working your contacts is always a great way to net big bargains and find out about special availabilities.

3. Book in advance. If you can, start searching for and book your wedding locations a year in advance. Most of the better spots, and

those priceless finds that not too many people know about, book up a year or two ahead. The earlier you start looking, the better deal you may find. Last-minute shopping, on the other hand, can cost you "desperation fees," meaning you'll pay more for an available spot . . .

Wedding Day Reflections

*W*e didn't have any connections in the restaurant business, but I do have an uncle who owns a great summer house in Newport, Rhode Island. We asked him if he would allow us to hold our wedding at his place, and we would count that as his wedding gift to us. He was thrilled to be of service to us, his new wife was thrilled to show off the house in such a way to the entire family, and we were thrilled that we were getting a drop-dead-gorgeous site for our wedding in one of the nicest outdoor wedding areas of the country for nothing!"
—Tania and Bill

any available spot. Another advantage to booking a site a year in advance is seeing the location in its glory at the time of year when your wedding will take place. You'll be able to experience the ambience, the gardens in full bloom, and the weather conditions as they affect your site.

Don't forget about alternate times. When you're dealing with availability of sites, those Friday night or Sunday afternoon weddings may still offer you more options than the quickly filled Saturday evening slots. Some specialty sites, such as museums and botanical gardens, open their doors to private events at times when their establishments are closed to the public. This gives you the added advantage of privacy for your affair, so ask about the availability and price dips for alternative times with all site managers. If you go by these sites' "open for business" hours, you might miss a golden opportunity.

Stay where you are. Holding your ceremony and reception at the same location, rather than at two separate ones, can save you a bundle of money. At an on-site wedding, you hold your ceremony in one area of your location—with chairs and an altar or trellis set up for the exchange of vows—and then move to another room or to the backyard or gardens for the reception. For couples who are not dedicated to marrying in a house of worship, this option eliminates the need for limousines or cars to take you and your bridal party from one spot to another. It also slashes your décor budget, since you no longer have to get flowers for the ceremony site *and* the reception site. Other savings factors are negotiable, but these are the big ones.

Sample Savings "Chop" List for Karen and Tony

When logistics prevented Karen and Tony from marrying in their hometown church, they added up the savings they earned by holding their ceremony at their reception site:

Two limousines at $50/hour for two hours (preparation time, traveling time, and ceremony time): $200

Flower arrangements for the ceremony site: $150

Florist delivery fee to church: $15

Church reservation fee: $45

Required pre-wedding counseling: $200

Officiant's fee: $100 (The mayor officiated for $50, rather than the priest's $150)

Church choir: $200

Organist: $60

Church curator: $20

Altar boys: $15 each

White aisle runner: $30

On-the-clock fees for wedding coordinator, who now avoids having to arrive early, set up the church, meet with the officiant for site setup rules, travel to reception site: $125/hour

On-the-clock fees for photographer's travel and waiting time: $110/hour

On-the-clock fees for videographer's travel and waiting time: $80/hour

Church or Estate?

Karen and Tony's experience (page 65) brings up a big issue. Yes, there are plenty of financial advantages to holding your ceremony and reception in the same place, but you might shudder at the thought of not marrying in a house of worship. If a church or synagogue wedding is a must-have for you, then these little savings are a moot point. As one bride said to me, "You couldn't *pay* me not to have my wedding in a church." Karen and Tony are in the minority on this one. In fact, the Association of Bridal Consultants says that 87% of all weddings take place in a church, chapel, or synagogue. That said, it's time to put your church to the criteria test, the same test I encourage you to use for your ceremony site *even if you're not marrying in a house of worship.* The same rules apply whether you're walking down the aisle at St. Patrick's Cathedral or walking across the lawn in your backyard.

Wedding Day Reflections

*A*nother big bonus, besides the money factor, was the fact that we were not limited by our church's particular rules. We belong to a rather strict church that would have fought us on our wishes for secular music, decorations, and even photographs taken by our guests in the church. The priest said the extra flashes would be distracting to him and potentially damaging to the statues. So, by choosing not to have our wedding in a church, we saved a lot of hassles as well as money.

—Karen

Ceremony Site Criteria List

- Is the site large enough to provide seating for all your guests?
- Will you have to rent chairs to seat your guests?
- Is the site available for enough time to hold your ceremony and take pictures afterward, or will you be hurried out after your first kiss so the next wedding (or funeral) can move in after you?
- Is the site climate-controlled? On a hot day, you'll be praising the air conditioner.
- What is the fee?

- What are the additional fees for the officiant and any other workers or performers?
- Is the site attractive?
- Is the site clean and well maintained?
- Are there restrooms at the site available to the public?
- Is there handicapped access?
- Is there adequate parking?
- What are the rules for the site? (As in, no photography, no secular music, etc.)
- Does the site allow you to decorate according to your own wishes?
- Does the site provide enough privacy?
- Is there a bridal lounge in which you can get dressed?
- How are the acoustics?
- Is the site wired with speakers to broadcast your vows, the musical performances, and the officiant's words, or will you have to provide sound equipment so that your guests can hear?

Any site you choose for your ceremony, whether it be a house of worship or the deck of a yacht, has to be a fitting location for you to make one of the most important commitments of your life. So please take the time to assess that spot thoroughly, ask questions, and make requests. Talk with the officiant about any pre-wedding interviews, applications, and classes you might need to take. Since your time is as valuable as money, ask yourself if you are willing to invest hours in premarital counseling, if it is so required by your house of worship. These are all individual choices, so make your best decisions.

Where's the Party?

Now we get to the fun part: choosing your reception site (or the site of your wedding and reception, if you so choose). Your girlhood dreams may have placed you at a glittering banquet hall, but your girlhood dreams never came with a price tag. Sure, that reception hall is always an option, if you strike the right deal, but you'll be pleased to know that a world of additional settings awaits your consideration as well. Take, for example, the wedding of Gina and Jeffrey, who married on a yacht that glided past the majestic New York City skyline, or Patrice and Alain who married in the gardens of a butterfly conservatory. Even though these couples didn't spend a fortune on their weddings, the backdrops they chose were worth a million bucks.

Use Your Wedding Coordinator

So where do you find that yacht or butterfly conservatory? How do you know which museum will let you use their elegant hallways for your formal cocktail party? Where do you call to book a private cove

The Top Four Reception Locations

According to the Association of Bridal Consultants, the top four choices for reception locations are:

1. Catering hall: 31%
2. Country club: 20%
3. Church or synagogue's social room or parish hall: 19%
4. Hotel ballroom: 15%

Ninety-eight percent of all couples will have an official reception, at an average cost of $4,217. Obviously, some brides have a budget higher than $10,000, so that might explain the country clubbing and the hotel ballrooms on the list. Your budget is different, and that isn't a bad thing, especially if it nudges you to find a more creative location than the same old ballroom everyone else is using. And *that* could make your limited funds a blessing, not a curse.

on a beach? Seeking out sites takes a bit of effort, but it's worth it when you find the perfect spot for your tastes, dreams, and budget.

I mentioned earlier that a wedding coordinator is worth her weight in gold, particularly when she reveals a little-known ideal wedding location, so check with your planner to find out alternate sites in your area. I spoke with Sarah Stitham of Charmed Places, (www.charmedplaces.com), an expert at helping busy couples find the perfect destination for their Big Day. "Most of the couples I work with are busy with their careers, their families, and their social lives, and they just don't have the time to travel to many wedding locations. I ask them their personal style and preferences, and then I point out some great locations for them to consider. It saves the couple time, and I've delivered several brides and grooms to gorgeous spots that just made their jaws drop."

Your own wedding planner can provide similar service, or you may be happier doing the searching yourselves. This can be one of the fun tasks that you do together. You'll spend a few weekends hunting for wonderful locations, visiting everything from wineries to restaurants' party rooms to cigar bars, until you find the one that feels right to both of you. Rather than strike out blindly, you might choose to start your hunt with an Internet search at the bridal Web site for your state or region. Many of these bridal sites rank companies (those that advertise on the site, in most cases) by affordability and rating, and there will certainly be a link to each location's Web site. Some of these Web sites use computerized 3-D visuals of their rooms or grounds, and you can take a virtual tour without even leaving your home. Remember, though, that the Internet gives you just a basic introduction. Never book a location based on pictures or supposed "happy couple recommendations." Always physically visit the site yourselves.

ASK AROUND

To expand your search, call your town's Chamber of Commerce for their list of estate homes, tourism and event sites, and other suitable locales. While you have the phone in your hand, dial up a few recently married friends to ask if they came across any interesting sites as they planned their weddings. Who knows? Maybe the newlyweds had to pass up that wonderful scenic overlook in favor of a more sheltered spot for their time of year. Maybe their guest list was too extensive to allow for a reception in that charming winery tasting room or at that lovely little Victorian bed and breakfast. What may not have worked for them may work for you. So ask around.

Ask someone in the business. The wedding industry is tightly interwoven, and many experts have the lowdown on the best wedding sites in the area. So, if you're starting to interview florists or caterers, why not toss in a question about the best or most charming places at which those professionals had the pleasure to work? And don't count out non-wedding event coordinators. Perhaps the company where you work regularly hires an event producer to stage your conferences, retreats, and holiday parties. Ask the event producer if she could suggest a suitable location for your wedding. Consider it a fringe benefit of your job.

Consider alternative sites that offer better per-guest rates and less stringent hiring deals than reception halls because they are *not* based primarily in the wedding industry. (As you'll see during your planning process, anything that's designated a "wedding service," a "wedding item," or anything else to do with weddings is usually going to carry a heftier price tag). If you got engaged by the ocean, perhaps you'd like to continue the theme by having an ocean-side wedding. If you're hopeless romantics and you drool over pic-

---

Simplify It

*S*earching for a great site on the Internet? Try these great time-saving Web sites for an introduction to the kinds of wedding locations near you:

www.CitySearch.com
www.DigitalCities.com
www.FieldTrip.com
www.Go.com
www.HereComesTheGuide
   .com
www.WeddingLocation.com
www.USACitylink.com
Your state's bridal Web sites, such as www.njwedding .com and the like

tures of weddings in English gardens, then perhaps a state arboretum in full bloom is perfect for you. Get ready to start visualizing. . . .

Anything but a Banquet Hall!
Top Alternative Wedding Locations

- Botanical gardens or arboretums
- Nature conservatories
- Zoos
- State aquariums
- Beaches
- Parks
- Scenic overlooks
- Marinas
- Gazebos
- Historic homes, mansions, and estates
- Ranches
- Museums
- Art galleries
- Country clubs
- University clubhouses or event rooms
- Waterside restaurants
- Seaside resorts
- Bed and breakfast inns
- Exclusive social clubs
- Elks halls, VFW halls, and Kiwanis halls—all can be rented and be miraculously transformed by creative decoration
- Historic landmarks
- Penthouse or hotel suites
- Jazz clubs
- Boats, yachts, and cruise ships
- Old schoolhouses
- Historic churches

Why Not Just Do It at Home?

The at-home wedding can either take place inside, using your living room and dining room, or outside in the same backyard where you played kickball as a child. The question often arises: Is an at-home wedding less expensive than a standard wedding at a banquet hall or alternative site? I wish I could say yes, but that's not always the case. As with any style or location of wedding, you can blow a huge budget, depending on the individual purchases and choices you make. An at-home wedding does offer you the chance to avoid site fees and to save on hiring affordable-yet-quality professionals, but it also carries added expenses. You may have to rent all sorts of supplies, from a tent to tables to napkins and knives. You may also need to rent one or several portable toilets, and you may have to arrange for that town permit to allow your guests to park on your street. Nothing's ever easy, is it?

Sure, the at-home wedding has its advantages. For one, you know it will be available on your wedding day. It also brings your celebration to the home where so many other meaningful events have taken place for your family. With the right planning, you can save plenty on the particular choices you make. So, if an at-home wedding is to your liking, simply follow the budget advice in this book to make sure you get all you can for your budget. (For a little extra help throughout this planner, I've added some special at-home wedding budget tips taken from my book *The Complete Outdoor Wedding Planner.*)

Reception Site Criteria List

Whichever site you choose, you'll have to put it to a lengthy Q&A test. Again, you're not just looking at a site in terms of its general beauty and size. You're also looking for its suitability for your day. Use the following questions to test your potential sites. You might find that a lovely site just doesn't have the parking space necessary for your guest-list size. Or the site doesn't have handicapped access. The uneven terrain may prove a challenge to your elderly guests, or that waterfall might be too great a temptation for your impish child relatives. I urge you to bring this list with you when you're touring reception sites, because the tiniest concern dealt with now can prevent a major disaster on your wedding day.

- Is the site large enough to accommodate your guests for the ceremony as well as the reception?
- Is the dance floor big enough?
- Does the site have an adequate number of restrooms, and are they clean and in good working order?
- Is there adequate parking at the site or close enough for use?
- Is parking free?
- Is valet service offered at the site?
- Can stretch limousines negotiate the driveway or fit through a curved driveway?
- Are the grounds attractive? (Look at the plants and trees that are in bloom in the month of your wedding, look to see that fountains are in working order, walkways are smooth and safe, and lawns are drained well)
- Do the grounds offer great picture-taking opportunities?
- Is there a separate room for the guests' cocktail hour?
- Is there a separate room where you and your bridal party can enjoy a drink and some relaxation before the reception?
- Is there a coat room?
- Is there a designated smoking area or is the site completely nonsmoking?
- Is the lighting adequate in the interior rooms?
- Is there a grand piano in the room for your musicians' use?
- Are the acoustics okay? Can you hear noise from another party in the room next to yours?
- How many other weddings will this facility book on your wedding day? (Ideally, yours will be the only one. This prime

"ownership" of the day prevents overcrowding of the parking lot and shoddy and rushed service, and gives you the clear attention of the owner, manager, or maitre d')

- What steps are taken to ensure privacy for your party?
- Is the staff professional, attentive, and of a friendly demeanor?
- What will the servers be wearing?
- Is the package all-inclusive, or can you select individual elements?
- Will they allow you to bring in your own caterers, cake, and liquor, or do you have to use the site's professionals? If you *can* bring in your own caterer, will the site slap you with a "caterer surcharge" for your caterer's use of their cooking facilities? (This is one of those nasty hidden charges that you need to watch out for. Those contracts can include some scary phrases that suck the nickels and dimes out of your budget)
- If you must use their caterer, can you sample the caterer's cuisine?
- Are they flexible about allowing you to create your menu, or do they have a set menu and limited choices?
- Do they offer options for guests with special dietary needs?
- Are you allowed to select or look over their linens, china, glassware, and silverware?
- Does the site offer the use of their own wedding coordinator?
- What are their fees for packages and selected extras?
- What are their extra fees?
- What are their minimum fees? (Some sites won't even book you if your wedding budget falls short of their mandatory minimum)
- For how many hours will you have use of the room or facility on the wedding day?
- What are their overtime rates, and what are their rules about overtime?
- Are they willing to negotiate on a set gratuity percentage? (Some establishments write in 15% to 19% or an even higher percentage gratuity to your bill. This is a good negotiating point when trying to save some money)
- Do they have a liquor license?

- Do they have fire, accident, and liability insurance? (Ask to see their certificates)
- Are there enough fire exits?
- Have they been fully inspected and licensed to operate? (Ask to see their certificate)
- Do they offer a complete, well-written contract?
- Do they let you make changes to the contract?
- Will they need any extra permits?
- Do union rules prohibit their workers from performing tasks you request?
- What are their restrictions with regard to noise, dress code, etc.?
- Do they have a cancellation/refund policy?
- Can you get a list of references?
- How did you feel when you toured the site?

Whew! That's a lot of scrutiny, but you'll find it's well worth it when you've chosen the best, most seamless location for your wedding. The more questions you ask now, the fewer you'll have to ask later. As always when asking questions, take good notes and get the manager's name. Let the manager know that you are working on a budget and see if he's willing to fulfill any special requests for reasonable discounts and the elimination of extra services that you don't want or need. Remember, if you don't ask, you'll never know.

For Rent

At-home weddings and some alternative wedding sites will require you to rent some items for your reception. You might need to rent just a few round tables for the church hall, or you might need to rent a whole house worth of items to transform a VFW hall or a barn into a truly dazzling dream setting.

Whatever your needs, begin by finding the right rental agency as listed with the American Rental Association (www.ararental.org). These hallmarked companies are registered for their fine service,

What Do We Need to Rent?

Tent (ask the caterer if she needs a separate tent for meal preparation and serving)

Chuppah

Tables (round or square, seating or buffet)

A table for the DJ

A table for gifts

A table for the guest book

Chairs

Benches

Linens

Table skirts

China

Silverware

Glassware, including crystal

Serving dishes and serving silverware

Butler-style silver platters for appetizer serving

Silver platters for display presentations of food

Wine fountains

Punch bowls

Coffee machines or dispensers

Espresso machine

Blenders for frozen drinks

Silver tea and coffee servers

Candelabras

Portable bars

Pedestals

Bridal arches

Podiums

High chairs and booster seats

Ice-making machines

Spotlights and decorative light machines

Chandeliers

Lighting fixtures for the restroom area

Lighting fixtures for the walkways and valet areas

Dance floor

Band platform

Ramps

Walkways

Fountains

Microphones and speakers

Heaters and air conditioners

Portable toilets

Extra table for the restroom area (if an outdoor wedding)

Clear-vinyl rug protector path strips (for at-home weddings)

Extra freezers or refrigerators

Power generators

Helium balloon inflation tanks for your own decorating uses

quality merchandise, and code of business ethics. Don't mess with an unregistered, unrecognized rental agency just because it quotes amazingly affordable prices. You might show up at your reception to find your guests dining at folding card tables with stained tablecloths and food-encrusted forks. Take the time to find a quality vendor and assess your needed items. Before you begin your search for a rental agency, be sure you know the specifics about your wedding—number of guests, the style of your reception, whether or not you'll have a buffet table, and any special items you know you'll want to rent, such as air conditioners, extra lights, etc. If you can answer his questions in detail, a good rental agent will assess your needs and advise you of needs you're not even aware of. Look at the list on page 76 to get your mind working on the kinds of items your day might require.

You'll see on the list that I mentioned lighting fixtures. This is one topic that might not have occurred to you as an important part of your day. But if you're holding your wedding at an alternative location, such as an estate home, Elks Hall, or even in a tent in your backyard, your setting might benefit from some special or extra lighting. Consider the wonderful look of tiny white lights gracefully lining your tent. Think about the elegant look of spotlights on your cake, the main table, or a portrait of the two of you at the entrance to the party room. Think also about lighting a dark or cobblestone walkway leading up to your tent or reception site for ambiance as well as for your guests' safety. Good lighting can accent your wedding, create a marvelous atmosphere, and provide a more secure environment. So consider lighting as an integral part of your day.

If your rental agency doesn't handle lighting, find a professional lighting specialist in the Yellow Pages or on the Internet, under Lighting Specialists or Theatrical Lighting.

Keeping Rental Costs to a Minimum

The key to smart budgeting when dealing with rental agencies is to prepare your order down to the smallest detail. Visit your site, take pictures, discuss your needs with all of your wedding professionals so that you know what you'll have to rent and, just as important, what they will provide. Your caterer, for instance, may prefer to bring her own silver platters and extra refrigeration unit. It would be a waste of money, and a shame, for you to pay to rent items that aren't needed.

On the other hand, don't *under-rent* in an effort to save money! One couple tried to skimp on wine glasses, and the bartender had to switch to plastic cups. Assess your needs realistically, and err on the side of caution by renting slightly more than you think you'll need.

To avoid any mishaps, talk with the rental agency's event planning specialist to determine how many glasses and plates you'll need per guest, and measure out how many people can *really* sit comfortably at a table for twelve. Smart ordering means smart shopping and the optimal use of your budget for this important segment of your wedding.

Setting Up the Goods

When placing your rental order, ask about the company's policies on delivery, setup, and cleanup after the party. Be sure you match the rental agency's schedule with the site manager's schedule for accessing the site itself! Your rental staff might want to deliver your tables,

May I Borrow That?

It goes without saying that you should always try to *borrow* some of the items on your needs list to avoid paying a fee to rent them. Ask around to see if anyone in your personal network system has an extra candelabra for the gift table. See if you can borrow a few children's booster seats from a friend's restaurant. You won't be able to borrow *all* of your rental needs, but you'll definitely shave a few expenses off what could be a pretty high rental price tag.

chairs, and other items the day before the wedding, and if you don't get the site manager's okay, you may wind up with a backyard full of tables, chairs, and boxes of china . . . and it will be up to *you* to deliver them and set them up on the wedding day! So, spell out the timing for delivery, setup, and cleanup with your rental agency and have a reliable relative or friend on site at that time to supervise the correct arrangements of your items.

Your Rental Contract

When you place your order, be sure to secure a solid and completely itemized order form and contract. This piece of paper ensures that you will receive exactly what you paid for, exactly when and where you want it. Be sure the rental agent writes down any style numbers for items that you have chosen after personal inspection of the merchandise at their store. Make sure that the contract states an exact delivery time (as in "By 12 noon on Friday, December 21), and that the *exact* return time and rules are spelled out. This last portion of information is vitally important, as many couples waste a lot of money because they (or their helpers) did not return the rental items by a specific time. Missing the "return-by" deadline by just a few hours can actually double your rental fees, because you wind up having to pay for another day's use of all that stuff. So ask specifically for the return-by time and know when the rental agency's staff should arrive at the site to disassemble and pack up your rented items. Again, assign a trusted and assertive relative or friend to stand watch as the items are packed up and shipped away, and give that person any tip money for the delivery staff.

Book 'Em

When sealing the deal on the location you choose, always be sure to get a clear, detailed contract signed by the site manager. An ideal contract will spell out the site location or the name of the room you have chosen, the date and exact hours of your wedding/reception, any special services or features you've purchased, and any items the site will supply. If you've negotiated special deals on payment or extras, get those in writing too. You'll find throughout the planning that insisting on stating such small matters in print will save you money in the long run. Too many couples report that what they agreed to was not delivered on the wedding day, and the resulting hassles and expenses put a damper on their wedding memories.

Put a deposit down on your site using a credit card. Now is not the time to dole out those $20 bills. Secure your reservations with plastic, and your investment will be better protected. Your contract should spell out the payment plan, including the manager's initialed note saying you placed your deposit as of that day's date. Your payment plan should be spelled out clearly with due dates on the contract, as well as the rules for any extra fees, service charges, included gratuities, and taxes.

As with all wedding industry dealings, be sure to call a few days before the wedding to confirm your reservations for that site as per your agreement.

Sample Budgets for Several Different Sites

To give you an idea of some site expenses, I've provided the following sample site budgets for a range of different wedding locations and styles. Please note that these are individual budgets provided by brides and grooms who negotiated their packages well and that the prices were valid at the time of this writing.

Grand Ballroom of Four-Star Major
Hotel Chain in Atlanta, Georgia

- Three-hour reception package, including hors d'oeuvres and carving stations, cake, and open bar: $86 per person

- Four-hour reception package, including hors d'oeuvres and carving stations, cake, and open bar: $98 per person
- Five-hour reception package with hors d'oeuvres, carving stations, three-course sit-down dinner, desserts and cake, open bar: $100 to $130 per person
- All packages include 20% service charge and 7% sales tax

Walt Disney World Pavillion, Walt Disney World, Florida

- Ceremony at the pavillion and four nights at the Grand Floridian: $4,900
- Supplement for more than eight guests: $500
- Afternoon tea party post-ceremony and later dinner for fourteen people: $1,200
- Tips: $75
- Use of photographer, videographer, and makeover stylists: $1,200

Backyard Wedding

- Site fee: $0
- Rentals: $750
- All vendors hired individually for total wedding budget of $9,600.

Cake Celebration in the Church Social Hall

- Use of social hall: $100 "donation" to church
- Cake: $130
- Coffee and cake-serving supplies: $40

Additional Money-Saving Tips

• Think about your own memberships. Your position in the company where you work might net you access to the executive penthouse at the nearby Hilton. Or your membership in a professional association could get you into a posh country club for less. One bride I spoke to said she became an active member of her local arboretum a year and a half before her wedding (she had a long engagement) and she got hefty discounts when she booked the arboretum's gardens and ballroom for her wedding. (And yes, she did continue as a member after her wedding—dropping out after she got the discounts would have been wrong. Integrity is important, even when wheeling for discounts.)

• Remember that some hotels mark up items and services tremendously in their all-inclusive wedding packages. Get clear, itemized lists of all charges, including the per-bottle wine charges and corkage fees.

• Compare wedding sites' offered services with prices you can get on your own by hiring your own professionals or renting your own items.

Is That a Vera Wang?

How to Find a Gorgeous Gown for Less

IT'S FANTASY gown time! No doubt your earliest visions of your dream wedding included a picture of you in a beautiful wedding gown. It may have been a flowing princess gown with a beaded bodice and a long train or a chic little sheath dress that shows off your hard-earned figure. Whatever your intoxicating self-image, you now have to absorb the sobering fact that your dream gown carries a price tag—sometimes a heartstopping, throat-closing price tag that makes the room spin. Yes, there are $5,000, $10,000, even $50,000 wedding gowns out there. Celebrities can drop $100,000 on a designer wedding gown without blinking a mink-lashed eye. You're in a different position, and you want a stylish and good-looking dress for a reasonable amount of money.

Don't Give in to Impulse

So many women flip through the pages of bridal magazines and take in all those gorgeous, glossy images of fantasy gowns, only to have the wind leave their sails when research reveals the astronomical

Wedding Day Reflections

*A*t first, I really resented that I had to look for a gown that was in my budget range. I was quite the brat about it, sighing dramatically that I wasn't going to bother looking for a gown in certain shops, because (SIGH!) I couldn't afford it. But then my maid of honor gave me a good wakeup call by pointing out that I was ruining my own wedding experience with my poor-me attitude, and she took me out and made a game of finding great wedding gowns for less. I changed my attitude—much to everyone's pleasure—and started enjoying the hunt for a beautiful gown at a reasonable price. Now, when I think about buying a gown for $8,000, I just laugh, because I found a designer dress at a trunk sale for just a fraction of what most other brides are paying for their gowns. I'm quite proud . . . and thankful to my maid of honor for showing me that it's far better to get your gown for less.

—Maria

prices. How do you get excited about shopping when your budget doesn't allow for the gown you really want? This is exactly where many brides make a cardinal mistake: They ignore their budget and buy the pricey gown. "I'm worth it," they say and then act like criminals, hiding the receipt from the groom and lying about the price they paid. Please don't give in to impulse buys when looking for your gown. Sure, if the gown is very important to you, then play with your numbers and give yourself a higher cushion to expand the types and styles of dresses you can consider. I have no doubt you can find an almost identical gown to that high-priced designer style for far less. You just need to know where to look. The Association of Bridal Consultants says that 45.5% of brides buy their gowns on sale. Hopefully, you will, too, as it's just plain ridiculous to pay full price for a gown when there are many wonderful budget-friendly sources out there. Your smart decisions at the outset and your willingness to keep a level head on your shoulders when shopping for this pinnacle item can turn you into a great bargain hunter, rather than a splurgy bride who doesn't exercise self-control.

In this section, you'll learn how to find your dream gown for less, what to look for, how to shop well, where to shop, and how to accessorize to complete the most amazing look for your Big Day. When you walk down the aisle in your lovely gown, your guests won't know that you didn't spend a fortune on it. They'll just sigh and say, "She's never looked more beautiful." Now *that's* the key to smart gown shopping!

What Kind of Gown Do You Want?

Before you start worrying about prices or where you're going to find that designer-looking gown, start off by deciding exactly what you're looking for. Lay the foundation for your gown shopping by knowing what style dress you want, whether traditional, formal, or a more kicky little strapless slipdress for your beach wedding (a la Cindy Crawford's oceanside wedding to Rande Gerber). Knowing ahead of time which cut, length, and style suits the formality of your wedding will save you much in the way of time *and* money. Clearly communicating such preferences as sleeve length and adornment will help the sales associate at a boutique or department store direct you to the gowns that fit the bill, so to speak.

An important part of finding your dream gown within your budget is choosing from among the types of gowns that are a "good fit" for your day. Ask the gown shop sales assistant to point out appropriate fabrics and styles for your style of wedding. A shiny fabric isn't best for daytime, because that's a more formal, evening look. Some fabrics are better for hot weather or outdoor weddings, and some fabrics hold a gown's shape much better than others. A good sales associate will show you the ideal samples for your described wedding, and she'll also help you find gowns that are in your price range. Take note, though: If the sales associate shows you gowns out of your price range and says, "But this is the biggest day of your life! You're worth it!" walk out of the store. A true expert will honor your budget and your requests, not try to pressure you into buying an inappropriate dress for your wedding or your gown allowance.

When you're shopping for gowns, you'll find that prices often don't depend solely upon the length, cut, or embellishments of a dress. A simpler style with fewer folds is not always less expensive than a more detailed dress. In fact, a sleek gown can be *more* expensive than a more intricate one. So, I'll leave it to you to discover the shapes and styles that work best for your body, your style of wedding, and your budget. What's the best way to do this? Start off by looking at pictures. Flip through magazines or search the bridal Web sites. Look at brides who have similar shapes and coloring as your own, and see what they're wearing. Does that fitted bodice make that lighter-on-top bride look more voluptuous (a la Gwyneth Paltrow in *Shakespeare in Love*)? Does that fuller skirt minimize a healthy-sized bottom (like Jennifer Lopez's princess ball gown)? Does that bride with muscle-toned arms like yours look good in lace-covered sleeves, or would a sleeveless style suit your wedding look (and the weather for the day)?

Don't stop with pictures. This search-and-find task is just step one. You should *always* try on gowns before buying them. Yes, you're sure to find fabulous deals and steals over Internet bridal Web sites. They show you breathtaking designs, expertly photographed, and invite you to click and buy. But what you don't know about professionally posed photographs is that the back view of the model that you don't see is often one of clips, duct tape, staples, and ties that make the dress a perfect fit. The real dress might be baggy, saggy, and shoddily made, even if the ad says it's a hot designer style right off the Paris runways. Your best bet is to save the picture and take it to your nearby shop. The gown specialist at the store will help you find a similar style to try on, so that you can decide if the design is right for you.

Finding the Right Shop Makes All the Difference

Where you shop is going to make *all* the difference with regard to the types of gowns you find and their prices. In the area where you live, you might have access to wonderful bridal gown shops that have been around for ages. You bought your prom dress there. Your sister bought her wedding gown there. These shops may carry a wide range of gowns that are to your liking and that suit the formality and style of your wedding. Those of us in the wedding industry, though, do caution you to expand your search beyond bridal specialty stores. Although they have beautiful options and often carry gowns that are specially priced, they are not always the very best bet for finding the gown of a lifetime. Word is getting out that some bridal shops inflate their prices, figuring that they have a captive audience in wide-eyed brides dazzled by the sheer magnitude and presentation of gowns and veils. In fact, the Association of Bridal Consultants' survey reports that only 1% of brides buy their wedding gowns at bridal boutiques. It seems today's bride has gotten the message that the real deals are found elsewhere.

Yes, you can find a bargain in a bridal shop, and you can have the time of your life doing it. That's why I'm *not* going to hold up a big red sign and tell you to run away. I am, however, encouraging you not to limit yourself to these stores. There are plenty of other locations that offer you surprisingly great finds, so I hope you'll take a day and seek out some other types of shops:

1. Department stores. Many top-name department stores have bridal sections or boutiques, and their wedding dresses sometimes feature big discounts. The real bargain, however, is in the department store's formal dress department. Especially in December, many stores stock hundreds of gorgeous formal gowns at up to 60% to 70% off. Brides who are flexible about style can find fabulous steals among the white, off-white, or pastel-colored gowns and dresses on display.

Simplify It

*F*or the best look at gown styles, plus a wonderful feature that lets you mix and match flattering tops and skirts to suit your own body shape and style preferences, visit www.DavidsBridal.com. Their design-a-gown feature allows you to scan their voluminous stock to find the right styles and even colors for your wedding-day wardrobe.

2. The prom-gown section. Whether you're in a department store or a teen clothing store, don't walk by those prom-gown racks. Today's high-school party goer has access to incredibly stylish gowns and dresses that are the new trend in prom attire. Poofy prom dresses from years past are "out," and red-carpet–worthy designs that make great wedding dresses are "in." I saw some amazing white strapless dresses and sexy side-slit gowns that would make fabulous wedding gown choices . . . for just $150. Compare that to a similar designer white strapless wedding dress for $700.

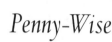

Penny-Wise

Prom gowns get marked down considerably in June, since stores are clearing out for the next season's stock. Those white or bride-appropriate dresses may still be on the rack for less. Just check them well for signs of repeated try-ons, and ask for a further discount for any marks you can remove.

3. That little hole-in-the-wall dress shop. I hear tons of stories from brides (in fact, I'm one myself) who took a chance on a charming dress boutique. Exhausted from fruitless hours in a bridal salon where nothing I liked cost less than $2,000, I passed a cute little shop on a corner. With nothing to lose, I wandered in, checked out the jewelry in the front case, and then head toward the dresses at the back of the store. They had maybe twelve or so wedding gowns all smushed into a crowded rack. I grunted as I pushed them apart to take a look, but there it was. The pretty Jessica McClintock dress I'd seen in a bridal magazine, with the eyelet, lace-layered bodice and the simple full ball-gown skirt, no train. Size 8. Perfect. I knew before I even zipped it up that this . . . was . . . the . . . one. And the price tag? Slashed from $400 to $150. Done. Bought. Paid for. It's my favorite "bridal budget coup" story. I encourage you to scout out the same kind of nonflashy, understated store for what might turn up a fabulous find.

4. Shops in a different part of town. If the bridal salons near you all seem to be located in the ritzy, upscale towns, then do a little searching for some charming and well-established bridal shops in less pricey

Your Dream Dress Is Coming to Town

Can I find a great bargain at a trunk show?

Trunk shows aren't as great an opportunity to find a bargain as a designer's sample sale or discontinued dresses on a rack. At a trunk show, held at a designer's showroom or at a bridal boutique, a sales representative presents the designer's complete new line of dresses. You show up, try on the designer's styles, perhaps find a bargain on a dress, and the designer or sales director stands by to advise you on the best style and fit for you. Since these are designer gowns, you might not find an enormous bargain to brag about, but you may receive a discount on the price, free alterations, some custom accent work, or even discounted accessories. Now, if you hear about a designer's *sample sale,* get in line and get ready to find bargains of 50% to 80% off as the designer clears away their old styles. Sample sales tend to take place during April/May and October/November, so if you can get to a major designer hot spot such as New York City during these times, you're in a good position to find a priceless designer style for a steal. You can locate an upcoming trunk sale or show by logging onto your favorite designer's Web site or by calling local bridal salons and asking to be added to their event mailing list. Also, look online for the *S&B Report,* which lists sample sales in the New York City area.

neighborhoods. The overhead charges may be lower, and the owner may have adjusted her stock prices to reflect her less affluent clientele. So cross the borders of your area and seek out small-town bargains.

5. Outlets. Sometimes when I walk into an outlet shop in Reading, Pennsylvania or Secaucus, New Jersey, I wish I were getting married all over again. Some of these outlet stores have amazing prices and

great one-day sales that can net you a deal. Designers such as Jessica McClintock and Demetrios run their own outlets in certain cities across the United States (check the Resources in the back of this book for these designers' Web sites), and you will find massive and well-known wedding gown outlet stores like The Gown Company (www.thegowncompany.com, 212-979-9000) in New York City. Outlets can give you some great finds on a wide variety of gowns, accessories, veils, and bridal jackets, so plan a day-trip with your sweetheart or your maid of honor to the outlet near you.

6. Antique shops. Don't laugh. No, the gowns aren't likely to be dusty and smelling of mothballs. Antique shops are often the lucky recipients of grand collections of formalwear acquired through estate sales and specialty purchases. Some antique shops show beautiful ivory lace gowns with a history, as well as intricate, hand-beaded dresses from the 1920s and 1930s. In many cases, these gowns are one-of-a-kind, and you might find a real bargain on a showpiece dress.

7. Missions, Salvation Army shops, and garage sales. Again, please don't laugh. While some brides wouldn't dream of buying their wedding gown at a garage sale, I can assure you that wonderful deals are available in those open garages on Saturday mornings and in mission stores. What do you think happens to the wedding gowns of women who changed their minds and called off their weddings at the last minute? What happens to the

Wedding Day Reflections

*W*hile cleaning out some old things after my divorce, I came upon the big white box that held my preserved wedding gown, veil, and accessories. I looked through the clear plastic window of the box and thought, "This is just too beautiful to sit here in the basement." I wasn't bitter enough to light it on fire, so I brought it to the Salvation Army store, where I knew that some happy young woman might find my $700 gown there, in perfect condition, for $100. I liked the idea that my gown would bring happiness to someone and that a woman who might not be able to afford a designer gown would get to wear one.
—Amanda

expertly preserved wedding gowns of women who got divorced? When the marriage ends before the dress yellows, these women sell their gowns. It may be through eBay, at a garage sale, or through donation to a mission. When they put up the For Sale sign, the women who opt to sell their gowns aren't likely to charge what they paid for it. Most charge one-half to three-quarters of the original price.

Click and Shop?

I mentioned earlier that you'll find a huge selection of wedding gowns over the Internet. You might shop through a well-known gown store's Web site, or a discount wedding-gown site. Whatever your choice, please practice safe Internet shopping. Only purchase through a site that has a secure server and a fail-safe return policy, plus a written and contracted guarantee on the delivery date for the dress. Check the stated fees for delivery and taxes to be sure this great buy will still save you money after you've paid all the extra expenses.

Remember that buying a gown sight unseen can be a recipe for disaster, no matter how great the price. Sometimes the risk is not worth it. If you must do the online shopping thing, then be as careful as possible. Allow *plenty* of time for delivery and returns, keep careful written records of your purchase, and shop only with a company with a street mailing address as well as a phone number. There are a lot of scams out there, and unfortunately, brides and grooms can be prime targets, lured by a too-good-to-be-true offer and then stripped of their money and trust.

Don't Buy It . . . Rent It!

If men can rent their wedding day outfits, why can't you? After all, you're only going to wear the gown once, right? Why spend a few thousand dollars on this purchase, only to wrap it up and store it

Simplify It

*F*ind local gown rental agencies through the Yellow Pages (under Wedding Rentals, Bridal Attire, or Costumes) or in an area Internet search. Brides who have rented their gowns say they were able to wear more elegant, designer gowns than they would ever have been able to purchase. With the trend in gown rentals rising, with more and more brides seeing nothing superstitious about wearing a used gown, and with more gown rental shops widening their selections as demands roll in, you may find that gown rentals are a bright idea.

away in the attic? If you're not the sentimental type who might want to save your gown for your daughter to wear someday, or if you don't have plans to use the material from your wedding gown to make a christening outfit for your baby of the future, then you might consider renting your gown for the day.

With renting, brides get not just a financial break but also convenience. Judy Brimer of Formals Etc. in Pineville, Lousiana says of her renting clients: "We give our brides more peace of mind. If their plans change and they need to scale down their wedding or change venues, they can easily walk in and completely change the style of the gown they'd like to rent." Don't worry about dropping food or spilling champagne on your rented gown. At this agency, they have a whopping $6 damage waiver that covers you for any harm to the dress. So it's not a "you break it, you bought it" situation. Ask any gown rental agency about their own damage waiver and repair policies.

Have Someone Make It

Another option that comes up frequently is making the gown yourself or having someone else make it for you for less than $300. Talented dress creators can buy or download a dress pattern (I like the offerings at www.Butterick.com), purchase the fabric for a discount at a craft store or even during a day-trip to the garment district of your local metropolitan area, and make the gown from scratch. I don't recommend this option for everyone, as it takes an exceptional amount of skill and experience to make a wedding gown of high quality and durability. Nevertheless, if you have a talented seamstress friend or family member, perhaps this lofty job would make a great gift to you.

Smart Gown-Shopping Advice

You will increase your odds of finding a great dress at a reasonable price if you take heed of some gown-shopping tips:

• Tip #1: Don't shop on the weekend. Most brides have full-time jobs or families to care for, so Saturdays and Sundays are prime times for hitting the crowded dress salons and department stores. If you can, plan your own shopping trip for an off-time, such as a weekday or a weekday evening. The key to finding great buys and great selections in a shop is having the trained eye of a true professional to help you along. If the three sales assistants are trying to help thirty brides at one time, you may be left in the dust.

• Tip #2: Make an appointment. To guarantee yourself time with a sales associate, call ahead and make an hour-long appointment at the store. This tip counts for department stores, as many of the top-name stores offer personal shopping services.

• Tip #3: Know what's *not* allowed. Some houses of worship don't allow brides to bare their shoulders or wear sexy wedding gowns. Before you shop, check with your officiant about any rules related to wardrobe.

• Tip #4: Keep an open mind. Sure, you have a good idea of the kind of gown you want, but as set as you are on that picture in your head that just screams *You*, keep an open mind when the salesperson brings dresses for you to try on. Remember, an experienced sales associate may have a great eye for gowns that flatter you most. So be open to suggestions—it's the stubborn bride who doesn't enjoy this shopping trip as much as she should!

• Tip #5: Try on lots of gowns. The only way to find the right style at the right price is to try on many different gowns. You might love the first one you try on, but if you stop there, you'll never know if another gown is better. The Association of Bridal Consultants says that brides try on an average of 12.5 gowns in total before selecting "The One."

• Tip #6: Allow enough time for shopping. On the average, brides spend ten months looking for the perfect gown. Ideally, you should start looking a year in advance of your wedding, to allow plenty of relaxed time for shopping as well as time for the gown to be ordered, created, delivered, and fit to your shape. If you wait too long, you could be forced into an unwise impulse buy plus costly rush fees of $100 or more.

• Tip #7: Don't shop for your future weight. It's the cardinal sin of gown shopping: buying a dress that's too small, because you're just *sure* you're going to drop those extra ten pounds before the wedding. Don't do it. Wedding planning can be stressful, and many brides report that they *gained* a few pounds during the process. How depressing would it be if the seamstress had to *let out* seams or add an extra panel of fabric to your gown because you didn't lose the weight you'd intended? Even worse, how horrifying would it

Simplify It

*W*hen on your gown-shopping expeditions, bring along a Polaroid camera. Have someone take a snapshot of you in each dress that you like and write on the bottom of the picture the store name, the design number, and size of the dress you're wearing. At the end of your shopping sprees, collect the snapshots and make your final decision. It'll be a snap to go back to the right store and find that dress. Too many brides have sad stories about "the one that got away"—and they're not talking about ex-boyfriends. Don't lose track of that great gown . . . smile and say cheese.

be if you had to suffer the double humiliation of having to buy another new dress off the rack because the one you ordered doesn't fit. Don't shop down. Order a gown for the size you are now, and know that it's a simple process (and an ego boost) for the seamstress to take in the sides.

• Tip #8: Make sure alterations are included. Some shops offer free use of their seamstresses, because alterations charges are included in the cost of the gown. Check out the itemized bill for included services and check to see that the shop has a full staff of on-site seamstresses. If alterations are not included in your gown package price, then ask for a written estimate of alterations fees from the shop's seamstresses or ask for a referral to an expert seamstress nearby. The alterations to your gown are so important, as they will make or break the way the gown fits you. So do think of alterations fees as a wise investment.

• Tip #9: Inspect the gown thoroughly before you buy. Especially if you're buying off-the-rack or a sample item from a bridal salon,

Watch Out!

Don't skimp on alterations expenses. A bad tailoring job can make your beautiful gown look *awkward* on you, even unflattering. I've spoken to several brides who regret "cheaping out" by having their grandmother or an aunt do the alterations on their gowns. The complaints ranged from "One armhole was lower than the other" to "My seams were falling apart as I was dancing." Don't be one of those brides who winds up crying in the bathroom as the site manager literally staples her dress back together. Find a good seamstress and pay her price to make the most of your gown investment.

check every inch of that dress. Look for loose seams, stains, and poor beading work. A good dress should be solidly constructed and free from any marks you'll have to remove. If you do see some lipstick stains on the inner edge of the bodice or black marks on the hem (all imperfections that can be easily removed), ask the salesperson for a discount. You never know.

• Tip #10: Don't shop when you're tired. Even if you have to cancel an appointment with a sales associate, don't shop when you're exhausted. Trying on twenty or so gowns and thinking objectively about each one takes a lot of energy. If you're not up to the task, don't risk making a rash decision just because you want to get out of there. Know the time of day that is best for you—are you more of a morning person?—and plan your gown hunt for that time of day.

• Tip #11: Don't bring a crowd. Too many opinions are likely to frazzle, not dazzle you. How can you make a smart decision on a gown when you have your mother, your sister, your mother-in-law-to-be, your maid of honor, and your five bridesmaids bringing dozens of gowns to you and calling out their subjective opinions that the dress makes your butt look too big? You might even be tempted to quiet the maelstrom by just buying the first gown that looks acceptable. For a better shopping experience, and a clear enough mind to ask the right questions and find the right dress, just bring one trusted companion with a camera who knows that your opinion is the one that counts.

• Tip #12: Get it all in writing. Everything from the gown number you've chosen to your exact measurements (all of them) to the payment plan should be spelled out clearly in a good contract and order form. Inspect this document carefully to find out the shop's return and cancellation policies, time of delivery, and alterations arrangements. Make sure the salesperson's name is on the contract and, again, pay with a credit card. Take the salesperson's card so that you can call and ask any further questions.

A Little Tuck Here, a Little Tweak There

We've already discussed how important good alterations are to the fit of your gown. Let's now get a little more detailed about choosing the right seamstress. The gown shop may have a stable of good seamstresses, and when you choose your gown, one seamstress is going to come out of her workshop in the back to pin and tuck your dress where needed. Choosing your seamstress may not even be on your To-Do list. However, if you're buying your gown off the rack at a department store, dress shop, or other location, you may be on your own finding a great alterations master.

Where do you find the woman with the golden straight pins? Many dress shops will recommend the seamstresses they use, and you can also get great recommendations from recently married brides. You might think you can save a few bucks by hiring the seamstress who works down the block at the dry cleaner, but I warn you: Performing "surgery" on a wedding gown is unlike most jobs a standard tailor is accustomed to. Indeed, wedding gown adjustments are a specialized art form, so do try to locate a seamstress who specializes or who has years of gown alteration experience.

Simplify It

*V*isit nearby dress shops, not to look at their gowns, but to collect the business cards of recommended seamstresses. Many of these shops keep little packs of nearby alterations experts for their clients' use. Just browse the store a bit, then look for those cards. It's unlikely that a shop will recommend a shoddy professional to their clients, so you can consider these cards to be a fair recommendation.

HOW TO JUDGE A SEAMSTRESS

Once you've found a few names of recommended seamstresses, it's time to interview them. Yes, this professional like any other in the wedding industry needs to be put under the microscope. You're entrusting a valuable service to her, so you want to be sure you hire the best professional possible.

Make an appointment for a consultation, and ask away:

1. How long have you been in business?

2. How many gowns are you working on right now? (If the number seems very high and if the seamstress seems frazzled and glassy-eyed, walk away from this overworked expert.)

3. Do you have a staff of additional experts and assistants?

4. How many fittings are included in your alterations package? (Aim for three or more.)

5. What is your pricing structure? (Does she charge a flat fee or a by-the-hour pricing plan. Flat fee is obviously a better bet, because you can control the final price.)

6. Do you have experience with a gown such as mine? (Especially useful if your gown has extensive beading, or it's a sheath dress.)

7. Do you offer pressing services for veils as well?

8. Where are the gowns stored? (Be wary of the seamstress with the basement workshop in a well-known flooding area. Gowns should be stored in an environment with climate and humidity controls.)

9. What are your shop hours? (*Very important!* Brides have complained to me that their seamstresses were only available for contact or appointments one or two days a week. These brides wanted full access to the seamstress on days that were convenient to them.)

10. Do you have insurance? (Again, very important. You'll want your gown covered by the shopkeeper's insurance policy in case of fire or other mishap.)

Just as important as these questions, are your observations of the seamstress and her working environment. Is she well-mannered and professional? Does she give you her undivided attention, or does she seem rushed and overwhelmed? Do you get a good feeling from her?

What is her workshop like? Size isn't so important, as a larger, flashy workshop might mean higher overhead costs for you. I'm talking about the organization factor. Does she have gowns piled up all over the place? Do things seem orderly? Are there stacks of unreturned messages on her desk? You can get a great sense of how effective this professional is by assessing where and how she works. I'm not going to advise you to walk away from a seamstress whose workshop seems a bit crowded or cluttered, however. That may simply be the seamstress's style of organization. Just be on the lookout for obvious signs that she's overwhelmed.

Trust your gut and hire the seamstress who's most likely to make the fitting process more comfortable for you.

Headpieces

With your gorgeous gown chosen, it's now time to select the finishing touch to your dream bridal look. Something about trying on a veil for the first time and seeing yourself in full bridal regalia may make your heart beat wildly. As emotional as that one moment is, the tears may really start flowing when you see the enormous price tag on that little satin headband and the layers of tulle that drape down your back. Yes, veils and headpieces can be very, *very* expensive, sometimes more than the gown!

You can find beautiful veils and headpieces at a fraction of full retail prices. If you shop for your veil in a bridal salon, you'll pay extra just because it's a wedding specialty shop. Browse through the offerings of veils, headbands, tiaras, and combs at your bridal shop just to get a base rate for the going prices. Then set out to find some bargains.

When considering styles of veil, headpiece, and hair pins, consider that detailed veils can be more trouble than they're worth. Pearl or applique accents can ruin the graceful, elegant line of the original design, and rhinestones and pearls added to the sides and front of a veil can make you look "spotted" in your photographs. So think about style, function, *and* price—and consider the plain designs.

A popular option right now is the jewel-encrusted tiara. This regal crown isn't just for beauty pageant winners. Today's tiaras are smaller and more delicate than the monstrosity that always seems to pull Miss Universe's head to one side or fall off onto the runway. Tiaras are intricate or plain and feature crystals, rhinestones, pearls, or colored gemstones. Also popular for informal or outdoor weddings is the simpler look of a single flower tucked behind one ear or into an upswept mass of curls, or a floral wreath crowning the head. These options are wonderful, and they can run you from $3 to $50, depending upon your design wishes. Compare that to the $1,000 diamond headpiece you saw in the bridal shop!

Try on as many different headpiece styles as you can, from headbands to bun wraps to combs and flowers, to see the designs and level of adornment that suit your tastes. If you have a "busy" gown with a lot of features in the fabric or design, you might choose a simpler

Like My Veil? I Made It Myself!

You'll see them in craft stores from coast to coast. The new rage in do-it-yourself wedding preparations includes kits to make your own veil for $20 to $30. Some of these kits come complete with a high quality, silk-wrapped headband and detailed instructions for attaching appliques and a veil. Some kits include pre-hemmed veil lengths, while others require you to do the hem yourself. Indeed, there is a wide range of quality within the make-your-own-veil offerings, so open that box, look at the materials, and judge for yourself if you can handle an important task like this one. For some brides who plan to wear their veil only for the ceremony and then whip it off for the reception, it's worth it to spend less on a headpiece.

headpiece to avoid overkill. Also, try on several different veil lengths to see if you can move well with so much material hanging from your head, and if the veils complement the design and style of your gown. While you're online looking for affordable quality headpiece accessories, you might want to check out the veil, tiara, and headpiece offerings at auction sites such as eBay. Bride Heather Peltier from Charlotte, North Carolina found her veil and other accessories for a steal on the online auction site, and she doesn't regret for a moment buying her items through this source. Indeed, many brides are happy to wear previously owned tiaras and headpieces . . . they receive far less wear than a used wedding gown, and there's less risk of a non-fit and a need for return.

> ### Penny-Wise
>
> *L*ike gowns, tiaras and headpieces can be rented, sometimes for as low as $20 to $30. Again, check the Yellow Pages under Bridal Attire, Wedding Rentals, and Costumes.

Another popular option for securing a veil and headpiece for less, one that's been recommended to me by countless brides across the country, is to ask a creative relative to make it as a wedding gift to you. You might present the request to a particularly clever aunt, or to a cousin or friend in fashion design school. One artist redesigned an existing headpiece, removing the veil and the appliques from a bride's mother's headpiece, adding hand-stitched beading to the silk lining of the band, and then attaching a shorter length of veil netting. Your handmade headpiece is not only a gift to you but a valuable portfolio item for a budding fashion designer. Remember to use your contacts with *all* areas of your wedding plans!

While getting your headpiece and veil for free is always a relief to your wedding budget, you can invite more relief by shopping for your hair décor at a discount jewelry shop. I browsed the pearl hairclip section of a department store jewelry counter and then headed right for an accessory store in my nearby mall. While a hairclip with real pearls costs $300 at the department store, an almost identical one at the

Take It from an Expert

I spoke with Kerry Trombetta, a hair designer at Salon Aurora in East Hanover, New Jersey to find out how she creates exquisite looks for brides who don't wear full headpieces or tiaras:

"If a bride is not using big accessories in her hair, I'll create a more stylish structure with a lot of the bride's hair hanging down the back and framing the face. The accessories are then just accents to the beautiful style of her hair itself. Or, I'll create a pretty upswept twist, accented with a classic rhinestone comb pushed into the center of it for a more dramatic look."

accessory shop (with fake pearls, of course) cost only $24. At that accessory shop, which admittedly is usually packed with high schoolers, I found pretty pearl hairclips, jeweled hair adornments, a wide range of simple white headbands, and—during the months before prom time in May and June—the widest selection of fun and pretty tiaras I'd ever seen, all for under $30 each. Don't count out the "teeny bopper" jewelry sources. They have some great accessories.

If the make-your-own-veil sets at your local craft store don't impress you, look at craft stores for their selections of faux pearl hairpins, combs, bun wraps, and other hair accessories. While some of the items did look cheap, I found some simple pearl hairpins in sets of six for $2.99. With the right French braid or sculpted, upswept hairstyle, that $2.99 can make a big impression when the pearl pins accent the right curves of a braid. Simpler hairbands ran from $4 to $12, and the more attractive bun wraps with tight clusters of pearls and gemstones carried a $12 to $25 price tag. Compare that to the $200 hairclips you see at the bridal shop!

YOUR HAIR

While we're on the subject of hair design, you might decide to skip the headpiece and veil completely in favor of allowing your beautifully upswept and sculpted curls to serve as your complete top look. Hair stylists create veritable masterpieces, and these lovely styles don't need to be covered by a traditional headband and veil.

If the Shoe Fits . . .

Stay away from those bride's shoes you'll see in bridal salons and gown shops. These pretty little styles with their beaded toe boxes and bows might look great in a display, but they're usually overpriced and something of a luxury even for the bride who's not on a budget. Instead, choose a plain white shoe (or shoes dyed to match your hued dress) with few or no adornments. Why pay extra for accents that will be hidden under your gown all night?

When shopping for shoe bargains, many brides hit the sales and discount shoe stores for great footwear. Some great stores to check are Payless ShoeSource, Marty's Shoes, Kmart, Target, Wal-Mart and Sears. Keep it plain, keep it simple, and go for comfort every time. Opt for lower heels that will be more comfortable for dancing, and, if your wedding will be held outdoors where you'll need to walk on grass, choose a wider heel. Thinner heels tend to sink into soft surfaces.

As for you beach brides, sure you might choose to go barefoot during your beachside ceremony, but if you'll move indoors for a

Penny-Wise

You can't beat a good shoe sale! Fall and winter shoes are at greatest sale value in November, at prices of 50% to 75% off. Spring- and summer-appropriate shoes are most affordable in June, with pricetags slashed anywhere from 50% to 70%. So, mark your calendar and shoe-shop at these great bargain times.

Slip These On . . .

What about ballet slippers? I've read that they're perfect for under-neath a wedding dress.

Ballet slippers can work well, but you'd be better off as far as foot support and durability with a pair of skimmers, which are a slipper-type shoe with a flat wedge bottom. These pretty little slip-ons usually cost under $30, and brides report that they allowed for more comfort during the many hours of standing, dancing, and conga lines on the wedding day.

cocktail at a nearby restaurant, you'll need suitable shoes for your dress. You'd look silly in flip-flops or sneakers, so purchase yourself a sensible pair of shoes for aprés-wedding parties.

NOTHING'S AS COMFORTABLE AS AN OLD SHOE

And what about wearing a pair of your own shoes? You can save $25 to $100 by *not* buying a new pair of little white pumps for your wedding day look, *and* you'll know that these shoes fit comfortably. So, if you have a pair of attractive white shoes already in your closet, why not pull them out and help your budget?

Accessory Heaven

You've heard the mantra of style mavens in fashion magazines and TV style segments: "Accessorize, accessorize, accessorize!" Sometimes, it's the perfect little accent that ties your entire look together, so think now about adding the finishing touches to your wedding-day image.

Jewelry

Fortunately, it's a common practice for the groom or the parents to buy the bride a string of pearls or a diamond pendant necklace, and most brides don't have to buy their own jewelry for their wedding day. However, if you feel strongly about choosing your own wedding-day jewelry, shop at discount jewelers or hit the sales at department stores.

If you're like most brides, you want genuine stones in quality jewelry designs, regardless of your budget. You might be thinking ahead to when you'll hand the diamond pendant necklace you wore at your wedding to your own daughter someday. If you're of this mind-set, please do follow your heart and buy the real thing. Use the advice in chapter 9 to help you find great deals on quality jewelry.

Gloves

Far less sentimental to you may be gloves. For ultraformal weddings, brides look amazing in elbow-length satin gloves, and their maids are quite complementary in their own pairs. However, when budget is an issue, those $20 to $50 pairs of gloves to match your outfits might be a great item to cut out. Gloves are not the necessity they were in yesteryear, and many brides are more comfortable without them.

Wraps

Especially if you're planning an outdoor wedding, don't forget to accessorize your gown with a matching jacket, shawl, or wrap. Bridal stores carry designer wraps, with some fetching prices in the hundreds of dollars. Again, try a regular dress shop or even the prom gown section at a department store to find a pretty, simple white or champagne-colored wrap to keep

---

Penny-Wise

*F*ine jewelry, such as diamonds, pearls, and other gemstones, goes on sale several times a year. You'll find good bargains during the alluring pre-Valentine's Day season, late summer, and also during winter holiday shopping time when 60%- and 70%-off stickers pop up in jewelers' windows.

you warm when the sun sets. Remember that the great holiday fashion sales in December also feature wonderful selections of wraps and jackets, so add these items to your winter shopping list. Or, get creative. Some brides do choose to make their own simple wraps, using their seventh grade home-economics skills to hem the edges of a simple two yards of suitable satin material bought on sale at a discount craft shop.

Penny-Wise

Will you have colored flowers in your bouquet? Pastel pinks? Bright reds? There's no rule that says your *jacket* has to be bridal white. If you open up the option of color for your jacket, you might find a great formal wrap in that pretty pink or romantic red in a dress store or department store. Without the "bridal" tag, it may be priced far lower than a white one at a dress shop.

Undies

Other accessories to secure for your wedding day include flattering lingerie, slip, stockings (try control-top for those fitted dresses), and your ever-important garter. Seek out the best buys possible on these items, avoiding overly expensive designer brands but aiming for quality construction, breathable materials, and the option of multiple wears. Good undergarments do affect the fit of your gown, so be sure to choose the right bra (strapless, racerback, etc.) for your gown's style and an appealing silhouette. Consider these undergarments an official part of your wedding-day wardrobe and wear them to your gown fittings each time. Your seamstress will do a better job of fitting your dress with the right undergarments under your gown.

As for your slip, ask your gown salesperson which kind of slip or crinoline you'll need under your gown. Many gown styles come with a built-in crinoline or lining system, and you don't even need a slip. Other designs do require a separate slip. These specialty slips, complete with boning and layers of tulle to add some fluff to your skirt, can cost as much as $200. To save this somewhat lofty expense, see if you can borrow or rent a specialized wedding slip, rather than shell out so much to buy one.

Sample Gown Budgets

FOLLOWING are some samples that show you how cutting just a few things down can make a huge difference.

BRIDE #1: FORMAL WEDDING AT RECEPTION HALL

Designer ball gown: $725

Tiara and veil from bridal salon: $350

White pumps: $70 from department store shoe department

Jewelry: Free, gift from the groom

Hosiery and undergarments: $120 from lingerie catalog

Gloves: $35 from catalog

BRIDE #2: INFORMAL WEDDING AT RESTAURANT'S PARTY ROOM

Designer ball gown, simple style: $450

Headpiece and veil from bridal salon: $200

White pumps: $35 from discount shoe store

Jewelry: Free, gifts from the groom and her parents

Hosiery and undergarments: $40 from One Hanes Place (www.onehanes-place.com)

Gloves: $0, not worn

Penny-Wise

*H*it the lingerie and undergarment sales at your favorite department or specialty stores. You'll find the best sales in the summer months, when undies go for 50% to 60% off retail prices.

BRIDE #3: INFORMAL OUTDOOR WEDDING IN BRIDE'S TENTED BACKYARD

White cocktail-length dress, found on bridesmaids' rack: $175

Headpiece: $10 worth of fresh flowers tucked into bride's upswept hair

White low-heeled shoes: $30 from discount shoe store

Jewelry: $45 from accessory store

Hosiery and undergarments: $45 from department store

White lace shawl: $29, found on sale at a nearby dress shop

Bride #4: Beach Wedding

Little white slipdress: $59, found on prom-dress rack

Headpiece: $0, bride wore her hair up without adornment

Shoes: barefoot for beach ceremony, $25 white slip-ons for indoor postwedding gathering

Jewelry: $100, delicate pearl set on sale at department store

Hosiery and undergarments: $49, no stockings, bra and panty set from Victoria's Secret (bride's splurge for her wedding day . . . and night)

Pastel-colored satin wrap for evening: $35, on sale at bridal shop

Bride #5: The Bargain-Hunter Bride

Designer gown: $100, found on eBay

Tiara: $30, found on eBay

Shoes: $0, wore shoes she already owned

Jewelry: $0, wore jewelry she already owned

Hosiery and undergarments: $40, from One Hanes Place (www.onehanesplace.com)

Wrap: $0, didn't need it for her early-hour wedding

Additional Money-Saving Tips

For Your Gown

Ask for discounts on gowns that have repairable damage to them. You might earn 10% to 15% off the dress.

Ask for discounts when you decide *not* to take a store up on its offered freebies, such as garment bags, discounted accessories, and the like.

Check the classified ads for gowns that have never been worn. Some brides who have canceled their weddings may be only too happy to get rid of the darned thing for less.

Ask about extra fees you see tacked onto your bill. Some slick shops will actually charge you a "trying-on" fee, an "accounting fee" to pay for the time it takes them to keep track of your deposits, and other service charges. If a charge seems ridiculous, ask to have it scratched from your bill. A quality shop won't try to squeeze in extra charges to begin with, but business practices vary from store to store. Some stores even charge extra if you need a gown over size 12 or size 14. Don't give in to these highway robberies . . . find another store that isn't out to get you.

> ## Penny-Wise
>
> *I*f you ask your maids to order matching shoes dyed to order, see if you can get one pair of the same style in white *for free.* A pair of strappy shoes for you is a nice freebie with your larger order of maids' shoes.

For Your Veil and Headpiece

Consider borrowing a friend's or relative's veil. She might not mind seeing her pricey tiara get a second use, especially if it's you wearing it.

For Accessories

Don't buy your bridal purse at a wedding salon where prices can run sky-high. Who wants to carry a purse with all those silk flowers attached to it anyway? You can find a great little purse (should you need one at all) at a department store during prom-shopping time and summer sales.

Please Don't Make Us Wear Purple Hoop Skirts!

Dressing Your Maids in Style for Less

WHEN YOU asked your sister, your best friends, and your closest cousin to be your bridesmaids, I'm sure they were thrilled. Nevertheless, deep down inside, they may have given way to a quiet fear: *Please don't make me wear a hideous dress.*

What is it about the bridesmaid's gown that can strike fear in the heart of your most beloved women friends? Many of the bridesmaids I spoke to said that what they hated most was wearing a gown that was chosen *for* them. Many also said they hated wearing a color that only exists in nature in the pumpkin and gourd family. Most said they hated paying *so* much money for a dress they knew they'd never wear again. As insulting as some styles can be, it's usually the ticket price that will stun your maids and make them wonder if you chose them to be a bridesmaid because you really *don't* like them.

In this chapter, you'll lead your maids toward finding the perfect gown for your wedding style and for their body types, coloring, and budgets. Today, the wedding industry is a help, not a hindrance, in this task, and there is a wide variety of bridesmaids dresses out there to meet any taste and financial level. The major designers have answered the call for more elegant and attractive bridesmaids dresses with better-detailed construction, plus great matching accessories. Your maids have great choices today. They just need to know where to look.

Who Makes the Decision?

It's a wise bride-to-be who invites her maids in on the gown decision. This is something you have to do in the right way. Just like when selecting your gown, too many opinions cause complete chaos, hurt feelings, and power struggles. So, as the leader of the women's wedding team, it's up to you to decide on the color of the gowns *and* on the formality level for your maids' attire. Like everything else, their wardrobe *must* suit the formality and style of your wedding, so that they are dressed appropriately for the event.

Stick to a Budget!

Do your maids a grand favor, and don't just pick gowns on appearance alone. Consider your maids' personal financial burdens and set a limit, such as "No gowns over $150." It's the much-loved bride who chooses a gown that won't clean out a bridesmaid's savings account or take the place of her spring trip to Cancun. I've heard from too many bridesmaids who are just spitting mad that the "inconsiderate bride chose a too [expletive-deleted] expensive dress that maybe she and her [expletive deleted] rich fiancé could afford, but who does she [expletive deleted] think she is?!" Yes, maids can turn into caged tigers when you tell them they'll be wearing a slim-fitting sheath dress, and oh, by the

Fitting Formality

Your maids' dresses must match the formality and style of the wedding, so try to follow these general guidelines:

For an Ultraformal Wedding
- Full-length, formal ball gowns
- Full-length, sleek sheath dresses
- White gloves and accessories
- Dresses in shinier fabrics for evening weddings, nonshiny for daytime weddings

For a Formal Wedding
- Full-length, formal ball gowns
- Full-length, formal sheath dresses
- Cocktail-length or beveled-length (slanted-cut) dresses
- Dresses in shinier fabrics for evening weddings, nonshiny for daytime weddings

For an Informal Wedding
- Cocktail-length gowns
- Knee-length dresses
- Slipdresses
- Floral sundresses

For a Beach Wedding
- Formal styles apply for a formal beach wedding
- Informal styles apply for an informal beach wedding
- Sexy slipdresses
- For beach goddesses at a casual beach wedding: matching color bikinis or bathing suits with a matching solid-color or patterned sarong tied around the waist

way, it's $600. Don't do that to your maids. Don't even think, *"But it's MY wedding."* Be considerate at this stage of the game, and do all you can to make this bridal party experience enjoyable for your chosen few.

Making the Decision

Once you've made the basic decisions of formality, color, and budget, then it's time to start looking through magazines, Web sites, and even dress shops to get an idea of what's out there. This is a fun task to share with your maid of honor. Grab a stack of magazines and head out for lunch or spread everything out at your place during an evening of wine, cheese, and beautiful pictures of your potential choices. Narrow your options down to the three that you'd like the rest of your maids to consider.

So, you've sent your maids their top three selections and asked for their input. Will it be the shiny lavender dress with the plunging back and the matching wrap? Will it be the sleeker, simpler, more conservative lavender cocktail-length dress, or the ultraformal beaded little black party dress? Your maids will let you know. Have your maids rank their choices, discuss why they do or do not love the style, and perhaps decide as a group on their own which one will be The One.

Now what happens if your maids are deadlocked? Two *love* the backless lavender dress, and the other three *love* the simpler style. Or, they all love the color, but they each have a problem with the bodice, the skirt, the strapless factor, or the beading. Your maids aren't being difficult. They have a right to request the gown that suits their bodies and their sense of personal style. You now have the op-

Simplify It

*R*ather than take on the task of trying to assuage your maids' egos and fears about which gown can't *possibly* be worn with a bra, ask your maid of honor to act as ringmaster for this tricky summit meeting. Allow your maids to come to a conclusion as a group and then let you know which of your chosen styles makes the final cut.

Help! My Attendants Are Scattered!

My bridesmaids live all over the country. We're not even going to see each other until a week before the wedding. So how do I organize sending all of them the pictures of the gowns they have to choose from? How do we make a decision as a group when we're all so far apart?

This is a common problem for a lot of bridal parties. Your friends may live all across the country—and in other countries—so the selection and ordering process is going to require some extra steps . . . plus the smart use of technology. Brides with faraway maids are either using e-mail to send scanned photographs of their most favored gown design styles to their maids, or they're directing their maids to the top three gown styles as shown on a wedding gown Web site. The maids then view the choices and send back an e-mail with their desired preference. We'll talk more about the "distant bridesmaid" issue when we get to the ordering stage, as that involves a few extra steps. At this stage of the selection process, share the images with your maids through the Internet. If you, or one of your maids, do not have access to the Internet, then make color copies of a page from a bridal magazine and mail it to your bridesmaid.

tion of allowing them to make their own choices. That's right. These days, brides are allowing their maids to choose a gown with the design elements they love in a uniform color. Just go to one of the major wedding gown Web sites, like www.DavidsBridal.com, to see the mix-and-match tools that allow your maids to choose the individual top and skirt styles that suit their bodies best. Your top-heavy maids might choose a more supportive halter top, while your less-endowed

Wear-It-Again Gowns

I'd really like my bridesmaids to be able to wear their gowns again after the wedding. But will they actually get a second use out of a blush pink gown? How can I make a choice that will better the odds of their getting some mileage out of the dress?

I spoke with several women who have served as bridesmaids or maids of honor in ten to fifteen weddings apiece. These wise women tell me that they didn't get multiple wearings from the pretty pastel dresses assigned to them. They did, however, make great use of the sexy black cocktail dresses, the fire-engine-red dresses from those Valentine's Day weddings ("It was great for the company Christmas ball!"), and the darker shades of navy and hunter green. They also made more use of cocktail-length dresses than full-length ball gowns. So, consider secondary uses for your maids' gowns, especially if you will be asking them to spend a slightly higher amount on them.

maids might go for the strapless look. Your more bottom-heavy maids might choose an A-line skirt, while your smaller maids might want a slimmer cut to their full-length gowns. The choice is up to them. So many bridal parties are going this route that it's almost become a standard in the industry. Brides love that their maids do conform to a unified look as far as color and formality, and they also love that their maids are happier in a more flattering gown of their choosing. The bridal party is clearly identifiable, and the pictures show the individuality of these lifelong friends and sisters. It's a win-win situation, particularly when your maids are free to choose the more affordable of the individual options.

Where Do We Look?

Again, you're not limited to the bridal boutiques. Sure, some of these shops offer more than 2,000 gown choices that take a full day of browsing through the racks, and you might find one that's geographically convenient for your maids and even offers an alterations package. These bridal shops do provide a wider range of styles in one color (a la the DavidsBridal.com selections), so they might offer your maids the happy task of choosing from many options. However, if the prices seem inflated, especially at the larger bridal shops, then grab your maids and head out for a day of dress hunting. Here are some of the most popular gown-scouting locations for great bridesmaids' dress buys:

> ## Simplify It
>
> Consider using the services of a department store's personal shopper just as you might for your own wedding gown. This type of service can save your busy bridesmaids hours of searching and narrow down the choices within your maids' stated budgets. Just call for an appointment and let the department store's staff save you all days of effort.

• Department stores. Your nearby department store's formalwear section will show a wide range of gowns and suitable dresses for your maids' inspection. Macy's, Lord & Taylor, and Bloomingdale's carry their greatest supply of formal dresses during the wedding season (April through July) and again during the pre-New Year's rush (November through January). If you have a larger bridal party to fit, hit these stores early for greater access to a wide range of sizes in each style. Sure, you can find more 30%- to 50%-off tags attached to these gowns after wedding season or New Year's, but you might not find the number of gowns you need in each style. (If, however, you only have two or three bridesmaids, then an after-holiday sale might be perfect for you.)

• The prom-gown section. Again, go to the prom-gown department for access to gorgeous, stylish, and sexy styles in a large range of sizes. In many cases, prices in this category of formalwear range from just $79 to $300, and I think they offer a far better selection than many bridesmaids' departments. Just be aware that high schoolers start planning their prom attire *early,* like in January, so find out from your nearby shops and department stores when they expect to receive the promwear collections.

• Well-known women's clothing catalogs. Many catalogs offer great selections of appropriate bridesmaids' apparel. Despite the added delivery charge, some of these catalogs offer great deals and a wide variety of selections, plus accessories. Some catalogs to look through: Chadwick's of Boston, Talbots, Spiegel, JCPenney, and Macy's. An added bonus to catalog shopping is that most of these sources provide a fail-safe return guarantee, which is rarely offered at a bridal shop that considers your order "custom" and therefore nonrefundable.

• Well-known Web sites. If you choose to shop on a bridal gown Web site for your maids' dresses, practice safe Internet shopping as described in the wedding gown section on page 91.

• Trunk sales and sample sales. Several times a year, the major bridesmaid-gown designers want to clear out their inventory to make way for next season's line. So, they plan a sample sale or trunk sale tour where they show off their dresses at a bargain. To find a great designer's sample sale near you, check designers' Web sites as listed in the Resources section in the back of this book or call your nearby bridal boutiques for their plans to host such events in the near future.

Can the Ladies Rent, Too?

Of course. The boom in wedding-wear rentals extends to maids as well, with conscientious brides offering the option of a one-time, low-money use of a pretty gown. So, if you favor a color or style that your maids aren't likely to want to own, or if you're aware that your maids are on tight budgets, consider investigating this option. Again, you can find gown rental shops through an Internet search, or through a look in the Yellow Pages under Bridal Gowns, Rentals, or Formalwear.

Smart Bridesmaids' Shopping

The rules for bridesmaids are the same as those you followed to find your own gown. They just get a little tricky when you add in several other people's orders. So please do refer back to the smart gown-shopping section on page 93, and add these bridesmaid-specific tips to your thought process when you start shopping for your maids' gowns.

• Start shopping early. Your maids will need an extended amount of time to order their gowns and have them fitted. So start looking at least nine months ahead of time to find the best deals and the right styles for your wedding's season. Shopping too late could cost your maids "rush fees" of an added 20% to 30% on top of the original expense for the dress. That's just money out the window. Another advantage to ordering early: That's lots more time for your maids to get their gowns altered and even fixed if they're inexpensive or poorly made.

• Inspect gowns for quality of construction. When your maid tries on a sample gown, encourage her to check the design for quality of construction. Are the seams well sewn, the zipper a smooth and effortless pull? (The sample may be a bit dingy from repeated try-ons from other bridesmaids, so judge the gown's color according to an official swatch of fabric and not the

Simplify It

*T*o find a great shop that rents gowns for your maids, call the tuxedo rental store and ask if they rent women's formalwear. If not, don't be afraid to ask them to suggest a local shop that does. Remember, the wedding industry is very accommodating to most requests—vendors want to keep you happy so that you'll recommend them to all your friends.

appearance of the gown your maid has on). I can't promise you that the gown that arrives after order will always be of the same sturdy design: Some companies do deliver shoddily constructed dresses that do not match the sample in quality. It is a sad fact within the apparel industry that there are some bad apples out there. All you can do is choose a very well-made gown and hope for the best when it is delivered to you.

• Advise your maids to order according to their measurements. Your maid might be a perfect size 8 in everyday fashions, but it's a well-known fact that bridal gown designers don't always adhere to the same sizing structure in use at the Gap. Your size 8 maid might fit into a dress a designer presents as a size 10. So don't let your women order by the numbers. Have them measured by a professional seamstress who writes their chest, waist, hip, leg length, and arm length (if necessary) on professional sizing cards. This is the best way to order a gown that fits and that will need minimal alterations.

• Have your distant maids send you their size cards. All of the bridesmaids' gowns should be ordered by one person, from one store or Web site. Even if your maids are scattered throughout the land, it's best to buy all their gowns in one bulk purchase from one source. This is a wise idea as far as organization is concerned, and it's also practical. Bridesmaids' gowns need to be dyed to match the color you've selected. Different factories in different parts of the country may have slight differences in their versions of dusty rose pink. Yes, you've ordered Color #2128, but the factory in Dallas might turn out a lighter version than the factory in Maine. So collect all of your maids' size cards by a specified date and submit them in one group order. An added bonus: You might receive a discount when placing an order for a larger number of gowns, and you can pass that 10% off to each of your maids.

• Encourage your tiny maids to choose petite sizes. Gown designers do offer petite lines that are designed to flatter smaller women. Plus, a petite gown may require less in the way of bottom hemming and wasted material. Just don't expect a petite gown to cost less than a standard size gown—that isn't always the case.

• Set payment plans in stone. Alert your bridesmaids that they will have to make a deposit of 50% on their gown right at the outset, and be sure they're clear on when the final payment is due. Be organized about this, and be sure your maids are well aware of any delivery fees, insurance fees, or taxes that will be added.

• Secure good contracts. When ordering your maids' dresses, be sure the order form and contract are completely detailed. A good contract will list the itemized orders of each of your maids (including their names, contact information, and sizing details), payment plan information, delivery date, and details on the shop's alterations policy or expenses. Read the fine print to learn about the store's returns or cancellation policies. Some stores, because gowns are custom ordered, do demand a no-return clause in their contracts, so don't be surprised if your shop doesn't give full refunds. A detailed contract, signed by the shop owner or sales associate who helped you, is an important record of your purchase, so keep close track of it.

> ## Simplify It
>
> *E*ncourage your faraway maids to Fed Ex their gowns and accessories (after alterations are complete) to your place several weeks before the wedding. This one simple step, even if it's an extra expense, takes away any risk of your bridesmaids' wedding-day wardrobe getting lost or damaged if they carry it when they fly. This way, you (and they) will know that their dresses are safe and secure, ready for the big day.

• Encourage your maids to pay with credit cards. As always, a credit card charge is far easier to track and protect than a cash transaction. So be safe and pay with plastic.

• When the gowns come in, be sure to deliver the right gown to the right maid, and do it through a certified, trackable sending service. Ask for delivery confirmation from the shipping company, and keep careful track of routing numbers. (Federal Express: 800-GO-FEDEX, www.fedex.com.) Or, track your parcels through the Priority Mail system of the U.S. Postal service (www.usps.gov).

• Alert your maids to the need for professional fittings. You can't force them; just encourage them to get professionally fitted wherever they are, and share the fitting advice from page 97 so that they can find the best seamstress possible. Encourage them to schedule multiple fittings, with one a few weeks before the wedding day itself.

She Who Has the Right Shoes Wins . . .

In most cases, particularly if your maids will be wearing cocktail-length gowns or slipdresses with their legs in full view, you'll want your maids to wear identical shoe styles and colors. That means searching for bargains.

Penny-Wise

*I*f you find great shoes at a discount store or department store that doesn't offer dyeing services, take all the shoes to a well-known shoe repair shop or local drycleaner with shoe repair service. A professional dye job, done of course in one dye lot to ensure consistent coloring, might run you around $10 per pair of shoes, perhaps less if you negotiate because of your larger order.

Sure, the bridal gown shop has a lineup of bridesmaid footwear, and some stores even offer discounts on group shoe purchases and dyeing orders. Do your homework to see if this is a good budget option for your maids. In some cases, it is. In other cases, you can beat the bridal shop's prices with a quick trip to a shoe outlet or a group visit to the local discount shoe store like Payless ShoeSource.

You can often find bridesmaids' shoes dyed-to-order in an organized bulk purchase with little hassle and lower prices on the Internet. I found a fabulous shoe site called www.myglassslipper.com, which offers a great selection of designer and discount shoes in classy and attractive styles. This site carries an extensive stock, including

Kenneth Cole, Vanessa Noel, Watters and Watters, Fenaroli, Peter Fox, and Dyeables, all the best names in bridal footwear. One stop here, and you won't even need to organize a shoe-shopping trip with your maids. Best of all, you can direct your faraway maids to order the correct shoe style and color right from the site. Sure, you have to pay a little extra for shipping, but I found great prices here that still added up to less than what I would have spent if I bought a pair of maids' shoes and had to dye them at a separate shoe-dyeing location.

Another great Internet resource for your maids' shoes (and perhaps your own) is Discount Dyeables (www.discountdyeables.com), which offers top-quality shoes dyed to order for less than half of what you might pay in a bridal shop. This company also offers dyed-to-match accessories, such as purses.

All the Pretty Jewelry

You might choose to give your maids their jewelry for the wedding as your gift to them at the rehearsal dinner. This option is a great token of affection and an assurance that they will wear appropriate jewelry on the wedding day. Your best bet is to search your local stores for pretty matching sets of beaded or faux pearl necklaces and earrings. One bride found lovely pearl chokers and pearl studs for her maids at an accessory store for less than $15 per set.

Another option for creative brides with a little more time is to make the jewelry sets. Craft stores offer easy-to-use, design-your-own necklace kits that you might choose for a rainy Sunday afternoon task. These kits allow you to create custom designs with just the right shade of coral when you haven't been able to find the right styles in a store. Each bride who has used these inexpensive kits tells me that as lovely as the finished product turned out, it meant even more to her maids that she had *created* these pieces for them.

If you don't give your maids jewelry, please do ask them to wear a certain type of jewelry on the wedding day. For instance, you might request they wear simple pearl or faux pearl studs and either a string of faux pearls or a simple true pearl pendant necklace. Tell them specifically that you'd like their jewelry to match, so you don't wind up in the awkward position of having to ask a style-impaired (or big social-statement-maker) maid to remove her big gold nameplate necklace or her sizeable yoga-inspired "Om" pendant. Be clear from the outset, so that your maids look great in your wedding pictures.

We All Need Support

Speaking of looking great, you might actually have to give your maids some undergarment advice. If the gowns you've chosen are strapless, are cut low in the back, or are panty-line nightmares waiting to happen, you may need to encourage your maids to purchase appropriate bras or thongs for the big day. How do you call up your cousin and tell her you're concerned about her being well-supported in her dress? Simple. Take care of the job quickly and efficiently with an e-mail suggestion and a link to a great undergarment shopping site such as One Hanes Place or even the sales at Victoria's Secret. Just tell your maids that you found truly supportive strapless bras and you-can't-even-feel-them thongs at a certain site, just in case they're interested. That's all you can do. Done.

And while we're speaking of undergarments, be *sure* to specify the exact brand name and color of the pantyhose you wish your maids to wear on the wedding day. It really does matter if one maid is wearing a suntan sandalfoot with her open-toed shoes and another maid is wearing shinier stockings with toe reinforcement. Believe it or

> ## *Simplify It*
>
> *A*void any last-minute headaches caused by snagged stockings. Ask your maids to buy and bring with them two pairs each of those L'Egg's suntan sandalfoots. Have a few extra pairs in stock for the maid whose engagement ring tears both sets.

not, this kind of tiny detail really does matter. Think about your wedding pictures. All of your maids are lined up on either side of you, smiling in their identical hunter green gowns, and it looks like someone colored every other maid's legs with a different brown crayon. You worked hard to avoid color discrepancies with the maids' gowns, so exercise care by specifying a stocking color and sheen level.

Gloves and Purses

What about gloves? For an elegant look at formal weddings, you might choose to ask your maids to wear elbow-length or wrist-length gloves. You can order them from your bridal shop, from Internet wedding sites, and even from some bridal-minded shoe shops. Take a look at the glove discount site Discount Gloves (www .bridalgloves.com, 800-479-4696), which will price advertised gloves for you at a significant discount. Just bear in mind that gloves are not a necessity and that you can cut one expense from your budget by skipping these elegant satin pull-ons entirely.

Another accessory that can be skipped is the dyed-to-match purse. Sure, it makes for a nice look while your bridal party is walking from the limousines to the reception hall, but that $30 dyed purse is only going to sit on or under the table during the entire reception. So cut your maids a break on this one and don't insist on their carrying matching purses. If your maids *want* them, however, check out the selection at www.discountdyeables.com for a wide range of dyed-to-match styles at affordable prices.

Wedding Day Reflections

*J*ewelry-making was a great way for me to let my flower girls help out with the wedding. At ages nine and ten, my nieces were adept at stringing the stones in the right order and handing the finished pieces to me for knot-tying and clasp-attaching. The girls were thrilled to tell everyone that they had helped make the necklaces, and it was so much fun to have one job that I could share with them."

—Kelli

Sample Budgets for Your Maids' Gowns

Following are some sample budgets that will put all of these elements into budget perspective.

Formal Wedding
- Designer full-length gown bought at a bridal shop: $400
- Shoes, dyed to match, bought at a bridal shop: $120
- Gemstone necklace and earring set bought at a bridal shop: $75
- Gloves bought at a bridal shop: $29
- Specialty undergarments (crisscross bra and thong to suit sleek dress): $40

Formal Wedding
- Designer full-length gown, rented: $75
- Shoes, found in matching color in discount shoe store: $29
- Gemstone necklace and earring set bought at an accessory store: $30

Semiformal Wedding
- Name-brand gown bought at post-New Year's formalwear sale at department store: $99
- Shoes, found at department store during post-New Year's sale: $19
- Gemstone necklace and earring set bought at accessories store: $30

Informal Wedding
- Off-the-rack dress, found at department store's postsummer sale: $35
- Shoes, found at discount shoe store: $25
- Bridesmaids wear their own jewelry: $0

Dressing Your Flower Girls for Less

It's the little ones that get the ooohs and ahhhs from your guests, so dress your flower girls in style. True, this is one expense that the bride doesn't normally take on, but it's a nice gesture for you to help the parents of your flower girls to find the best wardrobe choices for their little girls.

While the bridal shops feature lovely little dresses for your tiniest female attendants, you might do better to encourage the parents to shop at a regular children's clothing store, department store, or a discount children's clothing store. Hit the post-Easter sales for even better prices on fluffy little white dresses with colored sashes and pretty lace accents. In many cases, postholiday sales feature excellent prices on children's shoes and accessories as well.

For greater savings for the flower girls' parents, allow the girls to wear their Communion dresses or already-owned party dresses. Such a plain white dress can be accessorized with a sash or sew-on floral accents in a color that matches the rest of the bridal party. Total cost for this option: sometimes as low as ninety-nine cents for the ribbon. Get ready for that parent to hug you.

For jewelry, you can buy the child a pretty necklace or bracelet. If gloves will be worn by the entire bridal party, check department store display counters for great deals on children's gloves, or shop the Internet for such specialty items.

> ## Simplify It
>
> *F*or more specific nautical-themed kiddie clothes (great for casual beach or backyard weddings), log onto Katie and Co., www.katieco.com.

Men in Black

Dressing Your Men for Less

Even I have to catch my breath when I attend a wedding and see that lineup of groomsmen in their tuxedoes, greeting the wedding guests. The men always make a handsome bunch when they're gathered together and dressed sharply, whether it's a classic *007* look or a stylish Samuel L. Jackson ensemble with the long coats and the matching confident air. In this section, you and the groom will start off by deciding which look is right for your wedding day, and for your men themselves, and then you'll begin your smart shopping trip for everything from the tux to the shoes to the cufflinks. If you could take a before-and-after shot of your groom's best buddies, some small part of you might wish that you could choose their wardrobe all the time!

Style and Formality

As always, the general formality and style of your wedding will determine the outfits your men will wear. Obviously, a formal wedding calls for tuxedoes, while a more informal affair might find your men in chinos and crisp, white dress shirts for that Nantucket-inspired day overlooking the ocean. To help you narrow down your search, I've listed the general formality "rules" for wedding-day menswear. The tuxedo rental shop assistant can help you further define an appropriate look once you get the lingo down and know what you're looking for.

Rules for Men's Weddingwear

Ultraformal Evening
- Black tailcoat
- White waistcoat
- Wing-collared white shirts
- White vest
- White bow tie
- Black patent-leather shoes
- Shiny cufflinks
- Optional white gloves

Ultraformal Daytime
- Black or gray waistcoats
- Gray pants
- White wing-collared shirt
- Striped ties
- Black patent-leather shoes

Formal Evening
- Black tuxedo
- White shirt (or off-white shirt, to match bride)
- Black tie
- Cummerbund or vest, in black

- Black patent-leather shoes
- Cufflinks and other classy accents

  OR . . .

- Black tuxedo pants
- White or off-white dinner or cutaway jackets
- Black tie
- Black patent-leather shoes
- Cufflinks and other classy accents

Formal Daytime
- Gray cutaway suit, or . . .
- Gray jacket with gray pinstriped pants, or . . .
- Black or gray morning coat with gray waistcoat and black-and-gray pinstriped pants (very classy!)
- Light-colored or white jacket
- Ties or vests in color or coordinating print, such as a black-and-gray-striped tie
- NO WHITE SHOES, PLEASE!

Semiformal Evening
- Black tuxedoes or suits, or . . .
- White dinner jacket with formal black pants
- White or lightly hued shirts
- Black or color-coordinated bow ties, cummerbunds, and vests
- Black shoes

Semiformal Daytime
- Navy or gray suits, or . . .
- White linen suits, or . . .
- Gray or dark jacket with gray waistcoat
- White shirts
- Color-coordinated tie
- Suit-friendly shoes

Informal Evening
- Dark suits with white shirts and coordinating ties
- Dark shoes

Informal Daytime
- Dark blazer and white shirt with khaki pants, or . . .
- Gray or tan suit with white shirt (for spring and summer), or . . .
- White button-down shirt with khaki pants
- Solid or patterned, color-coordinating tie

Choosing the Style

Okay, so you have the formality rules down pat. Now comes the fun part: choosing the individual elements of your men's style. Before you head off to the rental store, let me ask you a question: What's the difference between a wing collar and a spread collar on a man's formal shirt? For details on men's jacket styles and a complete primer on all of the major menswear style selections, visit www.MarryingMan.com. Your rental shop owner will present the best selections to you, but you'd be well-served to acquaint yourselves with the many offerings out there before you shop.

Finding the Right Tuxedo Shop

Whenever I see an usher in an ill-fitting tuxedo, I know that he didn't go to the right rental shop. (Either that, or he's wearing his father's tux.) Choosing the right tuxedo rental shop—one with a long-standing reputation for great service and quality of merchandise—is wise, even if the prices are slightly higher. The reason for this is that good shops will have better designer and brand-name tuxedoes to rent, a wider variety of options, full lines of accessories, and—best of all—very savvy shopping assistants and rental agents who know their stuff. A good tuxedo stylist will interview you about your wedding's style and formality, perhaps take a look at pictures of your maids' dresses, and inquire about the setting for your event. Then he'll disappear into another room, emerging shortly afterward with a number of winning selections that fit right into your budget. A quality shop also offers custom-fitting sessions by well-trained tailors, plus advice on snazzy accessory and shoe choices.

So, you're looking for a shop that offers the finest in product and customer service. Where do you start? First, ask any recently married friends or relatives who live in the area to recommend a great formal-wear rental agency nearby and add that shop to your perusal list. Then continue your own shop-scouting to find the best store possible.

For formalwear shop referrals, as registered with the International Formalwear Association, check in at www.MarryingMan.com as well as at major wedding-planning Web sites, which provide shopping and style tips, and a list of recommended men's formalwear shops in your area.

When you decide on a shop, schedule a consultation with the rental agent. It's a good sign when the agent sits down and asks you some questions about the date, style, and formality of your wedding.

Check It Out!

It's a great sign when the rental agency you're considering is a member of the International Formalwear Association. This means that the shop is legitimate, and the stock is of the highest quality. To belong to such an esteemed association, shop owners and workers often must undergo training, and they receive special bulletins on the latest fashion trends and accessory lines.

Ask plenty of questions about the appropriate styles and fabrics for the weather during your wedding season, ask to see the fabric samples in the designers' showbooks or sample cards, and ask about any group discounts you might be able to swing. For orders of four or more tuxedoes, the shop might be willing to throw in the groom's tuxedo for free. For ten or more tuxedoes, they might throw in the father of the bride's as well.

Couples on a budget will be glad to know that nontraditional choices may earn them better prices. For instance, tuxes made from certain fabrics are less expensive. The best of tuxedo fabrics are marked "super 110s" and "super 120s," the number of threads per inch. These higher thread counts are usually an indication of better made, more attractive tuxes that hold their designs better and may cost more. The average tuxedo has a 70 to 90 thread count, but try to beat this number so your men don't look . . . well, average.

You're also likely to see that gray or white tuxedoes are less pricey than black ones. Don't be afraid to point out your budget wishes to the rental shop's stylist and to ask for his advice on getting the most stylish and attractive outfits at affordable prices. Your stylist will suggest designer name brands, colors, fabrics, and styles to suit your money needs.

Penny-Wise

In some cases, it's better to ask for free throw-ins, rather than a discount off the rental price. By free throw-ins, I mean shoes or bow ties or a free gift of cufflinks, pocket squares, or even a gift certificate for free boutonnieres. Many grooms say that these throw-ins are better deals than a stated discount off the price of tuxedo rental, as you're sure you're getting something for less.

Get Out That Measuring Tape

Once you've chosen the designer, style, and accents for your men's wedding wardrobe, it's time to ask your men to be sized for their outfits. Your nearby groomsmen can stop in at the shop for a professional

Give Them the Benefit of the Doubt

Don't scoff if your rental agent seems to be pushing the big-name designer tuxes on you. If you're hearing Perry Ellis and Ralph Lauren, don't automatically assume that your stylist is trying to make more money. I wouldn't trust a rental agent who didn't encourage you to rent the best quality tux out there and to avoid the cheaper, poorly made tuxes. Trust your stylist's input and consider these slightly pricier models for their great sheen, their great fit, and their great cut.

measuring session and have their vitals recorded on official size cards. Your faraway groomsmen also need to be sized professionally; ask them to be measured by an expert tailor and submit their numbers to the rental shop. These sizing appointments are generally free at the shop where you're placing the order, but faraway groomsmen may have to pay a nominal fee to a shop near them. One warning: Don't allow your men to take their own measurements in order to save a buck or two. Professional tailors know just which width of the chest to get, and they know just where to place a sleeve length for the most fashionable fit. So tell your men that this task is nonnegotiable.

Most shops use standard sizing cards, and this sample size card shows you the required measurements and info:

Men's Size Card
Name:
Shirt Size:
Neck Size:
Sleeve Length:
Waist:
Inseam:
Shoe Size:

For each man, order the size tuxedo that fits his largest dimension, whether it be his waist or leg length. Order toward the large size and have the tailor fix the fit. Because certain styles are more flattering to certain body types, your stylist can help you choose one that's more complimentary to all your men.

When you have the size cards from all of your men, including the faraway ones, it's time to put in your order and reserve those great tuxes, suits, shoes, and accessories for the Big Day.

Simplify It

A smart couple from Seattle shared this idea with me: They brought a group picture of the groom and his men to the rental shop so the rental agent could assess the men's best look. This photo was a recent one, not a lineup taken especially for this purpose, and it showed the men's personalities as well as their heights and general builds. The rental agent had a better idea of who he was outfitting than he could get just from the size cards, and he helped the couple choose the perfect wardrobe and accessories for those fun-loving men.

PLACING YOUR ORDER

Start searching early, and place your order as soon as possible . . . especially if your wedding will take place during the busy prom months of May and June or during the high wedding season of May through August. At these times when demand is high, the best deals will be snapped up in advance and the best stores booked to capacity. So waste no time in making your tuxedo or suit selections, getting your groomsmen to submit their size cards, and securing your reservations for those incredible Perry Ellis tuxes, at discount.

With those size cards in hand, place one group order at the tuxedo shop. Do not allow your men to order their tuxedoes individually. Your "bulk" purchase allows for control over the process, the assurance that the job will be completed, and perhaps the guarantee of a group discount or a free tux for the groom. With the expert help of the consultant, you will provide complete information when you place your order, including the style numbers and wardrobe and shoe sizes for each man.

Up to a week before the wedding, the men should go as a group for their final fittings. In some cases, your men may need an additional fitting, especially if your faraway groomsmen are trying on their suits for the first time. If so, tell the stylist that several of your ushers will be arriving in town three days before the wedding, and you'd like to request that their necessary last-minute fittings be exempt from any rush fees. Most stores will comply without argument. Your in-town men, however, should have their final fittings with plenty of time to spare.

Be sure the groom advises his men well. He should send them an e-mail or deliver a detailed message saying whose name the order is under, the style and price of the tuxedo itself, and *specific* instructions about the pickup of shoes and accessories. While he has his ushers' attention, he might remind them that they'll need *black socks* to wear on the wedding day. This is one of the most common snafus with men's wedding rentals. You wouldn't be the first bride to gasp at the sight of white socks or even Christmas-themed socks (I kid you not!) flashing into sight with each step. Micromanaging? Sure. However, you're better off mentioning nitpicky details like socks and plain white tee shirts, not printed tee shirts, worn underneath white dress shirts.

> ## Simplify It
>
> At the time of your tuxedo order or shortly thereafter, designate a dependable "Return Man" who will collect all the tuxedoes and shoes the day after the wedding and return them to the store. It's always best to have one person—the best man, perhaps—take on this task, so that the job is completed by someone you know (or hope!) will be dependable. Late fees could be charged to your credit card—and they're not cheap!—if you've placed and paid for the order yourself, so be sure this job is completed in your absence.

What If We're Not Renting Tuxedoes?

Informal and semiformal weddings may keep you from setting foot in a tux rental shop. If you're going the dark suit route, or if your men will be casually attired in khaki pants and matching white button-down shirts, then it's time to round up your men for a trip to the mall. Sure, you might feel a bit like a den mother if you run the outing, or you might load the groom down with instructions before he chaperones his buddies and your fathers to Macy's Labor Day sale. If dark suits are the order of the day, and your men don't have navy blue suits that look right as an ensemble, then this trip is a necessity.

For dark suits, try to shop the sales or the discount racks at men's clothing outfitters and outlets. At men's clothing shops, a salesman in a good mood may cut you a break when you bring seven men in to buy $150-suits. However, don't count on it. Retail stores are more likely to see each of your men as an individual entity, so you might not get the same discounts you'd find while renting.

For greater uniformity, also ask the men to buy the same style of dress shirts. Just telling them to wear a white dress shirt could turn up an array of collar styles and even variations of the color white. This request also prevents your thriftier groomsmen from slapping on a white dress shirt they already own and perhaps was stained in the past. The same goes for those khaki pants, which you can find in discount menswear shops at a bargain or through substantial sales at department stores or in catalogs such as L.L. Bean or Eddie Bauer.

You must ask all of your men to order new khaki pants, because "khaki" can range in color from light tan to dark sand to an almost brownish-green. To be safe, have all your men purchase the same khaki pants, the same style of white button-down shirt, and a tie in the style of your choosing. Then hit the discount shoe stores or department store sales so that the men can get a great deal on their matching shoes.

What About the Little Guys?

Ringbearers will certainly look adorable in whatever weddingwear look you choose, whether it be a mini-tux or a pint-sized version of your men in their khaki pants and white shirts. Just as with the flower girls, the ringbearer's parents will foot the bill for the child's wedding wardrobe, but it's best to cut them a break when you can.

Rental shops are usually fair about their children's-sized tuxedoes. As with the men, you're looking for great style and design *and* high-quality fabrics and construction. Even on a seven-year-old, the tux must fit well.

For many formal and informal weddings, you might be able to avoid renting a tux for your little guys. In some cases, it's fine to dress the boys up in black pants, a white shirt, cummerbund, and a bow tie. Some couples prefer to keep their child attendants away from a more adult look, and this option of skipping the rental allows for an acceptable and even more appropriate look for a little guy. So, consider your wedding vision, and see if you can allow the boys to skip those pin-striped trousers.

Stores

When shopping for a youngster's wedding day wardrobe, check out children's discount clothing stores and the sales at department stores for great name-brand styles for less. While some discount clothing stores do offer very inexpensive boys' party ensembles, look for quality of construction, appropriate fabrics, buttons that are attached well, working zippers, and stainless dress shirts. Sometimes there's a dark side to that $5 price tag. You may not be celebrating your budget victory on the wedding morning when the little guy's sleeves are different lengths.

Another source for boys' formalwear is the outlet shopping center. Check the outlets near you, found through the Internet, or ask the ringbearer's parents if they ever swing by a great outlet center during their regular travels.

Catalogs and Web Sites

Well-known catalogs and Web sites can also be a great source for finding stylish and affordable children's formalwear. In the back of this book, I've listed several Web sites for you to consider. Ordering from these sources is not nearly as risky a proposition as ordering a custom-made item like a bridal gown or bridesmaids' gowns. Kids' clothing catalogs have been around for decades, and many parents swear by their high quality. The key to dressing children is to make sure you will get a high number of wearings from each piece, so if a parent favors Lands' End despite a higher price (because the clothes are manufactured so incredibly well), then let her get her son's khakis there.

Keep Them Comfortable

Whenever you're talking about dressing children, remember that comfort is the key. A little one in an itchy or too-tight suit that is hot from too many layers and wearing a tie he hates is likely to fidget, pull a sour face in every picture, or even erupt into a full-blown tantrum. So make your childrenswear choices with the kids' comfort in mind. Choose the most breathable high quality cotton-blend fabrics with cotton linings, rather than nylon or other less aerated materials.

Formality Level

When looking at styles with an eye to formality, know that the little guys *can* match your men's styles exactly. If the men are in tailcoats, the ten-year-old can be in a tailcoat. If, however, you're comfortable with a separate, fun look for your boys, like a cute sailor's outfit for that four-year-old (please spare the nine-year-old this indignity!), then check out your options on the market.

Many couples like to have some fun with their child attendants' wardrobes, adding dashes of color to the little guys' look, such as using a coordinated but separate pattern for the tie, and even decking out the boys in cool sunglasses at outdoor weddings. Dressing the boys can be a lot of fun, and discount options are out there for the finding.

Shoes

As for the boys' shoes, don't bother renting a style to match the men's. Allow the parents to use the little guys' already-owned black dress shoes or encourage them to shop at discount shoe stores like Payless ShoeSource or Stride Rite, or in the generally well-priced children's departments at Target, Wal-Mart, Kmart, Kohls, and Sears. And do suggest a few breaking-in wearings so the soles are scuffed up and the shoe conforms to the child's foot without rubbing or blistering.

Additional Money-Saving Tips

- Choose all-inclusive packages that include discounts or freebies on alterations, accessories, and shoe rentals.
- Go with classic styles and stay away from hot new trends in men's fashion, which are often marked up due to their popularity.
- Consider using some color in the men's wardrobe. If the majority of the shop's customers rent basic black options, check to see if there's a better deal on colored ties, vests, and cummerbunds.

With These Rings

Saving on Your Bands and Stones

THE WEDDING bands. They're the enduring symbol of your marriage vows, the most important tangible part of your wedding day, and you'll keep them with you forever. While it's no secret that your wedding rings are going to claim a sizeable chunk of your budget, there are many ways you can get more ring for less. Your choices of metal, stones, and design are going to determine your base financial level, and—perhaps most important—*where* you buy your rings can make all the difference between finding a great steal and getting robbed.

Which Ring Is for *You?*

Before we start talking about platinum vs. 14-karat gold, diamond insets, stackables, and other wedding-band lingo, it's important that you decide which style and size of ring is right for you. Since you'll wear this ring every day for the rest of your life, it becomes a part of you. So, your rings need to fit your sense of personal style. Are you into small and simple jewelry and understated refinement, or do you prefer more dazzling, eye-catching looks? Do you want a simple platinum band, or do you want diamonds or gemstones embedded into your ring? You'll save yourself a lot of time if you predetermine what you're looking for, and you'll also save yourself from wanting a must-have dream ring that's just out of your budget range. So flip through those ads in the magazines, look at jewelry Web sites, and browse at some jewelry stores to get a look at what's out there. Just like when you shopped for your wedding gown, your advance decision of what you want helps you narrow your search and seek out the best choice for you.

Do you want two plain bands, or platinum sets with gold accents along the side? Some brides like to think ahead and choose these two-toned styles so their wedding rings will match any type of additional jewelry they might wear in the future. Your groom might want a plain gold band in a narrow width, while you might prefer a gold band with gemstone inlays. Just note: Plain bands can be less expensive than those ultra-detailed ones with the three levels of stones, the laser cutouts, and the transformer styles that flip open to reveal a ruby heart inside. Remember, it's the amount of workmanship on any wedding product that will raise prices significantly. So, if you're more into the meaning of your bands than the materialism, consider more plain bands before the more ornate.

Simplify It

To get a virtual look at ring designs, stones, and settings, visit www.BlueNile.com for its "Build Your Own Ring" interactive tool. You'll be able to "try on" a wide variety of ring styles and find the best style for you. Or, if you want to design your own ring from scratch and choose everything from the stone shape, size, and setting, use the ring design tool at www.adiamond isforever.com, and then print out or send an e-mail of the design to others. This is a great timesaver if you're planning to hire a ring designer to custom-make your rings.

The Wedding-Ring Primer

Before you head to the jewelry store, take a moment here to learn more about the world of wedding rings. Being well-informed about ring terminology, styles, and materials makes you a smarter shopper with better odds of finding a great ring buy. Those ring salespeople can dazzle you with trays of sparkling beauties, and they know just how to convince you that those pricey emerald insets bring out the flecks of green in your eyes. With the right combination of ring lingo, you'll know that those emerald stones are probably the most expensive choice you can make, and that the 24-karat band they're attached to isn't quite as durable as the 14-karat styles in the showcase to the left.

Platinum, Gold, or Silver?

Most of the ads you'll see in the magazines are for platinum rings. Right now, platinum is the hot metal of choice for its durability and shine (it is the strongest of the metals), and that demand also makes it the most expensive choice right now. While prices will be at the upper end of the scale, most couples find the investment to be well worth it, as platinum best protects your ring from nicks, dents, or wear. Made from a blend of 95% platinum and 5% alloys of iridium or palladium, platinum never tarnishes, and its natural state makes it 100% hypoallergenic and

Simplify It

*O*ne of the most important factors for choosing the right rings is making sure they fit into your lifestyle, career, and hobbies. A detailed ring with many ridges, laser cut-outs, details, and embedded stones might be in constant peril if you deal with messy materials, chemicals, and food on a daily basis. All those grooves can catch a significant amount of dirt or other debris, and chemicals can stain or compromise the strength of your bands. Everyday wear and tear may even loosen the stones if your hands are busy all the time. So, consider the ridged, detailed look with regard to practicality: Will you really want to take off your priceless wedding band before all of your work and hobby activities?

kind to the skin. You'll pay more for this metal, but you're likely to find that it's money well spent. If you've decided to go with the platinum, look for the markings "900 Pt," "950 Plat," or "Plat."

If platinum is out of your price range, but you like the look, consider 18-karat white gold. Both white and yellow gold are highly popular choices for wedding bands, and you may be able to afford a more detailed or gem-laden style of ring with this metal. When looking over any gold jewelry, closely inspect the piece to see that its finish is smooth and free of bumps or rough spots both on the outside *and* along the back of it. A well-made piece should be attractive even in spots no one will see.

Like platinum, gold does not tarnish or rust, but it isn't quite as durable as platinum. In fact, 24-karat gold is among the most malleable types of gold there is. Remember, the higher the karat number, the softer the metal. So, those 14-karat gold choices are more resistant to knocks and bumps than 24-karat styles. How does that work? Jewelry designers incorporate strong alloys into their ring metal mixtures, and durability increases as the numbers go down. Most jewelers will recommend 14- or 18-karat gold for wedding jewelry.

Sterling silver is a good choice for wedding rings, and it is sometimes the only choice for brides and grooms who may be allergic to gold and can't afford platinum. Silver in its pure form is also a soft and malleable metal, so again alloys are used during the creation process

Shop Wisely

We're talking future stress here. Silver jewelry is not the choice for you if you plan to spend time handling strong household cleaners or swimming in chlorinated water found in swimming pools and hot tubs. These chemicals can deteriorate the look and strength of your silver jewelry.

to strengthen it. Sterling silver is a mixture of up to 92.5% silver and 7.5% alloy, with jewelers recommending that the alloy of choice be copper, which adds strength without dimming the color of the silver. When shopping for silver jewelry, check for official quality grading marks such as "Sterling," "Ster," and ".925."

Settings

The setting that holds your stones can either improve the look of your diamonds or precious gems or take away from their luster. Some brides are quite resolute about having a low-set stone that won't catch on hosiery or knock on furniture, while others request a higher setting that allows the stone's cut to catch the light. Consider the following setting categories to find the style that works with the number and sizes of the stones you wish to incorporate into your bands:

• Bezel: Uses a thin strip of the band's metal (whether gold, platinum, or silver) to encircle the stone around the middle and hold it securely in place.

• Channel: A very popular style for wedding bands, the channel sets smaller stones in an equal line through the center of the band, and is held in place by two raised metal strips on either side of the stones.

• Cluster: The cluster gathers a group of stones in the same manner as a floral bouquet, with one larger stone in the center.

• Invisible: Gemstones are set in place very close together, with the binding metal hidden underneath.

• Pavé: Like a paved road, the ring presents the stones in an inlaid arrangement.

• Prong: These metal claws grip the edge of the stone to hold it in place. While jewelers do offer a six-prong setting, eight is more secure. A Tiffany prong setting will raise the stone higher off the ring band for

---

Listen to Someone Who Knows!

Michelle Orman of Jewelry Information Center says that choosing a pavé setting for your diamond wedding band is a great way to get more glitz for less money. The carefully arranged and well-faceted small stones create a sparkly, elegant look.

---

a more showy use of light, while a cathedral setting clasps the stone more closely to the band.

• Tension: The stones are held tightly between two rings of metal, using the tension between those rings to keep them in place.

DIAMONDS

Diamonds, rubies, emeralds, topaz . . . you might opt to incorporate sparkling stones into your wedding band, either to match or to complement your engagement ring. However, brides of all ages who want to include "a diamond is forever" sentimentality to their rings are selecting diamond-set bands to match their big diamond.

If you expect to make diamonds a part of your ring ensemble, consider the Four C's of choosing the best quality diamonds you can afford. All diamonds are certified according to a universal scale of Carat, Color, Cut, and Clarity, with the findings recorded in a Diamond Grading Report. Gemologists inspect the stones under high-powered microscopes and assign grading numbers or letters to "stamp" on the ring. The ranking affects the pricing, and it also shows the level of perfection in each piece. Always ask to see the grading certificate of any stone you're considering, as a good jeweler will provide an explanation of your ring's particular "DNA."

COLOR

Diamonds occur naturally in colors ranging from pure white to yellow. The pure white ones have almost no color at all and are the most valuable and of course more expensive. Colorless diamonds are graded D. Variations from there are indicated by letters moving upward from that point to Y and Z, the most yellow. Those D's are going to be most expensive, while obviously yellow stones are going to be very low-priced. Few brides want unattractive yellowish stones for their rings, so try to aim more to the middle of the scale for a beautiful stone and a moderate price.

CUT

The cut of the diamond determines its particular shape and angles, and therefore the amount of sparkle it gives off when its facets catch the light. The more facets a ring has, the more it sparkles. As you start to look at diamonds, you'll find cuts in the following shapes: princess (square-cut), round (the most popular choice), marquis, emerald, pear, heart, and other shapes. Cut is far more important than just whether you want a round or a heart-shaped ring. It's the cut, and the skill of the artisan who takes a raw chunk of diamond and creates its sparkly design, that determines its overall radiance on your hand. In fact, the cut of a diamond can affect its pricing by as much as 50%. A top-quality diamond can look like half its worth if the cut is not precise and complementary. So consider several shapes of diamond or gemstone cuts while searching for your ring accents.

Wedding Day Reflections

*L*ooking at the pictures in magazines, I was sure I wanted a round diamond. But when I tried on several different rings, I thought the round stone looked a little strange on my very small fingers. The jeweler helped me select from a variety of marquis-shaped rings, and the simple cut change made a world of difference. In fact, many of the fancier-cut diamonds were priced at less per carat than the round or emerald types I looked at.

—Laura

CLARITY

A stone's perfection is also graded according to a universal scale, with F1 being perfect (and far more expensive) and F13 imperfect (and therefore much less expensive). Your beautiful diamond may look flawless to the naked eye, but a look through a jeweler's magnifying viewfinder can point out carbon spots, chips, and many other imperfections. Internal flaws called inclusions and external flaws called blemishes should be noted on the stone's certification papers, as these kinds of defects can affect your ring's value. Smaller flaws, only visible with a microscope, are often judged okay by brides who would rather pay less for an "imperfect" stone (when no one will ever be able to see that teeny carbon spot inside). Larger flaws that are visible to the eye should eliminate that stone from your list. Don't pay a fortune for a visibly damaged stone.

Wedding Day Reflections

We very wisely went with a simpler style of white gold with tiny inset diamond chips for my wedding band because we're on a limited budget. My husband promised that five years from now, on our anniversary, he will "upgrade" my ring to a full circle diamond anniversary band.
—Jennifer

CARAT

The size of a diamond is its carat weight, with a carat weighing approximately one-fifth of a gram. Larger diamonds are, of course, more expensive than smaller ones, but the other three C's affect the pricing as well. A "full carat" diamond equals what is known as a one-carat grading; anything less is called a "light carat."

GEMSTONES

Diamonds aren't the only stones brides choose for a wedding ring. Brides of all ages are including their birthstones or other precious gems in their rings, and some brides who are mothers are using their children's birthstones in their bands. Some of the more popular gemstones used in wedding bands are:

- Amethyst: Purplish in color, readily available, moderately priced
- Aquamarine: Blue in color, the lighter-hued ones are more readily available and less expensive
- Citrine: Yellow in color, readily available, moderately priced
- Emerald: Green, among the more expensive of the gemstones
- Garnet: Usually red but occurs in a range of purple and orange tones with prices varying with color and other factors
- Ruby: Red, nearly as durable as a diamond, pricey

Keep in mind that gemstones do adhere to the same types of 4-C gradation scales, with toughness being an important factor in gemstone choice. Your ring may take some bumps and hits as you wear it through your lifetime, and you'll want to be sure the gemstones are tough enough to take this wear and tear. So be sure to ask your jeweler about the gemstone's grading on the "Moh's scale" (a scale that tests gemstone hardness), or other test of the stone's durability. As far as pricing, know that most gemstones in lighter-hued or muted shades may be less expensive than those in bright, full primary colors such as red, blue, or green. The reason for this is that many gemstones are heat-treated to intensify their natural colors—with heat, a paler blue becomes a deeper blue, for instance. This heat treatment makes

Birthstones by Month

January: Garnet	July: Ruby
February: Amethyst	August: Peridot
March: Aquamarine	September: Sapphire
April: Diamond	October: Opal
May: Emerald	November: Topaz
June: Pearl	December: Blue Topaz

the stone more valuable, and therefore more expensive. Always ask your jeweler if any stone you're considering has been heat treated—a reputable jeweler will offer full disclosure on this important factor. Heat treating doesn't only affect the price of the ring, it affects the *future treatment* and well-being of the ring. A heat-treated ring can be more susceptible to damage from knocks, ring-cleaning chemicals, even extreme temperature changes.

For more information on buying gemstones, contact the American Gem Society (www.ags.org, 800-340-3028), the Gemological Institute of America (www.gia.org, 800-421-7250), the Jewelry Information Center (www.JewelryInfo.org), or the American Gem Trade Association (www.agta.org). These Web sites include complete buying primers, plus thorough descriptions, histories, symbolism, and birthstone months of many of the most popular (and little-known) gemstones made by both man and Mother Nature.

Since fit is so very important, be sure you both have your ring fingers professionally measured and sized. You may know that you wear a size 6 ring, and you always have, but designs may vary in size . . . just like those wedding gowns. You'll want to get the best fit right off the bat, to avoid paying extra for resizing—or face the timing and expensive nightmare of having to order a new and better-fitting choice—after the rings come in.

Penny-Wise

*I*f you love the look of those high-priced gemstones, but you can't quite spare the expense, consider alternate gemstones that *look* like their pricier counterparts but actually cost up to 50% less:

Instead of *aquamarine,* choose *blue topaz* or *blue zircon*
Instead of *emerald,* choose a *green-shaded garnet* or *tourmaline,* or catch onto the new trend of glitzy green gems: *tsavorite.* Never heard of it? You will.
Instead of *ruby,* choose *red garnet*
Instead of *diamond,* choose *white topaz*

Your jeweler can show you additional gemstones that can double for loftier selections.

How Does It Fit?

One of the most popular styles of wedding bands is the "comfort-fit" band, which has more rounded inside edges designed for the comfort of the wearer. Many couples report that comfort-fit bands make their rings feel natural as soon as they first start wearing them.

INDIVIDUALS OR SETS

I wish I could tell you it's less expensive to buy a matching set of wedding bands, but that isn't always the case. Especially if your groom prefers a plain band and you want a more detailed one, you may be able to find better prices shopping for individual rings . . . perhaps even at separate stores. So, check the prices for both options, and choose the better deal both financially and for pleasing your individual tastes.

Where to Shop for Your Rings

As I mentioned earlier, *where* you buy your rings can make all the difference in the price, value, and style of the selections you find. A reputable jeweler, one with a sterling track record who has been around for years and hosts legions of loyal customers, will certainly be your best bet as you shop for your wedding bands. So ask your recently married friend, parents, and family friends if they have a jeweler they like. From quality of merchandise to ethical business practices and friendly service, a fine jewelry shop will meet your needs far better than a fly-by-night storefront you may find at the mall.

Jewelry Stores

When looking for your ideal jeweler, always check with professional associations such as the American Gem Society (www.ags.org or 800-346-8485) or Jewelers of America (800-223-0673). A jeweler who is registered and recommended through one of these associations has met the highest standards of professionalism and business practices. The Web sites for these associations contain narrowed-down lists of the best ring shops in your area. Take their recommendations as a green light, and conduct your research from there. Just as you did with your consultant and your gown shop, be sure the store has a long history of fine service to customers, has a clean record with the Better Business Bureau and the Department of Consumer Affairs, that their merchandise is plentiful and stocked beautifully, the store is clean and orderly, the staff is trained and knowledgeable, and the salesperson takes the time to listen to your questions and offer advice. The best ring shops make you feel welcome, and they make your ring-shopping experience memorable. They answer your questions, allow you to view your desired stone through the viewer, if possible, and they show you full documentation on your ring's authenticity. Their contract is complete, stating a firm delivery date, and they promise free fittings once the ring arrives. There's not a shady practice to be seen.

Penny-Wise

I've found great prices during the winter holiday months. Remember that the holidays are a prime time for engagements, so the department stores and jewelry shops often offer great discounts to holiday shoppers.

Department Stores

Department stores have wonderful jewelry sales from time to time, and the better ones offer complete grading reports on each of their gems and ring sets. I've found wonderful sales on wedding bands and gemstone band rings in department store sales for $200 to $600 off the original retail price. So do include department stores in your ring-shopping excursions, but buy only when a refund is offered, and be sure to get the ring appraised by an outside source immediately.

CATALOGS

What about catalogs? Believe it or not, you can find a quality ring at a discount, plus a no-fail return policy, in discount catalogs from Ross Simons, JCPenney, Macy's, and others. Many of these larger companies do offer specialty bridal catalogs where you may be able to find the perfect ring set at a fabulous price. Be sure to check the ring's materials and grading thoroughly, know what you're buying, and allow plenty of time for returns and full refunds, if necessary.

THE INTERNET

Some couples do swear by Internet shopping (while others have been known to swear *at it*). Many jewelry Web sites do offer fine selections

Words of Wisdom

Michelle Orman of the Jewelry Information Center suggests the following if you plan to buy your rings online:

- Use the same smart shopping rules you'd use for any ring store.
- Choose a Web site that has a legitimate street address, not just a Web address.
- Shop only through a Web site that offers a guaranteed return and refund policy.
- Ask for a fully itemized receipt that spells out the particulars of the ring you've ordered.
- Ask for an Independent Grading Report on any diamonds or stones to be used in your ring.
- Use your credit card, not a debit card, to secure your purchase. Credit card buys can be tracked and protected for your safety.

of wedding bands and diamond jewelry, with lovely full-color pictures and descriptions. Some couples have found amazing bargains on their rings or individual stones, and they trust the secure servers and delivery (always, always insured). If you'd prefer the convenience of Internet shopping, then practice smart Web shopping.

One bonus of Internet ring-shopping is that many sites serve as showcases for rings and provide a list of nearby retailers who carry them. Check the ring Web sites at the back of this book for a good start to your online ring hunt.

Other Sources

If you've been through the area ring shops and don't find what you're looking for, try several of the following sources, subjecting them all to the same background check and scrutiny you would for any other wedding professional. This is one of the most important purchases

Go Ahead . . . Fake It!

We don't have the budget to buy the incredible diamond-embedded ring that I'd like right now, but we're sure we'll be able to afford it in the future after we finish medical school. Is it okay if we use fake diamonds in my ring now and then change the stones later?

Of course! It would only be wrong if it felt wrong to you. So many brides are sporting fake stones now, and no one is the wiser. On a budget, this may be a great option, with the "real" diamond promised for your first anniversary. Faux diamonds are showing up in beautiful cuts now, and you're sure to find a lovely fake if you look in the right places. So, if you don't mind, who else could?

you'll make for your wedding and a lasting investment, so commit some time to finding the best source.

- Ring designers
- Jewelry design schools
- Antique jewelry stores
- Estate sales (you can find plenty of platinum ring styles here, as platinum was *the* jewelry material back in the old days)
- Auction houses
- Consignment shops

Engraving

The engraving of your rings is not an expensive proposition, except that most jewelers do charge by the letter. Often, you're allowed to choose the lettering, or font, that the jeweler will use to inscribe your words. Look at the font charts carefully, noting price differences between the most basic print or script and the more ornate, scrolled, or Gothic-type prints. Prices per letter can increase substantially depending on the font, so keep your font simple and let the sentiment do the talking.

Be sure to print your words to be engraved clearly on the order form, so that the artisan can correctly spell your loved one's name. And *double-check the wording with a careful eye when you pick up the rings.* Any mistakes caught now will prevent nightmares later on. One groom didn't notice that the jeweler had inscribed the name "Ann" on his wife's ring, when her name was Amy. Luckily, Amy had a sense of humor and the groom's mother (or worse, his ex) wasn't named Ann.

Insuring Your Rings

Insuring your engagement and wedding rings is *not* a frivolous choice made only by the fearful. Your rings are worth more than you paid for them, in every sense, and you would be heartbroken if they were ever lost or stolen, so it's wise to take steps to protect them. You have several options when getting your rings insured. First, check with your own insurance agent to see if your existing homeowner's or renter's policy covers fine jewelry. If it does, ask if your current policy states a value limit, as in "Fine jewelry above the value of $500 is not covered." If your policy has such a limit, ask for a rider to the agreement that raises the value to the cost of your rings. If your policy does cover pricier jewelry, ask your insurance agent to include your engagement and wedding rings within your existing policy.

Be careful about insurance terminology, though. If your insurance agent offers you a rider to your homeowner's insurance, ask specific questions about what the policy covers specifically. Does the policy cover you if the ring is damaged or lost outside the home? Would a floater or rider policy provide extra protection against outside-the-home occurrences? You have to be specific. Does it cover you if your ring is stolen, but *not* if you've misplaced it during a busy holiday weekend?

Be sure you understand the terminology in your policy. A *blanket* policy will cover your rings along with a collection of other jewelry and valuables, setting a dollar limit for each piece in the collection. A *replacement* policy covers the cost of getting an entirely new ring of the same stated value, provided your policy spells out all the tricky little have-tos, musts, and shoulds that insurance policies are known for.

Simplify It

*F*or the large amount of money you'll spend on your rings, it's important to have your purchases appraised immediately by a source other than the store where you bought them. A good appraisal will evaluate the worth of your rings and record the final tally on a certificate you will use to have them insured. A good appraisal will also include a closeup photograph of the ring, the dimensions and gradations of the stones, a description of the mount style, and a complete description of the stones' inclusions or blemishes. This is an important step to protect your investment and a solid practice for the smart consumer.

If your current insurance does not cover jewelry, then you will need to seek out an independent jewelry insurance source. Again, check with your married friends for names of the insurers and companies they use to protect their rings and then conduct a complete search for the policy that best suits your needs and budget. The American Gem Society (www.ags.org, 800-340-3028) offers a great free brochure on insuring jewelry. They and the American Society of Appraisers (703-478-2228) can help you find a reliable jewelry appraiser-insurer.

Additional Money-Saving Tips

• When you go on your ring-shopping trip, bring along a trusted friend who has some knowledge about fine jewelry or the ring industry. Your friend can advise you on questions to ask and which offers are better. Even better, bring a friend who is a certified, card-carrying jewelry buyer for a store or a privately owned ring sales outfit.

• Be prepared to bargain. You may be able to talk your way into a small discount or wangle extra services such as sizing, engraving, or comfort-fit bands for free.

• Shop jewelry sales *only* if the store's sale prices are lower than their usual prices. Avoid the common scheme in which jacked-up prices appear to be marked at a significant discount. Research at different times will reveal true bargains.

• If you're looking for diamonds, shop in the diamond district of your nearby metropolitan city. This is where the ring shop owners come to stock up on their merchandise, so you can share in their significant savings on stones and gems. Wholesale ring purchases can net you a diamond or bands for more than 50% off, but you might have to be accompanied by a registered jeweler or a registered, certificate-toting ring buyer.

• Use your contacts. If your cousin owns a jewelry shop, see if he can offer you a great deal on your rings. If he's ultragenerous, make it his wedding gift to you. If a friend works at a jewelry counter at a department store, see if she'll kick in her employee discount or kick her commission back to you.

• Shop at ring stores in different towns. Shops in the "richer areas" may offer their stock at much higher prices than reputable stores in moderately priced areas.

• Shop at antique stores, which may charge significantly less for a ring that has a wonderful history as well.

• Ask your friends and family to keep an eye out for jewelry sales at shops and department stores near them.

• Consider having your engagement ring merged into your wedding ring, such as re-setting your engagement stone into your wedding band.

• Don't buy rings at all! Instead, exchange family heirloom rings that have been handed down for generations, or . . .

• Have the stones from an heirloom piece—say, your grand-mother's wedding ring—re-set into a new platinum band for a fraction of what you'd pay for an entirely new ring. The cost for this option might run you $100 to $300 for the ring setting, as opposed to $900 or higher for the ring and the stones.

Simplify It

Keep copies of your official appraisal and insurance certificates in a very safe place, such as a safety deposit box at the bank, or in a safe in your home. These documents can protect your ring investments and may even help you redesign your precious ring to the smallest detail should the worst come to pass. Treating these documents like the valuable items they are will save you stress and heartache in the long run.

The Ceremony

The Most Important Part of Your Big Day

How interesting that *the* most important part of your day is likely to demand the smallest part of your wedding budget! Your ceremony is the reason for the entire event, and the expenses are probably going to be only nominal. In this section, we'll talk more about creating your ceremony than budget issues, as you can't put a price tag on the vows you'll take and the thrill of that first kiss as husband and wife.

Choosing Your Ceremony Style

The first step is choosing the kind of ceremony you'd like to have. If you adhere to a religious faith, there may be no question in your mind that your ceremony will be held in a house of worship and include Scripture readings, a Mass, or the playing of the "Ave Maria." If you're more the secular type, you might enjoy the freedom of choosing an interesting location (perhaps the outdoors or a great lounge at a historic home) as well as the individual readings, music, or vows that are short and sweet. Sit down with your sweetheart and decide on the look, feel, and faith of your ceremony, remembering that this most important decision is *yours alone* to make.

RELIGIOUS, IN A HOUSE OF WORSHIP

In many cases, houses of worship have set guidelines, if not strict rules, for the ceremonies they perform. When you speak with your officiant, you may learn that you'll need permission to play secular music and that your vows must be read by the book. Some houses of worship restrict the use of cameras and videotape, and you must use their musical performers. Of course, rules vary from one house of worship to another, but I urge you to ask about any rules at the outset. If you're granted some leeway with the readings, then choose your favorite passages from Scripture, books, poetry, songs, or letters.

RELIGIOUS, AWAY FROM A HOUSE OF WORSHIP

Many religious officiants will venture outside their houses of worship to perform a ceremony in another location. If you have your heart set on that gorgeous bluff overlooking the ocean, call around to see which of your favorite officiants will agree to perform on site. Many couples who choose a nonreligious setting appreciate the freedom to include religious elements within their day, without the look and feel of a church setting. With personal faith so important to many, this option is often a strong solution for the couple with divided family beliefs.

NONRELIGIOUS

As mentioned earlier, you have the option of hiring a nonreligious officiant to perform your ceremony. From the mayor to superior court judges to a licensed captain of a ship, you might choose a secular officiant to lead you through your simple and personalized ceremony, allowing yourselves complete freedom to choose the elements and structure of your own rituals.

Questions to Ask Yourselves

As you discuss the style of your ceremony, use the following questions to design the ceremony that's right for you, for your beliefs, and for the style and budget of your day.

- Do we want to include religious rituals during our ceremony?
- Do we want to include family members in our ceremony? In what capacity?
- Do we want to include any special, secular songs in our ceremony?
- Do we want a simple ceremony with just vows and a reading, or do we want a longer, more formal, more traditional event?
- What are the dream elements of our ideal ceremony?

Stand Your Ground!

Very often, couples get pressure from their family members regarding the level of faith included in their chosen ceremony style. Parents may push you to have your wedding in a church as they did and as your sister did—and you may get a good dose of expertly applied guilt for claiming that you want your ceremony held away from a house of worship. Don't get pushed into a ceremony you don't want. Whatever your chosen style and location, state your preferences clearly and assertively, but diplomatically. Family ties do get strained when the couple's choices depart from the parents' expectations, and you might find yourself in a whirlwind of opinions. If your parents resort to the oldest known control tactic in wedding history—the dreaded, "We're paying for it, so we say what goes"—stand your ground and explain with great calm that you want your ceremony to reflect who *you* are. Hopefully, your parents will be big enough to accept your choice and support you as you create the ceremony of your dreams.

Choosing the Officiant

If you're holding your wedding at a house of worship to which you belong, your search for an officiant may be quite simple. You will just make an appointment with your favorite pastor, priest, or rabbi and begin the process of "interviewing" him or her for the position (see questions on page 166). If you do not belong to a congregation, then begin calling around the area to find the best house of worship for you. Allow plenty of time for this step, as officiants and churches or synagogues do get booked up early, with their available Saturdays and other weekend days snapped up a year or so ahead of time.

When you begin to call religious officiants, start right off with the "deal breaker," if you've chosen to include nonreligious elements in your wedding. You'll save yourself a ton of time if you get right to the questions, "Will you allow us to play secular music?" or "Will you allow us to skip the Mass?" For a secular ceremony you may be able to find a religious officiant who is willing to conduct a ceremony that does not include Scripture or other religious references, but more often than not a secular ceremony will be conducted by any of the following, according *to your state's certification rules.*

> Town Mayor
> Town Deputy Mayor
> Town Committee Chairperson
> Federal District Court Judge
> United States Magistrate
> Municipal Court Judge
> Superior Court Judge
> Tax Court Judge
> Retired Superior or Tax Court Judge
> County Clerk
> Minister in any religion

Will You Marry Us?

We'd like to hire a secular officiant to preside over our wedding ceremony, but we want to make sure he's legal! How do we find out who's licensed by the state to perform ceremonies?

To find an officiant who is recognized by your state to perform marriage ceremonies, just call your town hall or county courthouse for a list of the judges, magistrates, mayor, or town council members and their phone numbers. Be sure to start this search as early in the process as possible. Mayors and judges especially have very booked schedules, so be sure your potential officiant is available to serve on your day.

If you'll hold your entire wedding from start to finish at an established wedding hall, botanical garden, or other site that regularly hosts weddings, the site manager may simply hand you a list of recommended officiants. Some sites actually require you to employ their regular officiant. So ask about any officiant rules when you speak to your site manager, request a list of their favorites, and be clear on their rules about ceremonies in general. Your chosen officiant will need to know the location's requirements as well, as he might not be willing to perform an outside ceremony for his own personal reasons. Leave nothing to chance when completing this crucial step of your planning process.

Take a Number! Interviewing Officiants

Your officiant is every bit as important as your caterer, your florist, your DJ, or your coordinator, right? So, you'll have to interview him

Wedding Day Reflections

We were kind of shocked when we went to meet with the pastor, and he handed us five pages of essay questions! His church required every engaged couple to fill out their answers on such topics as "Where and how did you meet?" "Does your family support your decision to marry?" and "What are your plans for raising children?" I was a little put off, but we completed the questionnaire together. When I asked the pastor why we had to provide so much information, he said, "I take my job seriously. I will not bestow the blessings of our church on a couple who's marrying on a whim, and when I do believe in a couple, I want to help them create a ceremony that's right for their beliefs." I realized that this pastor was simply upholding his version of job integrity. That we were given the okay proved to us, as well as to him, that we were serious about our vows and our commitment to one another.
—Lila and James

or her with the same mind-set of searching for experience, quality, and friendly demeanor that you'll use with every other professional involved in your wedding plans. A quality officiant will invite your questions, answer them fully, explain his rules and preferences, and let you know just how much creative control you'll have over your event. So, devote a good block of time to this step, know that the quality of officiant you choose will determine your satisfaction with the ceremony, and get the full story on what you can expect from each person. Don't forget to ask about any fees or donations that are required and any travel expenses that may be involved.

Here are some topics to approach with your potential officiants:

How many weddings have you conducted?
Have you conducted any weddings like ours? (important if you're planning an interfaith, nonreligious, outdoor, or other alternative style of ceremony)
Are you available to work our wedding?
What are your fees, as well as any extra fees for your house of worship?
May we see a list of your establishment's wedding rules and restrictions?
Will we be allowed to design our own wedding ceremony?
What will you be wearing on the wedding day?

What is required of us, as far as documentation, interviews,
classes, etc.?

For the best choice, be sure that both of you meet with your contenders, in person. This kind of face-to-face encounter will tell you
more about the type of person you're about to entrust with the
sacred responsibility of joining you together as husband and wife.
During that meeting, remember that the officiant is also interviewing
you. Many religious advisors, judges, mayors, and other leaders do
have personal preferences about whom they will marry. So don't
be surprised if your prospective officiant asks you a barrage of questions about how you met, how long you've been together, even what
your parents' marriages are like. These questions aren't meant as an
intrusion on your privacy but rather serve as the officiant's way of getting to know you and perhaps considering your choices of ceremony
elements.

THE OFFICIANT'S FEES

Another piece of information your officiant is likely to request is your
marital status. If you have been divorced or widowed, you will have to
present full documentation of your divorce decree or a death certificate for your departed spouse. I know this isn't the most cheerful of
tasks, but it is a legality that must be addressed. Save time at your initial consultation with the officiant by bringing all your paperwork
with you.

Now, since your budget is a concern, let's talk about officiant's
fees. According to the Association of Bridal Consultants, the average
cost for an officiant and use of a house of worship is approximately
$140. Some officiants do charge a nominal fee for their time and ser-
vice, and others may ask for a kind donation to their house of worship. Freelance secular officiants might ask for a bit more money,
perhaps $50 to $150, and they might charge you for their travel. If
you're inviting the town mayor to serve as your honored officiant, ask
what his or her fees are upfront. Again, these may only be nominal,

Minister for a Day

I've heard a lot about people becoming "ordained for the day" in order to perform a family member's ceremony. How can we find out more about this?

Each state has its own rules about residents applying for a one-day ordination to perform a valid marriage ceremony. To be safe, ask your town hall's marriage registrar or your state's marriage bureau for information on legitimate ordination services. Plenty of Internet "Get ordained now!" sites exist, but you'll need to make sure you're adhering to the laws of your state and not succumbing to an Internet ad that has no authority in your area. So make some calls and compare the cost to your other officiant choices.

but every part of your budget needs to be recognized and recorded. This may be the most important $140 you'll spend for your wedding.

Choosing Your Ceremony Elements

Now is the time for you to design your ceremony as a true reflection of who you are, what each of you will bring to the marriage, and which musical choices will enhance your entire ceremony from approach to departure. This is by far *the* most important part of all your wedding plans. It's where you make your ceremony *you*, where you include your loved ones, and where you join together in matrimony. Hopefully, you've chosen a location and an officiant that allow you to add your own touches to the wedding rituals and not require you to echo standard promises by rote. You don't want a cookie-cutter ceremony, right? So let's get started building your dream elements now.

Your Wedding Vows

Your vows are the public declaration of your commitment and a fine chance to say what's in your heart as not only a promise, but as a gift to your beloved. Wedding vows are perhaps the most emotional part of the ceremony, and it's the task that demands the greatest part of your attention.

If you will be writing your own vows, allow plenty of time to compose the right sentiments, the right promises, and perhaps a little something extra to personalize your expression to your partner. Many of the couples I spoke to happily volunteered parts of their own vows for your inspiration:

> "I promise to be faithful to you for all the days of my life, to always keep you in my heart as my best friend above all else."
> "I promise to love you, to adore you, to make your happiness as important to me as my own, and to hold your hand forever as we walk through whatever the future may bring us."
> "From the moment I saw you, I knew that real happiness was possible. You have brought me so much joy, so much comfort, so much faith. I promise to bring the same to you for as long as we both shall live."

You're not just bound by the traditional rendition of "in sickness and in health, for richer, for poorer, 'til death do us part" anymore. Today's couples want to write their own promises and include their own personal touches. I've heard about taking a portion of the vows in the bride's second language, so that her family could also understand what was being said. I've also heard about the couple's children taking vows of their own, promising to support their parents as a united family. There was also the couple who inserted inside jokes into their vows, with their guests none the wiser. "We wanted to use a little inside joke about the first time we said 'I love you' to one another, but we couldn't be graphic in front of our guests," wryly smiles one bride as she recounted her steamy story to me. "It was important to us to include that moment with some kind of reference, and it turned out to be that one little something that was just ours alone, while the rest of our wedding was shared by everyone else. In that moment, it was just the two of us."

Whatever your wishes for your vows, start early and write them either together or apart, promising to surprise one another with your written promises at the wedding. Most of the couples I spoke to said that they agreed ahead of time to a word count or time limit, so that one partner wouldn't feel outsentimented.

You might be required to run your vows by your officiant, especially if he or she will be reading them out loud for you to repeat. If you and your partner wish to surprise one another with your vows, then make separate appointments for the officiant's review.

Penny-Wise

This has to be one of *the* biggest wastes of money I've ever heard of: One couple actually paid a professional writer $800 to pen their vows. They found the writer through a professional association, asked her to "make it romantic," cut her a check, and then probably went on to spend $6,000 on a wedding cake. It's not the money that's so troublesome . . . it's the fact that the couple surrendered the most personal part of their ceremony to a stranger because their money allowed them to.

READINGS

If you wish to include several readings in your ceremony, decide who will receive the honor of performing the readings—whether it be your officiant, your maid of honor, the friend who introduced the two of you, or your own child. Select from a wide assortment of religious psalms (ask your officiant for suggestions—most have a booklet or preprinted page of suggestions), famous or little-known poetry, great quotes from luminaries of our time, or even pages from your love letters to one another.

Music

Music sets the tone for your entire ceremony. From the lovely classical music you might have playing as your guests are being seated to the trumpet voluntary that announces you as husband and wife, the music you choose will enhance your ceremony and make lasting memories for you all.

This is the part of the ceremony that might affect your budget a bit. If you'd like to hire your house of worship's singers or musical accompanists, ask about the fees for their services. Most houses of worship allow you to use their organist for a nominal fee, and they may also invite you to make a donation in exchange for a number performed by their choir. They may restrict you to a list of their officially recognized musical artists, or they may allow you to bring in your own soloist, pianist, guitar player, or flutist.

If you do plan to hire a musician, start by checking with the American Federation of Musicians (212-869-1330) for the names and contact numbers of the types of musicians you seek. Try to hire local musicians, so that you do not have to pay a mint for their travel expenses and mileage, which can add up. Once you get the names of the best matches for your wishes, it's question time again. Ask your musicians the following to find the best artist available:

- Are you available on our wedding day?
- Are you willing to travel to our wedding site?
- What are your fees for the stated playing time?
- What are your extra fees, such as travel expenses?
- What are your overtime fees? (Yes, this is important to know, even if it's unlikely that you'll run into overtime. Ceremonies do get delayed, whether because of a glitch in the site's schedule,

Simplify It

*T*o find wonderful quotes on marriage, love, and other wedding topics, visit www .quoteland.com, which provides a wealth of suitable sayings for your ceremony, or visit your library to find appropriate quotable writings by your favorite poets and authors.

the delayed arrival of the bride or bridal party, or any number of other unforeseen occurrences.)

- How many weddings have you played?
- What is your musical education background?
- Can you play our wished-for music in our desired repertoire?
- Are you willing to learn our wished-for songs from sheet music we will provide?

- What are your fees for learning these new songs? Hourly? By the song? Flat fee?
- What will you be wearing to the ceremony?
- How many weddings will you be working that day? What is the time period allotted between them?
- Do you offer a contract for our working agreement?

Of course, you should always audition musicians in person. An audio or videotape just doesn't cut it when your guests will be hearing live music on your wedding day. If possible, ask your ceremony site manager or officiant if you can use the church or synagogue one weeknight evening to audition your musical acts. The acoustics of the site may affect the sound of the performance, and it's best to get a feel for how the music "works the room." One couple decided at such an audition that the music of a single flute just wasn't enough sound for them, so they changed to a Spanish guitarist to match the Spanish style of the cathedral where they were to marry.

Devote careful time to finding, interviewing, and auditioning your musicians, so that you get a flawless performance on your wed-

Wedding Day Reflections

We hired our local high school's chamber singers for our ceremony, for just a $150 donation to their fund-raising drive. Thrilled at the low cost, we added their marching band's award-winning trumpet soloist to announce our arrival. It was a big savings, it made our ceremony more musical, and since we both went to that high school, it was a nice personal touch for us to incorporate a little of our history together.

—Daniela and Paul

ding day. Ask your musicians to play the songs you'd like to hear during your wedding, and judge them on a level playing field.

While professional musicians are always the best choice in terms of value and quality of performance, your budget might not allow for a pro's higher fees. In this case, why not hire a music student to play on your Big Day? You can find great performers at a nearby college's music department. These students appreciate getting the extra experience, exposure, and pocket money, and the best of them possess talents that rival the professionals. Call your local college, or even high school, and ask the music director if he or she can recommend a talented violinist, cellist, pianist, vocalist, or other type of musician. This option might save you 50% to 60% of what you would pay a professional.

Another great idea for finding an affordable and talented musician is to hire a friend or a member of the family. If your cousin is bound for the San Francisco Symphony Orchestra in the fall, why not ask him to play a song at your wedding as his gift to you? If your niece is an aspiring singer with true talent, invite her to sing a few songs as the guests arrive. This is another lovely way to include your loved ones in the wedding, and it also saves them having to buy you an expensive wedding gift!

Post-Ceremony Flourishes

After your ceremony and photography sessions, you'll dash out through the crowd of happy well wishers to your waiting car.

Tradition still maintains that the bride and groom are showered—okay, pelted—by some variation of birdseed, confetti, or rose petals. Since you'll have to supply your guests with the chosen toss-it—*as okayed ahead of time by your ceremony site!*—think ahead to the cost of these little items. Sure, a box of birdseed is going to be inexpensive, but you might not want to get these tiny missiles down the front of your dress or stuck in your hair for the rest of the night. That said, think about the wealth of post-ceremony toss-it options out there today. No doubt you've seen those great little bottles of wedding bubbles, and that might be your choice for your day. Or, you might choose to have your guests ring little bells with their good wishes, rather than throw anything at you.

Whatever you choose, be sure to look in the right place for your supplies. Some of the major wedding Web sites advertise "great rates" on wedding bubble bottles or tulle-wrapped birdseed packets, but you can do better than that price-wise. I visited several craft stores, including Michaels and Treasure Island, and I found great prices for wedding bubble bottles and bells. On another shopping trip, I happened upon a dollar store, where I found the same lower prices.

The key to more affordable toss-its is your willingness to do some of the work on your own. Have some fun flexing your creative muscles by making your toss-its from scratch. Ask your mother and your bridal party over for some wine and cheese and then sit down as a group to assemble little birdseed pouches from squares of tulle tied with a pretty ribbon in your wedding's colors. If you have a great

Or . . . Don't Spend a Dime on Toss-Its!

You don't have to have the birdseed, the bubbles, or the bells as you run for cover to your limousine. In fact, some sites don't allow toss-its at all. As a replacement, try these free post-ceremony flourishes:

Have your flower girl hand out cards instructing the guests to serenade you with a chosen song as you pass by.

Have your bridal party start a big round of applause for you.

Have your bridal party start a rousing chant, such as your names.

Ask to have the church bells or carillon played for your departure.

source for tiny plastic bottles bought in bulk, then buy a dozen or so inexpensive containers of bubble solution and fill those tiny bottles with a matching pastel-colored solution. Add a pretty ribbon bow or label the bottles with personalized stickers made on your home computer. The creative options here are endless, and you can have a lot of fun putting these little packets together for your guests. You can save anywhere from 15% to 30% off the cost of ready-made toss-its from a catalog or Web site.

Birds and Butterflies

The release of doves or butterflies is a beautiful flourish at the end of a wedding ceremony. For some brides, it may be the one dream image they allowed room for in their budgets. Check carefully with your wedding site for permission to release live animals before you start researching companies. Many sites do not allow such releases for both practical and belief reasons. For instance, environmentalists do say that it's a bad idea to release butterflies in a region where they cannot survive. Other groups warn against dove releases in areas where there is a lot of airport traffic overhead.

Research local companies well, and provide them with the information *they* will need to suit your order. Most dove release companies will not let their birds fly in sunset hours, as the birds need daylight to find their way home. There are many considerations to take into mind when thinking about live bird or butterfly releases at your wedding, so ask plenty of questions of the companies you contact.

Additional Money-Saving Tips

• Research the religious elements of your ceremony on your own, in the library, or on the Internet. Don't pay a $75 religious adviser's fee to explain the rituals to you.

• Get your own copies of your divorce decree, late spouse's death certificate, or other documents. Don't pay the house of worship to send for these papers at a fee. Often, you can secure notarized copies of your own documents for a nominal fee, or even for free at establishments like your own bank.

• Limit the number of songs performed by the musicians. Not only will this help your budget, but it also makes your ceremony shorter and more comfortable for your guests.

• Make or borrow a ring pillow or chuppah for use during your ceremony.

• Ask if your house of worship will allow you to borrow one of their chuppahs, aisle runners, or other common wedding supplies.

• Shop in a craft store for a pretty candle that will work as a unity candle. Don't pay high prices for an ornate bridal unity candle at a bridal shop or Web site. A plain white pillar candle can be jazzed up with faux-pearl pushpins and other accoutrements as found in a craft store.

• Use your favors in place of toss-its. No, I don't mean allowing your guests to throw Godiva chocolates at you. Instead, have an honor attendant hand out little engraved bells for your guests to ring festively at your departure and then take home as keepsakes.

Planning the Reception

Smart Budget Moves for a Stylish Celebration

I F YOU'RE like most brides, you've allocated a significant chunk of your budget to making your reception something very special. On the average, couples devote anywhere from 22% to 45% of their budgets to the celebration event, wanting to thrill their guests with a party to remember. Even though you're on a budget, you too can create the reception of your dreams by prioritizing your funds to get more reception for your money. By following the cost-effective planning ideas in this chapter, you can make your reception *look and feel* as if you didn't have a budget at all.

These ideas will help you make the smartest use of your money, leading you through the many decisions and creative options you'll encounter in planning your celebration. My favorite experts have lent their professional opinions for your use, and couples from all over the country share their own success stories as well. You're planning the party of your lifetime, so let's get started setting the foundation and then fulfilling the dream elements of your perfect wedding.

What Do You Want?

Of course, your first step is naturally going to be a brainstorming session to decide what you want your dream reception to look like. Do you want an elegant cocktail party for your informal event? Or do you want the cocktail party, the sit-down dinner, four hours of dancing, and then a jaw-droppingly gorgeous cake wheeled out to the oohs and aahs of your guests? Do you want white-gloved butlers strolling about, offering crudités on silver platters and then snifters of Grand Marnier after the meal? How formal do you want your reception to be? These decisions— these visions—determine the style and type of your ceremony plans, so that you can find the right professionals to make it happen. Not only do you need a plan at the outset, but you also need a backup plan in case your dreams don't fit realistically within your budget.

The initial "what do we want?" discussion is so crucial for planning your reception. Matching your much-wished-for elements to the style and formality of your wedding will help you fit your dream reception to your budget and give you a great advantage when you approach your vendors. Couples with a solid idea of what they want are less tempted to spend more on their receptions than couples who walk into a caterer's office with blank slates and no set boundaries to their plans. Clearly, knowing what you want saves you time, money, and frustration down the road.

Use this section to record your wished-for reception elements, allowing yourself some flexibility throughout the process. You may find as the process rolls on that your priorities will shift as the true prices come in.

Again, this worksheet is just to get your thought process running and some of your highest priorities set on paper. Your caterer or banquet hall manager will make great use of these lists to help design the right menu for your budget and for the style of your party. The key at this point, of course, is to find the ideal caterer who's best suited to take your wishes, your money, and her own talents and resources,

Worksheet: Reception Food

What we want for the cocktail hour (for example, passed hors d'oeuvres; ten-item buffet; open bar vs. passed glasses of champagne or wine, etc.):

What we want for the sit-down dinner (for example, four courses; no salad course; one meat entrée and one fish entrée; no sit-down dinner at all— we want a five-hour cocktail party buffet and that's it, etc.):

What we want for beverages (for example, open bar with full stock; just wine; beer and soft drinks; limited specialty drinks like martinis and vodka tonics; we'll supply our own liquor, etc.):

What we want for the cake and dessert (for example, three-tiered cake simply decorated with fresh flowers; smaller decorated cake; Grandma's making the cake; full Viennese table and the cake; just cake and chocolate-covered strawberries, etc.):

Additions to our reception menu (for example, ethnic foods; child-appropriate menu option; no ice sculpture; have leftover food donated to homeless shelter in town, etc.):

Important menu restrictions (for example, vegetarian options; sugar-free options; kosher options; etc.):

mix them all together, and present the reception menu of your dreams. . . .

Finding Your Ideal Caterer

So where do you find the menu designer who's going to be the answer to your prayers? Your reception hall may have its own staff of caterers, chosen for their years of experience, expertise, and perhaps even award-winning service. These pros will sit down with you and help you devise an award-winning menu of your own. In many cases, reception halls, banquet halls, country clubs, even restaurants do use their own catering staffs for the entire meal, including the cake. So ask your reception site manager about the caterer's experience, style, and knowledge of any special menu requirements you may have. And set up an appointment to talk with the chef.

If your site does not have its own catering staff, you'll have to seek out a qualified professional to work your event. The site may have a list of qualified caterers whom they favor. Ask recently married friends whose caterers did a magnificent job on their wedding for a referral and any inside scoop on what it was like to work with that vendor. Sure, those mini-lobster quiches may have been the highlight of the party and the talk of guests for months afterwards, but few guests if any would have heard about the chef's demanding and unreliable behavior throughout the process. Don't just judge by what you saw or tasted at your friend's wedding. Ask for the *real* story.

If you have no references to go by, then start your search with a source far more reliable than those big ads in the Yellow Pages or flashy Web sites on the Internet. Contact the National Association of Catering Executives (847-480-9080, www.nace.net) for qualified members in your area. As you know, membership in a professional association can mean that your vendor is well-screened, well-trained, and possesses years of experience with weddings and events similar to yours. If your wedding will be smaller, you may opt to hire a personal chef, found through the prestigious national association Personal Chef (www.personalchef.com, 800-644-8389). A personal chef might be just the expert to provide all of the appetizers and entrées for your event.

Another option is to ask your personal network of friends, family, and colleagues for any recommendations they'd like to hand along. One couple reported that they found their perfect catering candidates through a colleague who regularly planned the office Christmas party. Her years of experience putting that bash together led her to establish great contacts among very talented but little-known caterers in town.

While I always recommend that you hire an experienced professional for an event as important as yours, you might want to try your luck with a beginner. Check with culinary institutes in your area for the names of any soon-to-graduate chefs or cooking students who could use your great event as a portfolio builder. These beginners love testing their skills, and they're often every bit as talented and highly trained as longtime experts with staffs of their own. If you choose a beginner, be sure to interview well, taste-test their offerings (as you should with any cooking expert), and judge whether or not you think this beginner can handle a party of your magnitude. This option might be best if your guest list is small and you want a standard menu—this means less pressure on your student chef and not as much risk to you.

When interviewing caterers, remember that you're looking for more than just cooking skills. Just like with your coordinator and other vendors for your day, you'll need to judge your prospects according to how professional they are, how willing they are to listen to you and incorporate your ideas whenever possible, how quickly they return your calls, and how well they present themselves as well as their dishes. This professional will be your partner, and you're entrusting a large responsibility to him. So be sure you've spent the time and energy to select the right caterer for you.

Questions to Ask Your Potential Caterers

For *any* caterer, cake baker, or other professional who will contribute the food to your wedding, always conduct a detailed interview, a taste test, and a viewing of their previous wedding spreads. This is one of the most important vendors you will hire, the one whose work will be the most evident to your guests, and the one who can literally make or break your wedding. So ask the following questions and judge your prospective caterers well.

1. Do you belong to a professional association?
2. At which culinary institute did you receive your degree or certification?
3. For how many years have you been a caterer?
4. How many wedding receptions have you catered?
5. Do you have much experience with a wedding of our size or style?
6. How many weddings will you be catering on the weekend of our wedding?
7. Do you have any other weddings to cater on our scheduled wedding day?
8. Can you provide the types and styles of food that we desire?
9. Do you have a fixed menu, or are you willing to add new dishes to a menu according to our requests?
10. Do you specialize in any types of menus or ethnic cuisine?
11. Do you charge extra to bring your own cooking equipment to the site?
12. Do we need to rent any extra tables or items for your use?
13. Which serving items do you provide as part of your package and which will we need to rent for our guests' use? (i.e. serving tongs, platters, heating trays, etc.— don't just assume that the caterer automatically brings these types of items).
14. How many assistants and servers will you provide on the wedding day? (As a general rule, you should expect one waiter per fifteen to twenty guests for a seated dinner reception, and one waiter per twenty-five guests for a cocktail reception or buffet.)
15. How much time will you need to set up at the wedding site, and how much time will you need to clean up afterward?

16. Do you offer a refund or cancellation clause in your contract?

17. Do you have insurance?

18. Can we come in and sample your menu offerings? (Please remember to sample two or three items from each course, to get a solid feel for the caterer's skills.)

19. Can we visit one of your actual wedding setups to view the presentation on site?

20. Can we see pictures or a portfolio of some of your buffet or food presentations?

21. Can we review your standard list of per-guest consumption for each item on our menu, or each item you will provide for our use? (Important—you'll need to know if the caterer has estimated that your guests will eat an average of three shrimp cocktails each. Ask her about her estimation rules, and see if you can negotiate larger or smaller amounts according to what *you* believe your guests are likely to consume.)

22. Can you provide letters of referral from satisfied clients?

23. Will you view the site ahead of time in order for us to discuss your needs on the wedding day?

24. Do you take on the responsibility of setting up the buffet dishes or other items, or will we have to arrange for site staff to do that?

25. What are your fees, including extra fees or overtime?

26. What kinds of packages do you offer in our price range?

27. Do you guarantee these prices as written in the contract? (Be sure to confirm this one, especially if you book a year ahead. Many brides and grooms find themselves subject to price raises a year later . . . and the contract included wording that allowed them to do it! Make sure you stipulate in writing that this price is guaranteed.)

28. Are gratuities for yourself and your staff included in the package deal, or do we have to tip your staff individually?

29. Are gratuities figured before or after taxes?

30. Please itemize your labor costs. (Labor costs are included as a percentage of the catering fee. Ask to have these labor costs explained, as in "these costs apply to my staff's setup, serving, cleanup," etc.)

(continues)

31. Do you receive a commission from the site or from any other wedding professionals you recommend to us?

32. Will you be present at our wedding reception to oversee the serving?

33. What will you and your staff be wearing?

34. Please describe your staff. (Important! Ask the caterer if her staff is comprised of apprentice caterers or apprentice wedding coordinators who have experience in the event industry, or has the caterer hired high school students at a lower wage and with little or no training? The servers and catering staff are crucial to your day as they interact with your guests, handing out hors d'oeuvres and clearing plates efficiently during the cocktail hour. A quality caterer has a well-trained staff.)

35. When is our final guest head-count due?

The Chat with Your Caterer

Once you choose the best professional for your day, it's time to sit down and devise your reception menu. Schedule a consultation that includes a full-disclosure conversation during which you share with your caterer your wish list from page 179, show him or her a picture of your reception site (if he or she can't travel to the site in person), discuss the formality of your event, provide a picture of your gown, and talk about the menu options you have in mind. With this information, your caterer will get the all-important feel for the kind of reception you want, which options suit your visions, and which decisions need to be made from the outset.

At this point, you will remind the caterer of your budget limitations and your need for the best expertise in creating wonderful menu choices and serving station setups with price in mind. A quality caterer knows just how to stretch a budget and still impress your guests. This discussion may bring you some rude awakenings, however. Many of the couples I spoke to said their jaws practically hit the floor when they selected menus according to itemized price lists. Their original plans for twelve different passed hors d'oeuvres had a much larger price tag than expected, and they were forced to cut down to eight menu options. While this exposure to true dollar amounts is never the most enjoyable part of planning, it is important that you rein in your expectations and do the best you can with your budget.

I spoke to several catering managers and chefs, and they shared the following Budget-Stretching Rules for your reception menu:

For the Cocktail Hour

• Skip the buffet table and have the waiters pass the hors d'oeuvres. Most caterers agree that this limits the amount of food consumed by guests, resulting in a lower per-person price for this portion of the event.

• Choose fewer hors d'oeuvres. Serving eight wonderful options rather than twelve can cut your costs by 10%.

• Get creative with hors d'oeuvres. Look over the caterer's menu options and choose more affordable items. Vegetable and cheese mini-quiches might cost less than crabmeat miniquiches, for instance.

• Skip the raw bar. Ravenous wedding guests often wolf down oysters, shrimp, clams, and crab legs. Save the more inexpensive sea-food for the entrée or for accents at pasta serving stations.

• Skip the cheese tray at the cocktail party. Very often, this tray is one of the biggest leftovers at any affair. (Plus, many people are hesi-tant to eat cheese that's been left out for four or five hours.)

• Have fewer food stations at the cocktail hour. Your guests don't need to eat *that* much before the actual meal.

• Stick with pasta or seafood stations, which are less expensive than carved meat stations. Your caterer can certainly suggest wonder-ful, unique recipes for pasta/seafood or even ethnic dishes at this time of the party.

• Buy the appetizers yourself! Hire a caterer only for the preparation and serving of the entrées, while you find great savings on appetizers at a discount food store.

• Choose less elaborate presentations for appetizers. Don't pay more just to have your shrimp cocktail attached to a heart-shaped frame. Just dump the shrimp into a bowl and garnish with greens and lemon slices.

• Negotiate to have server's fees removed or lowered from your package. While it can be a savings to have those hors d'oeuvres passed butler style, you might get socked with a server fee that erases any savings! Ask if this fee can be counted as part of the labor fees in general.

For the Entrées:

• Create combination platters. Instead of filet mignon or lobster tails, provide three grilled jumbo shrimp and a few flavorful beef medallions. Guests love having *both* options, instead of one.

• Select in-season seafood. Depending upon where you live, various seafood options are available at lower prices at certain times of the year . . . particularly if you live near a location where fish and shellfish are caught. A friend of mine says he can buy large lobsters for a pittance right off the trawling boats at the harbor in Providence, Rhode Island! At market, seafood is always subject to going rates for the time of year, weather conditions, and the economy, but your caterer will be able to advise you right up until a few days before the wedding as to the most economical and impressive choices for your meal.

• Consider a meat dish other than prime rib or filet mignon, for a savings and as a new taste for your guests. Try a loin chop, a pork dish, a lamb chop, even ostrich or buffalo for some new flavor. Australian lamb is the new hot flavor for wedding menus, so ask your caterer for different meat ideas.

- Limit the meat dishes. Your vegetarian, vegan, and health-conscious guests will love you for the meatless lasagna, seafood, and vegetable dishes. The savings could round up to 15% off per guest.

- Skip a course. Many formal weddings include an appetizer, salad, soup, pasta, entrée, and dessert, all coming *after* the cocktail hour! If it looks like the food options are too plentiful, ask your caterer to skip one or two courses. All you really need after your guests have scarfed down their hors d'oeuvres at the cocktail party is a salad or small pasta appetizer, the entrée, and desserts. Again, skipping some courses could shave 10% to 20% off your catering bill.

- Serve smaller portions. Ask your caterer to show you a presentation by size of the courses you've selected. If that plate of baked ziti is enough to feed a linebacker, ask the caterer to provide half portions of that course. If a ten-ounce cut of meat costs too much, try an eight-ounce or a six-ounce portion.

- Consider the prices of ethnic selections. Ask your caterer if you can provide your own ethnic specialties, rather than have her make the pierogies or bratwurst. Very often, you can find more affordable food through an ethnic association or specialty food store.

- Negotiate lower prices for kids' meals. Your caterer may allow you to pay significantly less for ten children's meals, rather than have you pay the standard $50 per-guest price for kids who are only going to munch on carrot sticks and mashed potatoes.

- Negotiate lower prices per person for the vendors you'll be feeding. Your photographer, videographer, and entertainers won't partake in the cocktail hour, for instance, so why pay the full $50 per head as if they were guests? Ask instead for a special meal, or just the appetizer and entrée, to be served to your vendor guests. You might save up to 40% for each of these people.

• Don't assume that a buffet is cheaper. Just as with the appetizers, portion control through specific serving sizes can save you a fortune.

Sample Menus

Three-Hour Cocktail Party at Four-Star Hotel

Hors d'Oeuvres

Salmon mousse on toast points

Crab tarts with dill sauce

Fruit platter with dipping sauces

Food Stations

International cheese platter with bread and cracker selection

Vegetable crudités

Spring rolls

Cold pasta station

Carving station with sirloin or ham

Open bar with premium liquors, beer, wine, and soft drinks

$80 per person

Five-Hour Full Reception at Four-Star Hotel

Hors d'Oeuvres

Melon with prosciutto

Crab tartlets

Bacon-wrapped scallops

Potato puffs

Shrimp cocktail

Cheese display

Sushi display

Fruit platter

Food Stations

Marinated vegetable station

Hot hors d'oeuvres

Carving station with beef tenderloin, honey-glazed ham,
   or beef sirloin

Dinner

Mesclun salad or Caesar salad

Tri-style ravioli

Stuffed chicken breast

Salmon fillet, flounder française, or filet mignon

Open bar

Dessert

Wedding cake and Viennese table

$110 per person

Cocktail Hour Reception at Restaurant's Party Room

Passed Hors d'Oeuvres

Shrimp cocktail

Cheese tartlets

Cucumber-stuffed endive

Marinated beef strips on miniskewers

Mini vegetable quiches
Cheese and fruit display with breads and crackers

Food Stations

Pasta station
Salad station
Seafood station with grilled shrimp, grilled scallops, clams oreganato
Open bar for four hours

Dessert

Cake and one dessert option

$45 per person

Full Dinner Reception at Restaurant's Party Room

Passed Hors d'Oeuvres

Shrimp cocktail
Cheese tartlets
Cucumber-stuffed endive
Marinated beef strips on miniskewers
Mini vegetable quiches
Cheese and fruit display with breads and crackers

Food Stations

Pasta station
Salad station
Seafood station with grilled shrimp, grilled scallops, clams oreganato

Dinner

Pasta appetizer

Stuffed flounder, chicken marsala, or beef sirloin tips and
grilled shrimp combo platter

Open bar for five hours

Dessert

Cake and chocolate-covered strawberries

$65 per person

At-Home Informal Cocktail Party

Buffet-Style Appetizer Lineup

Crostini with marinated tomatoes

Mini cheese, vegetable, and seafood quiches

Minimeatballs

Shrimp cocktail

Mini-Reubens

Potato pierogies

Salad

Marinated vegetable antipasto with garlic bread

Cheese spread and cracker display at the bar

Liquor bought at wholesale distributor

Dessert

Wedding cake

$40 per person

Clearly, you can plan an extravagant menu for your day, or you can choose more economical options. If you have a smaller guest list, you might choose to include more lofty menu choices at your celebration. A $75-per-head expense isn't so bad when you only have twenty or so guests to feed. If your wedding will be larger, then aim for menu choices that will lower your per-guest expense. Your caterer will guide you through menu-by-price considerations, so that your reception expenses remain grounded.

The Dessert-Only Reception

This is a popular trend for couples on a budget. Rather than spend $20,000 on a full-blown reception, some couples choose to skip the fanfare and host a more intimate, casual gathering of their friends and family. At this event, far different from the average wedding, guests are served fine champagne and a selection of wedding cake and desserts. One couple I spoke to smiled from ear to ear when they reported that their elegant dessert-only reception cost them only $12 per guest.

Think You Can Do Better?

Brides and grooms with lots of helpful assistants (think: parents, bridesmaids, and family members) can often beat the prices of caterers by purchasing and preparing the wedding meal on their own. Of course, you'll give up the convenience of having someone on site do all the cooking, stand by a hot oven, and coordinate the servers to get all that food out while it's hot. Fortunately, many families are willing to help out. Mothers and fathers are willing to spend an hour or so in the kitchen if it means their little girl will be able to afford more of the wedding of her dreams.

If you're willing to go the do-it-yourself route with the menu, consider the following tips:

• Shop for your appetizers and menu options at a discount or wholesale bulk food store. For instance, I found great party platters at

Costco and Sam's Club for low prices . . . and I know from experience that their catering trays are always delicious. To find warehouse stores near you, check out Costco (www.costco .com), Sam's Club (www.samsclub.com), and BJ's Wholesalers (www .bjswholesale.com). It might be worth a short ride to another town when you see the savings available at these superstores.

• Plan your menu around inexpensive food choices, such as chicken, pasta, and in-season seafood for even greater savings.

• Use recipes you know and love, rather than take risks with an untried recipe.

• If you have plenty of time and want to try some new recipes, check great new cookbooks you find in the library, or try out the recipes listed on the Food Network's complete Web site at www.foodtv.com. Your Cajun wedding reception will be a blast when you serve Emeril's recipes!

• Include several cold dishes in your offerings, to ease the pressure on whoever's in charge of getting food out of the oven and served hot to your guests.

• Comparison-shop among great food sources like the local Italian deli in town. I found lower per-person prices at my hometown pizza place than with the caterer I researched.

• Check out your supermarket's catering department. At a Super Foodtown, I found great catering trays and even a fabulous baked goods at reasonable prices.

> ## Wedding Day Reflections
>
> We're not the partying type, so we didn't want the five-hour bash and all the expenses that went along with it. To us, what was important was the ceremony and having all of our friends and family with us to witness it. We didn't need music, we didn't need to do the Macarena. We just wanted to celebrate quietly. So, we bought great champagne and stocked a Viennese table with incredible desserts. Our guests loved it, because it was something different from what they were used to.
> —Linnae and Tom

• Garnish your platters of hot appetizers with sprigs of parsley, rosemary, lemon and lime slices, pimientos, or other colorful foods. These decorative accents make your platters look more professional.

• Place potted plants and flowers on your buffet table to fill in blank spaces and make the offerings look more plentiful.

• Copy the presentation tips at restaurants and hotels: Place your platters on several different levels, held up by platforms or pedestals for a more attractive look.

• Finally, reward your volunteer cooking staff with a nice gift or a bottle of wine at the end of the reception and pay them tribute at the wedding with a toast or a song dedicated to them. (If you don't want your guests to be "in the know" about your home-cooked meal, then just thank your volunteers for "helping to create our day.")

Would You Like Something to Drink?

Your beverage tab is another big portion of your reception expenses, and it's also a place where you can find great savings with the right decisions and right resources. Many established reception sites and hotels do offer an open bar with your choice of premium liquors or a more limited selection of drinks, and they remain in control of the price per bottle. At your reception site, ask about the types of liquors available, the vintages chosen, even the number of bottles opened. One of the most colossal wastes of money at any reception is when the bar staff opens too many bottles of wine or other liquors, and at the end of the night, even though they weren't used, you still have to pay for them. On your dime, the wait staff might be sipping your Chardonnay and gulping down the cheese platter after the party ends.

Clearly, you can save a bundle by talking with the reception manager, caterer, or bartender to establish clear guidelines on the liquors you'll stock at your bar. Take a look at their itemized order list, ask them to explain their estimates of how much each guest is likely to drink (they have it down to a science), and state your preferences for the uncorking of bottles of wine. Most couples request that bottles be opened on a need-only basis and that they not be charged for all unopened bottles. This keeps the "corkage fees" to a minimum.

Your first concern might be which kinds of drinks to offer. Many open bar arrangements do allow for unlimited use of premium or top-shelf liquors, several different kinds of wines, soft drinks and fruit drinks for mixes, and bottled water. Don't just accept a site's stated list of liquor in supply; ask to have some say in what's offered and what's not. One couple saved a fortune and prevented misbehavior by their younger guests by instructing their bartenders not to serve shots of hard liquor. Mixed drinks were fine, but no shots. Their theory was to stop their younger guests downing shot after shot of vodka or tequila and get them to slow down their pace with larger, mixed drinks. Their strategy worked and earned them a lower bar tab and more in-control guests.

One of the smartest things you can do before you sit down with the bartender or reception hall manager is to learn a bit about the price ranges of liquors, wines, and champagnes. You don't need to take an expensive wine-tasting course to find out the real price

Wedding Day Reflections

*F*riends of ours were recently married, and we learned from them that we have to watch the bartenders carefully on the corkage-fee thing. Our friends lost a bundle when the site manager showed them ten uncorked and unused bottles of wine standing behind the bar at the end of the night. We learned from them, and we stated upfront to our reception manager, that we didn't want bottles opened en masse ahead of time, and we wanted the bartender to stop opening bottles an hour prior to the end of our reception. That limited any waste, as our guests chose to finish off that bottle of Merlot rather than open another Pinot Grigio. We asked one of our ushers to serve as "bottle-master," checking to see that the bartender was fulfilling his promises, and we saved about $100 at the end of the night by avoiding alcohol waste.

—Tamara and Charles

range for a good California Chablis or a good Riesling. Just visit www.winespectator.com for a complete primer on wines, champagnes, and liquors; view some reviews and price ranges; and even receive updated lists of the best-rated vintages around. You might find some great suggestions for tasty fumé blancs under $15 per bottle, with your guests being none the wiser on the actual price.

Once you have your lists in hand, see if the reception hall manager can order some of your chosen vintages as replacements for his list. In some cases, the site may allow you to bring in your own supply of liquor rather than use their stock. This can add up to some great savings if you go about it the right way. Ask your bartender for an outline of how much liquor you'll need for your guest list and then seek out great choices and great prices at a discount liquor store or wholesale liquor supplier. Buying in bulk may net you even greater savings. This is a great job for the bridal party to help out with, as you'll certainly need the extra bodies to carry those cases of wine and liquor into your reception site.

> ## Simplify It
>
> You won't want to ruin your wedding by offering your guests wines that taste like the $5 you spent on them. So, test out those great suggestions from Wine Spectator at a casual wine-and-cheese party with your bridal attendants a few months before the wedding. Have your maids and ushers rate their favorite choices, and choose the winners to be served at your wedding.

CHOOSING ECONOMICAL BUT PLEASING BEVERAGES

I spoke to several wine merchants and liquor suppliers for their top tips on choosing more economical, but still pleasing, beverage options for weddings on a budget. Here are their responses:

• Serve top-shelf liquors at the beginning of the evening and then serve call bar, or less prestigious, liquors the rest of the night. "Your guests won't be able to taste the difference once they have a few good drinks in them."

• Limit the menu of drinks, offering only a few top-shelf liquors such as vodka, gin, and rum, and only a few selections of white and red wines.

• Put a restriction on the types of mixed drinks your bartender will prepare. Drinks such as Long Island Iced Teas and Cosmopolitans use more liquor than most choices, so leave them off the drink menu. Print up a list of drinks the bartender will make, such as martinis, gin and tonics, and the like.

• Find great-tasting yet inexpensive wine vintages during a thorough search at your liquor store. A well-trained wine expert can help you find the best choices at a discount.

• Offer microbrew beers instead of big-name imports and watery domestics.

• Serve after-dinner drinks by way of a strolling waiter in tuxedo, who pours the cognac or Grand Marnier right from the bottle with a white-gloved hand.

• Limit your international coffee bar to include only espresso, cappuccino, and standard coffee. Eliminating the more exotic Chai teas and Jamaican and Irish coffees will cut down on your supply expenses.

• Offer a wide supply of nonalcoholic drinks for your teetotaler friends, underage guests, and children.

• Close the bar during dinner, and close it for good an hour or two before the end of the reception, while the coffee is served.

• Be sure your site has a liquor license before you stock up on wines, beers, and champagnes! Double-check so your purchases don't go to waste.

• Have a nonalcoholic reception. Some couples choose a liquor-free reception if they have major budget concerns, religious beliefs, or

No Line at the Bar

We're having our wedding at an inexpensive hall, and we'll have to hire our own bartenders. What's the rule for how many bartenders we'll need?

Ideally, you'll be well-served by hiring one bartender per seventy-five guests. If your guest list reaches 100, it would be best to hire two bartenders to keep the drinks flowing well and your guests from having to wait in a long line.

they're supporting a relative who has stopped drinking. In place of liquor, provide pretty punches and soft drinks.

• Skip the champagne. Guests can toast you with whatever drink they have in their hands.

Most weddings do have open bars, as it is an insult and very tacky to make your guests pay at a cash bar at your reception. It's also an insult to expect your guests to tip the bartenders. Tell your bar staff ahead of time that they are *not* to set out a brandy snifter stuffed with dollar bills as a hint to your guests that they need to fork over a buck for every drink. Assure the staff that you will tip them at the end of the night, and be generous if the bartenders have done their jobs well.

Your Wedding Cake . . . and More!

Few jobs within the wedding planning process are as much fun as this one. Scouting out cake bakers, flipping through their glossy pages of masterpiece confections, and tasting little samples of wedding cake to find the right flavors has to be one of the most enjoyable parts of the process. The prices, though, can make all that sticky sweet icing sink to the bottom of your stomach.

Wedding cakes are big business these days, with some bakers charging $1,000 or more for the most beautiful of cake designs. The most lovely, architecturally sound cakes piped to lacy perfection can cost more than your first car. So read up here before you fall in love with a true piece of wedding cake art and find out how to buy the wedding cake of your dreams for less.

Finding the Right Baker

The right cake baker can make a world of difference in the appearance, taste, and cost of your cake. So invest some time in scouting out the best cake baker for you. You might choose to hire the professional at the bakery where your family has gone for special family cakes for years. You know they make great desserts, so you trust them to create the cake of your dreams. I encourage you to add this well-known professional to your list of contenders, subjecting this baker to the same kind of interview process you'll use for other bakers. After all, making a wedding cake is an art of its own, and even though you know your favorite bakery makes a mean French roll and a cannoli to die for, you'll need to be sure that their wedding cake will meet the high standards you expect for a purchase of this magnitude. Your other contenders might come from recommendations from recently married friends, your coordinator, and recent wedding guests who rave about a cake they've just enjoyed at one of *their* friend's weddings. Just ask for a referral to the baker in question.

It's All in the Effort

Those structured wedding cakes with four balancing layers and miles of piped-on icing in intricate patterns always cost more than a pretty, stacked cake with pristine white frosting and fresh flowers as décor. With cakes, you will always pay more for the amount of time and

Questions to Ask Your Baker

- How long have you been in business?
- How many wedding cakes have you made?
- Can we view pictures of your wedding cakes to select our design?
- Can we schedule a sample tasting of your cake flavors and fillings?
- Which flavors, fillings, and icings can we choose from?
- Can we order a cake with different flavors and fillings on each level?
- How many wedding cakes will you be making during the week of our wedding?
- Do you make your cakes fresh, or do you use frozen sections?
- Will you decorate the cake using fresh flowers, or does the florist have to do that?
- Will you deliver our cake to the reception site?
- What is your delivery fee?
- May we see a copy of your contract?
- Do you have insurance?
- Do you have a current, valid license? (Ask to see a copy.)
- What is your cancellation/refund policy?

effort your baker spends on the design. So keep your choice simple and elegant, pass up those rolled fondant covers and the sugar-paste, hand-rolled flowers and cherubs. Your guests will be just as thrilled by the sight of your beautiful cake cascading with flowers as they will at a cake that looks like the Taj Mahal. Keep it simple, and your price tag will be simpler as well.

You might want to reconsider offering a wedding cake whose tiers balance on pedestals. These designs can cost more, and they're trickier for shipment, arrangement, and stability throughout the reception . . . especially if yours is an outdoor reception where rising temperatures could cause melting and tipping of your cake. Choose instead to have the layers rest directly on top of one another for a more sound structure.

Since the greatest expense with wedding cakes is the time it takes to decorate them, why not order a plain round or sheet cake and do the decorating yourself? Some brides do have the time and talent to actually bake the cake on their own or have a relative do it, but I find that it's not too much of an expense to get a professionally made sheet cake and do the labor-intensive accents yourself for far, far less. If you'd like to decorate your own wedding cake, at a savings of up to 50% depending upon your choices, you have several options:

• Visit a florist to find out which fresh flowers are safe to use as décor on wedding cakes. Then place an order for a selection of fresh flowers to be picked up and arranged on the cake on the day of the wedding.

• Take a cake-decorating course at a local adult night school or culinary school to learn how to pipe sugar-frosting accents onto your cake, create lovely flowers or pearl drop designs, and master other decorating methods.

• Ask a friend with proven cake-decorating skills to perform her artistry on your cake as her wedding gift to you.

It's What's Inside That Counts

When you order your wedding cake, ask the baker for his or her list of the different types of cake and fillings available. Couples today are making their wedding cakes extra special by choosing cannoli cream or chocolate mousse fillings, or almond-flavored cake instead of the standard white cake with strawberry filling. View price sheets for these options to be sure any extra expense for these choices is manageable.

And to Top It All Off . . .

Don't spend a fortune on your cake topper! Some of those pretty little bridal Web sites and bridal stores will show you figurines and other décor that can cost from $20 to $150! Skip the porcelain bride and groom dolls, and top your cake with fresh flowers, sugared fruits, seashells ($5 for a bag of twenty at a craft store!), or figurines you already own or can borrow from a parent or relative for free.

• Buy a cake decorating kit from a master and celebrity cake designer. Gail Watson Custom Cakes offers easy-to-use "Cake Kits" that offer a wide selection of prepared cake accents and design materials. Check out the supplies at www.gailwatsoncake.com.

• Forget the piped-sugar roses or rolled fondant sculptures and decorate a plain store-bought cake with thoroughly washed and dried objects that fit your wedding theme. Some ideas: seashells, mini conch shells, starfish, crystal wedding bells, porcelain figurines, and even flags from your country of heritage. These personal touches are very inexpensive and make great conversation pieces for your guests.

• Decorate a plain, store-bought cake with your favorite candies, chocolates, or even inexpensive chocolate-dipped fruit. The cost for this might be $20 to $40, rather than $100 and up (way up!) for a standard wedding cake.

LET THEM EAT CUPCAKES!

A hot trend at casual weddings is (surprising enough): cupcakes! I know, I wrinkled my brow when I first heard about this. It brought me back to the days of grammar school birthday parties at the roller rink and a box lined with foil holding a lineup of sprinkled cupcakes.

Things have evolved. The little cakes I've seen at fabulous backyard weddings—and as featured in the top style and wedding magazines—are adorable. You can top them off with a smooth, thick layer of scrumptious frosting and décor of fresh flowers or hand-sculpted sugar flowers or other shapes, sugared fruits, or even traditional candies. At one wedding I attended recently, the bride used a stencil and piped hers and the groom's initials with colored frosting on some cupcakes and sifted chocolate powder on others. The artistic effect was wonderful and so was the effect on her budget—$30 in total for all her baking needs, including that $2.50 stencil she used.

If you think cupcakes would work well for your informal wedding, practice putting the frosting on ahead of time. Your cupcakes shouldn't rest on top of one another, so save the decorations by experimenting with silver platters held above the serving table by pedestals of different heights. You might choose to use Styrofoam circles of differing diameters in order to frame out a wedding cake shape, with your cupcakes lining the outer circles and top in true wedding cake form. Or you might line your dessert buffet table with your wedding cupcakes all in a row. The choices are yours, so get creative!

The Groom's Cake

In some regions of the country, a groom's cake is always offered in addition to the traditional wedding cake. If a groom's cake is a must at your wedding, check different bakers for the best cake within your budget or ask a talented baker friend to do the honors for you. Especially if you have spent more on your wedding cake, a groom's cake makes a great wedding gift from a much-loved relative or friend.

Serving Charges

One thing I want to warn you about with regard to your cake is the equivalent of that corkage fee for your beverages. Some establishments actually *charge* you money to slice up and serve your wedding cake. I kid you not. The price might range from twenty-five cents to a few dollars per slice! If you see a cake-cutting service fee in your contract (see how important it is to read the fine print!) try your best to negotiate this fee right out of your agreement. After all, the staff is already getting a mandatory and perhaps included 18% gratuity. This extra charge for normal duty is just a rip-off!

ADDITIONAL DESSERT OPTIONS

You might not want to stop with wedding cake as the closer to your meal. Many couples choose an extravagant Viennese table filled with delectable cakes, pies, tarts, fruit flambées, mousses, and truffles in order to really impress their guests, please the taste buds, and cap off their event with a flourish. I attended one lavish wedding where the Viennese table had an entire room to itself, with a velvet curtain dramatically draped back to reveal a fifteen-foot-long table filled with every kind of dessert you can imagine. Of course, the bride's family spent close to half-a-million dollars on this wedding, so this presentation didn't shock me at all. On a budget, the same kind of display can be arranged, minus the velvet curtain.

Talk with your baker about the most economical choices for additional desserts. Most couples on a budget do skip the lineup of cakes, mousses, and anything set on fire before eating. You might choose to offer a simple bowl of big ripe strawberries dipped in chocolate, with a bowl of freshly whipped cream on the side. A tray of minipastries or truffles can also be a wonderful end to your meal. At an outdoor or informal wedding, why not provide an exotic fruit tray with a great presentation of pineapple, star fruit, kiwi, and berries as a healthier option to that white chocolate-frosted wedding cake with the chocolate mousse filling? It is possible to provide a second dessert option without too great a hit to your budget. Just talk to your baker and your caterer to discover ideas that might work for you.

Stop and Smell the Roses

Choosing Your Wedding Flowers for Less

So, WHAT do you have in mind for your wedding flowers? Are you picturing a beautiful, big bouquet just bursting with gardenias, lily of the valley, stephanotis, and tiny white rose buds? Would you like your maids to carry lovely pastel bouquets, and your mother to wear her favorite orchids as a corsage? Do you envision a sea of dramatic floral arrangements at your reception site, with a solitary white rose at each table setting? Indeed, your fairest wedding dreams may include such splendor, but the sobering reality is that wedding flowers and arrangements are *expensive*. Especially if you want that sea of floral arrangements and those pricey flowers in your bouquet.

Don't throw this book across the room with a frustrated, "I give up!" and a sorry vision of carrying a bouquet of flowers picked from alongside the highway. You *can* create a great floral look on a lower budget. You just have to know a bit about the business of horticulture and the art of bouquet and arrangement-making. This chapter will help you design your floral look for less and reveal little-known secrets for spending 50% to 60% less than you'd pay if you weren't wise enough to read this book.

Penny-Wise

*A*ccording to the Association of Bridal Consultants, the national average amount spent on floral pieces for the wedding day is between $200 and $500. A mere 2.5% of brides out there will spend over $2,000 for their flowers. You can laugh at them now.

As always, I encourage you to begin your floral design session by imagining what you'd like your wedding-day bouquets, centerpieces, and accents to look like. When you begin your search for a floral artist, it will help you tremendously to have your own limits in mind, so that you don't overspend when tempted by glossy portfolio images of bouquets you can't afford and never even dared to dream of. Arming yourself with a set vision and allowing for some flexibility with new knowledge you'll glean from a solid professional is the best way to stay on track and not walk out of the floral shop disappointed. Realistic expectations are the key to success.

Find the Right Floral Artists

Of course, it takes the right floral designer to make your arrangements, bouquets, and décor come out as lovely as possible. A quality professional will guide you through the planning process, point out budget-saving options, and plan your designs with allegiance to your floral allowance. These artists can work magic with the many varieties of flowers and greenery available to them, and your wedding as a result will be all the more beautiful.

To begin your search, ask recently married friends and relatives to recommend the florist who designed their wedding-day flora. You can even check with major hotels near you for their list of most-referred florists, as the event industry is very loyal to its own. Don't limit yourself to florists who advertise that they are wedding-day specialists, as a true floral expert will be well-versed in creating pieces for corporate, charity, and other nonwedding events. Check with either the Society of American Florists (703-836-8700, www .safnow.org) or the American Institute of Floral Design (410-752-3320, www .aifd.org). The recommendation of a local floral designer from either of these professional associations means the professional has a

Know Your Stuff!

Before you contact individual floral designers, be sure you're ready to provide the crucial information this person will need to help you design the perfect look for your wedding's style and budget. The details to provide are:

- The formality of your wedding
- The exact locations for your ceremony and reception. Your florist may have worked there before and thus have knowledge of the best designs for the rooms.
- The size of your wedding
- The size of your bridal party, including child attendants
- What your gown looks like. (Take a picture so the florist can design a style of bouquet that compliments the cut of your dress.)
- What your bridesmaids' gowns look like
- What your men will be wearing (some boutonnieres are more appropriate for certain kinds of lapels)
- The color scheme for your wedding
- The theme of your wedding, whether a beach wedding or English garden
- Your must-haves, such as gardenias in your bouquet or a special arrangement in memory of a departed loved one
- Your budget, so the designer knows the range of possibilities

top-notch reputation, years of experience, and continued training within the floral design field.

When you start calling florists, you can save a lot of time by asking right away if he or she will even take on a job at your budget level. Some of the more upscale, busier shops do state a budget minimum for weddings they will take on. So be clear at the outset that your wedding is going to be on a more moderate scale.

Always stop in at the shop to meet the designer in person, take a look at the condition of the store in general, view their designs as featured in the refrigerated cases, perhaps even view the design studio. Meet one-on-one with the florist you're considering and ask the same questions I have been suggesting you ask your other wedding vendors, so that you can get a true feel for how this person does business. When you meet the right designer for you, you'll know.

First, Know Something About Flowers

It will help tremendously if you learn, with your floral designer's help, a bit about the flowers you'll have to choose from. Some types of flowers are more expensive than others, depending on their rarity, the season, and whether or not they need to be imported. This kind of knowledge is crucial to the grand total of your floral expense. I spoke with Kimberly Aurora Kapur of RomanticFlowers.com about which flowers are less expensive at certain times of the year. Kimberly explained that the growing conditions and local availability of certain flowers varies depending upon regional access. "Basically," says Kapur, "most flowers can be obtained all year round, depending on where you live in the country." Availability and ease of delivery do affect prices, so consider Kapur's list of flowers that are generally more abundant (and perhaps better-priced) at certain times of the year:

Spring: tulips, daffodils, hyacinth
Summer: cosmos; dahlias; zinnias; sunflowers; herbs such as rosemary, sage, and thyme

Questions to Ask Florists

- Are you available on our wedding date?
- Do you do weddings for our budget level?
- What are your fees? (Ask for an itemized breakdown of approximate bouquet, centerpiece, boutonniere costs, and accept that prices will vary according to your specific floral inclusion wishes, sizes, etc.)
- How many years of experience do you have?
- How many weddings have you done?
- Do you do our type of wedding (important for outdoor wedding plans)?
- Have you designed any weddings at our particular location before? Similar locations?
- How many weddings are you working that weekend?
- Are you working another wedding on that same day?
- To which professional associations do you belong?
- Can I see pictures or reviews of your work?
- Can I visit your workshop to see live examples of your arrangements and bouquets? (Hint: Visit the shop on a Friday when the floral expert's staff is putting the finishing touches on the next day's bridal bouquets and centerpieces.)
- Will my flowers be arranged by you, a trained member of your staff, or an assistant? What are your assistant's qualifications?
- Can I rent other items from you, such as aisle runners, a chuppah, pedestals, potted plants, or fabric swags for the cake table?
- Do you deliver? If so, what is your delivery fee?
- Will you be present at the wedding site to arrange the floral décor? Will a member of your staff be assigned that role? If so, what are the assistant's qualifications?
- Do you have insurance? (Ask to see a copy of the policy.)
- Do you offer a cancellation or refund policy?
- When are deposits due, and how much is due at each deadline?

Autumn: zinnias, kale, fall foliage, berries (such as viburnum), rose hips

Winter: hollyberries, snowberries, paperwhites, magnolia greenery

Year-round: carnations, mums, roses, baby's breath

Simplify It

Since you're opening up another working partnership here, always consider the floral designer's personality, willingness to listen, professionalism, and the general "vibes" you get from her. You'll need to work well together to create your ideal floral plans, and that will take a high level of communication and trust. After all, you're entrusting her to create the most visual aspect of your day (besides you in that gorgeous gown!), and she's counting on you to describe exactly what you want. She wants to please you as much as you want to be happy with the final outcome.

This is just a sampling of the flowers you'll find available at peak times. Speak with your own floral designer in your area to find out which flowers will be at peak or more affordable when you'll need them. If you'd like to do your own research, I highly recommend you spend some time browsing through www.AboutFlowers.com for an extensive listing, descriptions, and pictures of the many flowers you might consider for your day. You might just find a new favorite bloom as well!

Aside from the types of flowers you choose for your pieces, you need to know that the florist's *time and labor* make up the bulk of your floral expense. Ornate and complicated bouquets and arrangements that require lots of extra effort in securing and creating each look are going to cost you more. So pick out your styles of bouquets and centerpieces (or centerpiece alternatives!) with a devoted thought toward the complexities of the work involved. For instance, a hand-tied bouquet is often a simpler and less time-consuming style than a carefully arranged Biedermeier (tightly clustered round bouquet). With just a simple switch from one kind of bouquet to another—using the same exact types of flowers—you might be able to save 10% to 20% on the cost for each item on your list.

Creating Wedding-Day Bouquets

Designing your bridal bouquet is one of the highlights of your wedding planning process. No doubt you'll flip through page after page of sample pictures to find the right bouquet for the style of your wedding, for the cut of your dress, and for your budget. Know that the trend is moving towards color in brides' bouquets, making for attractive arrangements and more affordable prices if you make the right design choices. Floral experts tell me that an all-white bouquet actually requires more flowers to make a visual impact, while some bursts of color create volume of their own and therefore require fewer blooms. You might opt for pastels or brights or perhaps a delicate shading of blush pink to make your whites pop. The choices are up to you, and you'll certainly have much to choose from.

Now here's where we get into design. As mentioned earlier, a less labor-intensive bouquet style may mean significant savings on the cost of the piece. Try a hand-tied bouquet or a nosegay bouquet. These are both popular styles chosen by brides who favor smaller and less expensive styles. The Biedermeier and the breakaway style are far more labor-intensive and therefore more expensive, so consider your budget when your floral designer shows you these types of elegant designs. Your floral designer may need to look over pictures of your gown and your maids' gowns to find the right style of bouquet for you. She should certainly discuss the prices of differing sizes, differing

Simplify It

*R*ight from the very beginning, review your floral design priorities to decide what's a must-have and what you can live without. Paring down the nonessentials will allow you to devote more of your budget to creating gorgeous bouquets and centerpieces. Your "I can do without" list might include flowers on the pew bows, arrangements for the ceremony site, arrangements for your buffet table, flowers for the cake table, rose petals for your flower girls to sprinkle, and other significantly priced options. Your savings here can run up to 10% to 30% of your floral budget. Just don't cut too deeply, or you'll be disappointed with your meager floral choices.

flower choices, and the natural look of incorporating more greenery into your collections.

Flowers for Men

It's not a given that your men will wear roses as their boutonnieres. If you don't consider other options, you might be losing an opportunity to save a good chunk of money. While boutonnieres may not be the largest expense in your wedding plans, they still occupy a place in your floral budget where you might get a great, unique look for less. I've interviewed several floral designers and spoken to hundreds of couples to find the most popular boutonniere flowers today. Some of these are: carnations, chrysanthemums, cosmos, dahlia, delphinium, lily of the valley, phlox, and ranunculus. Nearly all came in as comparable or less expensive than the standard rose lapel flower, and all garnered appreciative high marks from guests and the men's dates.

If you're not one to insist on uniformity for your men's look, you might opt to have each man wear a different flower in the same color family on his lapel. Couples are having fun with their boutonnieres now, using great colors and even including flowers that have a special significance to them.

Centerpiece Ideas

If you are looking for some breathing room in your budget, you can open up wide savings by choosing simpler centerpieces. Those enormous traditional wedding centerpieces can run anywhere from $50 to $150 each! Why spend that kind of money when you can center your tables with equally elegant and way more affordable alternatives? Following are some tips on designing your centerpieces with money in mind:

FLORAL CENTERPIECES

If you really want the look of a floral arrangement but don't want to drop $150 each for them, shave a significant portion of the expense right out of those arrangements! Use only a few bold, beautiful, and moderately priced flowers and fill in more affordable blooms and greenery. One low-priced option shared by Kimberly Aurora Kapur is to include flowering branches for a dramatic, tall, and eye-catching look. "Branches give depth and volume to your arrangement, so consider cherry blossom, moss-covered branches for an earthy look, and ilex branches which are holly branches without the leaves. In the spring, consider quince and forsythia branches as well." Even branches of brightly hued fall foliage can make a statement for your centerpieces.

A wonderful and inexpensive option whose elegance belies its expense is the glass bowl holding floating flowers and candles. You can find highly affordable prices at craft stores for your bowl and floating candles, while your flower order may be as simple as twelve single gardenias or ranunculus, with one bloom set for each bowl. Surround the bowl with several small votive candles (just ninety-nine cents each at craft stores), and sprinkle some rose petals on the table to extend the color. Kimberly Aurora Kapur regularly creates these centerpieces for her budget-conscious brides, with the expense approaching just $90 for six tables' worth of centerpieces.

Simplify It

Visit your florist's shop a year before your wedding date in order to see for yourself the kinds of flowers and arrangements that are most plentiful, bright, and infused into the lovely arrangements the shop is producing. One fall bride said that she discovered bouvardia, cosmos, cyclamen, and pink yarrow—all flowers with which she was previously unfamiliar—during a fifteen-minute stop at her florist's in October. "And I thought I'd be stuck with just mums at that time of the year!" she said, filling her order with these unique and beautiful (better yet, affordable!) flowers for her day.

NONFLORAL CENTERPIECES

How can you beat the look of elegant white pillar candles of varying heights set as centerpieces? Candles give each table a more intimate atmosphere, and the grand view across the room becomes one of unerring elegance. Again, seek out great sources for pillar candles, candle platters and trays, and even floating candles for those glass bowls. I visited a well-known décor store and found white, pear-scented pillar candles for $25 each. Then I went across the street to a craft store and found the same style of candles without the pear scent for just $7 each. You have to hunt around.

Some other ideas for inexpensive, nonfloral centerpieces:

- Collections of wedding day favors, arranged for your guests' taking

- Framed photographs of the two of you

- Framed photographs of other family members on their wedding days

- A lavish bread basket, filled with different types of breads and spreads, tapenade, garlic butter, and olive oil decanters

- A bowl or basket filled with exotic and colorful fruits such as star fruit, kiwis, pineapples, and mangoes. For a brighter look, cut some of the fruits in half to show off their juicy insides.

- A basket filled with lemons or limes (great if pale yellow is your wedding color!) bought in bulk at a warehouse store or farmer's market

Wedding Day Reflections

*L*ily of the valley is my birth flower, and Tom's mother has wonderful lily of the valley plants in her backyard. We not only used the flowers from her garden as our lapel flowers, honoring her green thumb, but we loved the symbolism of incorporating my birth flower as well.

—Marguerite and Tom

• Beautiful crystal decanters filled with sangria, iced tea, water with lemon, or water with a rainbow of cut fruit slices

• For beach weddings: a glass fishbowl filled with sand, seashells, and starfish (just a few dollars for a bagful of shells at a craft store, or free from nature if you spend a few weekends collecting pretty shells at a nearby beach)

The Floral Contract

Your floral order is an involved one and will itemize numerous purchases of certain types and styles of bouquets and color specifications. Since you'll want to be absolutely sure you wind up with what you ordered, you'll need to secure a contract that spells out your wishes to the smallest detail. Beyond the basics of your bouquets, broken down by number of roses included in each and the like, also include the date and exact street location of the wedding site, a phone number at the wedding site, the delivery time and location, the deposit and payment amounts, a refund and cancellation clause, and the designer's signature on the contract.

If it is your preference, have the floral designer state in writing that he will be the one to deliver and set up your floral accents, centerpieces, and pew bows at your wedding sites. Get every detail in this crucial document, so that in case of non-delivery or delivery of the wrong items you can receive your refund with little fuss. It's also wise to include a "time is of the essence" clause that guarantees delivery of your flowers to the right locations by a specified time. Brides and grooms who secure this wording are more likely to receive their shipments punctually, and to receive prompt refunds or discounts if a delivery was late or incomplete.

Worksheet: The Complete Floral Shopping List

Use this worksheet as a checklist to keep your floral budget in order. Note the number of items you'll need to buy, rent, borrow, or make:

Your Flowers

❑ Your bouquet
❑ Flowers for your hair

The Bridal Party (Women)

❑ Maid/matron of honor's bouquet
❑ Bridesmaids' bouquets
❑ Flower girls' bouquets
❑ Rose petals for flower girls to sprinkle along your path
❑ Flowers for the maids' hair
❑ Flowers for the flower girls' hair

The Bridal Party (Men)

❑ Groom's boutonniere
❑ Best man's boutonniere
❑ Ushers' boutonnieres
❑ Ringbearers' boutonnieres

Personal Flowers

❑ Bride's mother's corsage
❑ Bride's grandmothers' corsages
❑ Groom's mother's corsage
❑ Groom's grandmothers' corsages
❑ Corsages for godparents
❑ Corsages for readers, candle lighters, performers, wedding coordinator, other special female guests
❑ Boutonnieres for readers, candle lighters, performers, other special male guests

- ❏ Flowers for new stepchildren
- ❏ Memory flowers

Ceremony Site Flowers and Décor

- ❏ Pew bows
- ❏ Floral bunches for backs of each chair
- ❏ Altar décor
- ❏ Candles
- ❏ Floral arch
- ❏ Chuppah
- ❏ Aisle runner (optional)
- ❏ Floral arrangements on pedestals
- ❏ Flowers on guest book signing table
- ❏ Greenery garlands

Reception Décor

- ❏ Centerpieces for head table
- ❏ Centerpieces for all guests' tables
- ❏ Centerpieces for buffet tables
- ❏ Centerpieces for gift tables
- ❏ Centerpieces for guest book table
- ❏ Centerpieces for name card table
- ❏ Centerpieces for favors table
- ❏ Centerpieces for bar
- ❏ Floral arrangements for restrooms
- ❏ Flowers to decorate the cake
- ❏ Flowers to "sprinkle" around candle centerpieces
- ❏ Flowers for the getaway car
- ❏ Throwaway bouquet
- ❏ Accent potted plants
- ❏ Floral garlands to wind around stairway handrails, deck railings, ship masts, etc.
- ❏ Other flowers

Sample Floral Budgets

Following are some examples of what couples have opted for depending on their budgets and tastes.

MANDY AND DAVE'S TOP-SHELF WEDDING

Mandy and Dave were lucky enough not to be on a budget. Their floral designs were upscale, all-inclusive, and fulfilled by one of the most popular florists in town.

> Bride's bouquet, Biedermeier in all white: $175
> Seven bridesmaids' bouquets, smaller Biedermeiers with pastels:
> $100 each
> Ten single rose boutonnieres: $30 each
> Two corsages for mothers: $40 each
> Ten floral arrangement centerpieces: $75 each
> Six flowers for pew bows: $15 each
> Rose petals for flower girl's sprinkling: $35
> Memorial flower arrangement for departed family members: $185
> Total: $2,315.00

THERESA AND LARRY'S SMART BUDGETING WEDDING

Since Theresa and Larry were paying for the wedding themselves and handling their student loans and car payments at the same time, they exercised great spending control with their flowers, sought out ways for their florist to save them some money, and still designed a lovely floral look for their day.

> Bride's bouquet: $60 for simpler, hand-tied bouquet in bright
>   colors
> Four bridesmaids' bouquets: $50 for similar hand-tied bouquets
> Six boutonnieres: $12 each for small sprig of stephanotis
> Two corsages for the mothers: $15 each for smaller, simpler styles
> Ten centerpieces of single gardenias floating in bowl of water:
> $140 total for flowers and bowls found at craft store

Plain tulle bows as pew décor: $20 for lengths of tulle and $6 for
    faux pearl accent pins

Skipped flowers for head table, as bridesmaids would set their
    bouquets in front of them

Total: $518 for a look that rivaled Mandy and Dave's wedding

Additional Money-Saving Ideas

• Expect higher prices on flower-giving holidays such as Valentine's Day and Mother's Day.

• Use nonbridal flowers. Most brides use white roses, gardenias, and orchids in their bouquets, and the prices for these blooms increase during peak wedding months. Instead, consider using other attractive flowers that are priced reasonably.

• Use more expensive flowers, like stephanotis or orchids, only as accents to larger, more economical arrangements.

• Use more foliage in your arrangements. Great greenery choices include: eucalyptus, pittosporum, asparagus ferns, salal or "lemonleaf," evergreen, and leatherleaf.

• Use branches, berries, fruits, and other inexpensive nonflower choices to build beautiful centerpieces for less.

• Shop for inexpensive potted flowering plants at your supermarket or warehouse store.

• Invest in topiaries and other potted plants that you will use at the wedding and then at home in your garden or in porch flowerboxes.

• Consider ordering flowers from a wholesaler and making your bouquets and centerpieces yourself. Stick with easier-to-master bouquet styles like the hand-tied method. Rent potted flowers and plants to decorate your reception and ceremony areas.

• Have your maids set their bouquets at the center of each guest table, making their bouquets do double duty as centerpieces.

• Check with your ceremony site to see if the room will already be decorated. Especially at Christmastime, Easter, and other religious holidays, houses of worship are wonderfully decked out with holiday plants such as poinsettias or Easter lilies. If the site is decorated, you don't need to do it yourself.

• To be safe, check with your officiant to see if you can decorate the ceremony site at all. Some sites do not allow décor by outsiders.

13

Capture the Moment

*Photography and Videography
for Less*

O<small>F ALL</small> the areas of wedding planning, pictures trip up budget-conscious couples who don't have their priorities in line. These well-intentioned couples slash away at their photography and videography budget—they even go so far as to *not* hire a professional but instead ask a friend to take the pictures—and as a result they make one of the biggest budget mistakes out there. Your pictures and video are way too important as a lasting, tangible record of your day, and of your loved ones who share in it, to be considered an unnecessary luxury. Sure, the prices are high, even astronomical with some experts. But you will regret cheapening out in this area when your pictures come out rotten, or your cousin Ed missed videotaping the cutting of your cake because he was outside having a cigarette. My advice to you is to hire professionals for these important tasks and be cost conscious within the specific plans you set for them.

Finding Your Photographer

The key to the success of your wedding photographs is the professional you hire. Wedding photographers are trained to capture the best moments of your day and provide you with a finished product that becomes more valuable over time. As you start exploring your photography needs, know that this investment is not one to be taken lightly. So, research your vendors well, view plenty of samples of their work, ask for modifications to their standard wedding-day packages, and don't waste money on unnecessary extras.

Your Yellow Pages, Internet searches, and the full-color wedding section of your local newspaper will certainly feature beautiful ads touting the services of professional wedding photographers, and you can certainly use these to collect your list of contenders.

Since first-person experience is the best way to judge a photographer, ask your recently married friends who they hired, how they really felt about the work, the time they waited for delivery of their pictures, and whether or not the photographer met their expectations *and* investment. Be sure to flip through your friends' albums, judge the content and quality of the photos, and ask plenty of questions about how cooperative and professional the photographer was.

For a thorough check on your photographers, contact the two major photography associations for their referrals on the most experienced, best-trained, and most reputable pros in your area: Professional Photographers of America (800-786-6277, www.ppa-world.org) and Wedding and Por-

Wedding Day Reflections

*I*f we could do one thing from our wedding differently, it would be to hire a good videographer. The footage my brother's friend took got shakier and more erratic as time went on, since he was getting more and more drunk throughout the night. At one point, he mistakenly left the camera rolling while it lay sideways on the table. Now, we have lots of sideways footage of people lining up at the bar and getting their drinks instead of our guests dancing to the music. We call it the $1,000 Savings of Shame.
—Carrie and Ed

trait Photographers International (310-451-0090, www.eventphotographers.com). A high rating from these organizations means that a photographer meets high standards and may therefore be worthy of your significant financial and emotional investment in his work.

QUESTIONS TO ASK THE PHOTOGRAPHER

While you can save plenty of time inquiring over the phone about your contenders' availability for your wedding day, basic package explanations, and price ranges, you should always conduct your interviews in person. Go to the expert's studio, view his sample albums and framed portraits, and see how he presents himself and interacts with you. Again, you'll be forming a close working partnership with this expert, so consider your rapport—the photographer's willingness to ask questions of you and listen to your answers, explain whatever technology he uses, and generally just make you feel comfortable. Remember, this is the vendor you'll be sending into your crowd of guests, the vendor who will be speaking with your in-laws and friends. Be sure that he presents himself well, has a friendly demeanor, and knows his stuff. Most couples said the photographer they finally hired was the one who put them at ease, who possessed a quiet level of competence and wasn't talking a mile a minute trying to make a sale or push his "creative vision" on them. As you assess your top contenders for their expertise and rapport, ask the standard questions you now know to ask, as well as the following specific questions:

1. Can we see an itemized price list for the picture sizes, reproductions, and albums we might want?

2. Are we free to customize your packages in order to get the shots we want?

3. Do you offer a budget package? What is included in it?

4. How many hours of work are included in the package we want? (The average package is four or five hours.)

5. How many photographs will you take in total? (On average, a good photographer will take between 250 and 300 pictures over the course of four to five hours.)

6. Can we get some photographs in black and white?

7. Will you be taking our photographs, or do you plan to send a staff photographer from your studio? If so, can we meet with that photographer, see his samples, and learn his professional credits?

8. What will you be wearing to the wedding? (Important: Inform the photographer about the formality and dress code for your wedding, so that he will fit in with the crowd.)

9. Will you be working with an assistant? Several assistants? (Important: Find this out, since the assistant will also be included in the caterer's head count.)

10. What will the assistants be wearing?

11. What kind of camera do you use, digital or 35-millimeter? (Ask the photographer to explain the advantages and disadvantages of his chosen form of equipment.)

12. Do you have backup cameras, batteries, and equipment?

13. What time will you arrive before the ceremony?

14. How long will it take to shoot the post-ceremony pictures? (Important: Specify a time limit, such as an hour or half an hour, so that you can arrive at your reception on time.)

15. How long will it take to get the photographs back?

16. How long will it take to receive our albums after we place our order?

17. What kind of touch-ups can we request for our pictures?

18. Can we see the proofs on CD or online? (Ask if the photographer is registered with a view-it-and-buy-it service like Pictage.com, which creates a password-sensitive area where you or a guest can view

all of the proofs, and purchase those you like. This service saves you a bundle when you can show your guests the pictures online rather than ordering albums for them.)

19. Can we keep the proofs? (Some photographers will allow you to keep all of your proofs, which allows you to create mini-albums for family members and friends, if you choose. The savings here can run you $200 to $400.)

20. Can we buy the negatives from you? (Some studios will *not* let you buy the negatives. They keep them, copyright them, and therefore make a *lot* of money when you need to have extra copies made. Still, some companies do have a policy of selling negatives to the couple. It's best to ask.)

21. How long do you keep the negatives?

22. Where do you store the negatives? (Ideally, the photographer will keep the negatives in a fireproof safe or vault, perhaps even off site from the studio.)

23. Do you digitize the negatives?

Placing Your Order

With your expert chosen, it's time to put together your photography package with equal attention to expense *and* the important emotional value of this investment. Together, you'll decide on the amount of time you'll have the photographer on duty, the number of pictures he'll take, whether you prefer posed portraits or more candid shots throughout your day, how large you want your albums to be, how many albums you'll order for the parents, and any extra-special considerations you have. Many couples on a budget can save a fortune with the right decisions made at this point, and a quality photographer will even point out additional ways for you to save.

As important as it is for you to state what you want, hand over a list of your most-wished-for shots (your grandmother dancing the Peabody with her sister, your bridesmaids drinking a toast to you, etc.), it's equally important to let your photographer know at the outset what you *don't* want. You can save a ton of time—and time is money— if you can say you don't want a posed picture of all your wedding guests taken on the steps outside the church after the wedding, or that you don't want table shots at the reception, or a picture of your recently divorced parents who aren't speaking and are not willing to call a truce for your wedding day. Your photographer doesn't want to waste your time, either. So spell out your wishes to be sure you get exactly what you wish for.

Next, choose the number of pictures you want to include in your album and start thinking about the types of pictures you might like to feature. Some couples create a more formal, official album with their posed pictures and then a second, more casual album that contains fun pictures of their guests celebrating. This second album might be comprised of those free proofs or the pictures from your guests' throwaway cameras.

Mix up your selection by ordering some 8 × 10s, some 5 × 7s and know that there will be a ton of candid photos being taken during the event.

Wedding Day Reflections

*B*oth our sets of parents are divorced and remarried to other people, so with the addition of our grandparents and our godparents, we would have had to order eight official albums for all of them! To save the $600 it would have cost in total, we just used our proofs and our candids, ordered copies of a few of our favorite formal photos, and assembled the gift albums using pretty photo albums we found in a craft store.

—Nina and Trey

Here's where I'm going to encourage you not to cut too deeply, to spend a little more than you might at first consider. You might think you're making a smart money move by ordering the smallest number of pictures possible, thinking you'll only really want a few great shots for your albums and for a framed portrait. However, once you see the proofs come in, you're going to be very, very sorry that you didn't allow yourself more in your budget. These pictures are full of meaning, full of emotion, and you're going to look great in them. If you signed a contract for a package that includes only a handful of prints, then you'll have to pay *extra* for the additional pictures you want. So err on the side of ordering too many, allowing yourself a greater expenditure for this important part of your wedding memories. You can always use the extra shots for those gift albums, for framed pictures to give to your bridal party as thank-you gifts after the wedding, and to send to faraway guests who couldn't come to the ceremony. In this case, less is not more.

Hiring Your Videographer

Your wedding video, too, is an investment that increases in value over time. So don't trust this important record of your day to just anyone. A true professional can capture your wedding for posterity, with complete coverage of the most important moments and even those once-in-a-lifetime shots that only a masterful expert knows how to find. Wedding videography is an art form, so you can do yourself no greater favor than allowing room in your budget to hire a professional . . . if only for a short time.

Start your search for the best videographer by again asking your recently married friends for their recommendations. They can tell you if their videographer was right there to capture the greatest moments of the day or if he was bellied up to the bar while the bride danced with her new father-in-law. They can tell you if the videographer's microphone system fritzed out, or if they didn't receive their edited video for six months, or if the videographer did a rotten job of editing their footage.

Your photographer can also give you some names, as most photography studios employ a stable of highly reputable video artists on call. A big benefit here is that your photographer is *not* going to refer you to an untested expert. The video pro he suggests is a reflection on his studio, and you can be sure the video vendors he presents to you possess excellent credentials and a solid reputation.

QUESTIONS TO ASK THE VIDEOGRAPHER

Of course it's important to view samples of the videographer's work, seeing as many different tapes as you can watch, but it's also important to subject your video pro to the same questions and rapport-assessment you used for your photographer. Your video expert, too, will be mingling through your crowd, interacting with your guests, and holding the vast responsibility of capturing the essence of your day on film. So don't choose a pro based on one nicely edited sample tape. Make some calls, visit his studio, and get out your number-two pencil for the next important interview of this process. Again, ask the general availability and contract questions I've suggested throughout this book and then ask these specifics:

1. Have you shot our particular kind of wedding before? (Such as a beach wedding, boat wedding, a night wedding where special light considerations will have to be discussed.)

2. Have you worked with our photographer before?

3. Have you worked at our wedding site before?

4. What kind of videography equipment do you use? (Ask for an explanation between his digital camera technology and his standard VHS camera. In many instances, VHS will produce a great image for less, depending upon the vendor's price differentials for equipment.)

5. Will you bring a backup camera along?

6. How many backup battery packs do you bring along?

7. How much footage will you shoot?

8. Will you be working our wedding, or will you send another videographer from your studio? If so, can we meet with that professional and view his samples?

9. Will you bring a lighting assistant along on that day?

10. What are the extra charges for your lighting assistant?

11. What will you be wearing on the wedding day?

12. What is your editing process?

13. How long will it take you to edit the footage and deliver the tape to us?

14. What are your basic package rates?

15. Do you have a budget package, and what is involved in that?

16. Do you have a time minimum, such as a "four-hour minimum package?"

Wedding Day Reflections

We considered not having a wedding video at all, since we were on a tight budget and had already booked a big photography package. However, a recently married friend told us that her wedding video was priceless to her now, as it was the last footage she had of her mother while she was alive. Her mother was diagnosed with cancer four months after the wedding, and she became very ill very quickly. That wedding footage was the last time her family saw her mother absolutely radiant and laughing, dancing, having the time of her life, and it is now a truly invaluable keepsake. Knowing that a wedding video can be your last and best look at a loved one, and even a way to show your kids departed family members in the future, we decided to invest the money in hiring a professional to capture every moment of our day.

—Dana and Tyler

17. Can we customize your plan to suit our needs?

18. Can we have a list of itemized prices?

19. What is your overtime fee?

20. Can we have a photo montage added to the beginning of our tape? What are your extra charges for this service?

21. Can we select the musical background you'll add to the tape?

22. Do we get to select any special effects for our tape?

23. When are deposits due, and how much is due at each payment?

24. What do you charge for making duplicate copies of the tape? (I recommend that you get the expert to make copies for your family members; even though it costs more, the quality of the tape is unrivaled and you won't risk damage to your own copy.)

25. Do you deliver the master tape to us, or do you keep it in storage?

When discussing the quality of the expert's equipment, one term you're likely to hear is *digital cameras.* You've seen them, you may have used them, and now you're left to wonder if this kind of camera is worth the extra money it costs for your expert to use it on your wedding day. While digital cameras continue to move into the mainstream, video experts say that this technology is not at 100% yet. The same goes for the option of having your wedding video streamed onto DVDs. Since these technologies aren't quite refined yet and as only time will tell if digital footage fades over the years (as experts fear it will), skip the ultra hi-tech equipment and go with the tried and true: VHS. Take some time and ask your chosen videographer to explain his camera and film stock plans to you. You might decide that you're willing to risk the potential unknowns of the digital camera world. The choices are yours.

Your quality videographer will assess the audio during taping, and to get good sound he'll attach tiny, unobtrusive microphones to the groom's lapel. This discreet wiring job will capture your vows loud and clear, and it will also pick up the whispered affections that come right from your heart when you first stand face-to-face. Your guests may not be able to hear your groom tell you that you look beautiful, but you'll have that moment on tape forever.

How your videographer puts your footage together makes all the difference to the final tape. A smooth edit will be seamless, flawless, and make the most of the individual moments of your day. Here's where we get technical again. Now, the trend in the industry is toward

Try Another Angle?

My videographer asked me if we wanted one camera, two, or three. He explained that having several cameras allows him to capture several different angles, and it makes the wedding video come out better. Is it worth the extra expense to have more than one camera?

Having more than one camera does allow for better angles and some variety in your footage. Perhaps your videographer will set up a stationary camera in the church balcony to get a wide overhead shot of you walking down the aisle, and then he'll be up close with a hand-held camera to capture the two of you taking your vows. While this option does provide additional dramatic views, it's often an unnecessary expense. A good videographer can shoot a wedding quite beautifully with one camera. Save your money on this and buy some additional copies of the tape for your family members instead.

nonlinear editing, in which video footage is transferred onto a computer program, edited to perfection, and then transferred out to a tape or CD-ROM. This system allows more editing and refinement options, a greater range of special effects, and the capturing of more details. See if the video pro works with a nonlinear editing system, and ask about his level of experience with that system. Some new programs are out on the market, and you don't want your pro "practicing" on your tape.

CHOOSING YOUR VIDEOGRAPHY PACKAGE

Standard videography packages offer three to five hours of taping during your day. That means you're on the clock from the moment your cameraperson shows up. Since time is money, you can instruct your video pro to show up at the ceremony site, ready to go, rather than kill an hour taking shots of you getting ready at your house. Instead, have a family member record your brunch, salon, and veil attachment moments on your own camcorder and hand that tape to the videographer for insert editing.

You're on Candid . . . Microphone

Here's a tip the groom should know about wearing a microphone clip-on: It's easy to forget that you have it on, especially if the videographer attached it to you a fair amount of time before the ceremony. So be careful what you say to your best man while the guests are being seated! My microphone even picked up the unmistakable sound of a nervous groom taking a big swig from a flask of bourbon right before the ceremony started!

—STEVE BLAHITKA, VIDEOGRAPHER, BACK EAST PRODUCTIONS, EAST HANOVER, NJ

The videographer will shoot your footage on a master tape or on a series of tapes, which in normal circumstances he will take back to his studio for editing. However, if your budget is bending and you don't place a high priority on getting an edited version of your tape suitable for entry into the Tribeca Film Festival, you can save a bundle by asking your videographer to simply hand over the tapes he's shot at the end of the night. When you use this option, you're accepting the "raw footage" of your day as your finished product, and you might save hundreds of dollars by avoiding the time-consuming and laborious editing process. Sure, the footage may roll on for hours and be less palatable than a two-hour period focused on a special moment, but you'll have all of the images of your day taken in real time.

Simplify It

*A*gain, draw up a complete contract with your videographer's instructions, the details of your order, your payment plan, and the specified date of delivery. This contract will ensure that your investment will be worth the expense and that your expert will fulfill his obligations.

If you'd rather have the tape edited, talk to your expert about saving money on the process. One choice might be to limit or eliminate special effects. Do you really need a graphic of dancing bunnies hopping through footage of your guests doing the Macarena? Or, do you really need that introductory montage of your baby pictures and snapshots from your courting days set against an original rendition of "Sunrise, Sunset?" Skip the pricey extras and shave down your budget.

Additional Money-Saving Tips

• Hire your experts for a shorter, action-packed period of time. Instead of that five-hour package, go for the three-hour package and save hundreds of dollars. At your reception, cut the cake earlier in the evening, so that the photo and video pros can leave shortly afterward.

Your guests can then take the fun candid shots with their own cameras or throwaways you provide.

• Don't pay for proofs. If your photographer will not allow you to keep the proofs, then don't pay to have 200 pictures developed. Ask to view your photos on contact sheets or CD so you can view them at a lower cost.

• Buy a more affordable album. Some of the fancier varieties are leather-bound, with detailed photo inserts and gold lettering scrolled on the cover. Downgrade to a simpler bridal album for a savings of $30 to $75.

• Thin out your album. Limit the number of pages in the album, choosing perhaps twenty pages rather than thirty or forty.

• Shorten your videotape. Your videographer may charge you less for a one-hour tape than a two-hour tape. The condensed version is often more enjoyable to watch, as the highlights of the day are wonderfully edited together and the slower moments eliminated.

> ## *Simplify It*
>
> *T*o keep your videographer on track, let him know about any special tributes, toasts, dances, or footage you want him to catch. Also, provide him with CDs of any particular songs you'd like included on your tape.

• Provide your guests with throwaway cameras, bought in bulk at Costco, Sam's Club, BJ's Wholesale, Kmart or Wal-Mart. You can often find better prices at these sources than at camera shops and bridal Web sites.

• Only use one throwaway camera at each table (some brides supply two) or put disposables at every other table and encourage guests to share the honors. Each throwaway camera might yield twenty-four pictures, so you do the math for your twelve guest tables! One ingenious couple I know prevented duplicate pictures from their guests and professional photographer by having the wait staff place throwaway cameras on the guests' tables *after* the professional photographer's departure and right when the dancing fun started. The couple didn't waste money on fifty shots of them cutting the cake, and the candid shots were a big success!

• Negotiate to purchase your negatives. It might cost a high amount, but it will save you a fortune in the long run if you own your own pictures and can reproduce them at will . . . without those high copy and enlargement fees through a studio.

• Use technology. Rather than order 100 or more wallet-sized bridal portraits to hand out at your wedding, have the photographer provide the image on disk, which you can then send as e-mails to your guests. Also, send e-mails of your bridal portrait to friends and relatives who couldn't attend the wedding. This gives them a look at you on your day and allows them the option of saving the image forever. And you don't have to pay $15 for each print!

• Use technology again! This is one of my favorite finds: For about $25 each, you can create photo DVDs that showcase up to fifty of your wedding photos in a virtual wedding album, complete with music and rolling credits, through www.shutterfly.com. (Also at this site are fun gift items that incorporate your wedding photos onto calendars, mugs, tee shirts, and other items.)

14

Let's Dance!

Saving on Entertainment for Your Reception

Y OU WANT your guests to have a wonderful time at your wedding, right? After the delectable food and desserts, guests remember a great wedding for the entertainment you provide. A top-notch DJ or band will invite your guests onto the dance floor, spin just the right songs for your most sentimental slow dances, and lead the party with great personality. In this section, you'll start your search for the perfect musicians and entertainers for your event, without spending a fortune.

What Do You Want?

The style and formality of your wedding will determine the type of entertainment on your wish list. If you're having a traditional, formal wedding, then you might be looking for a DJ or a full band to play everything from Top 40 music to the classics of the 1940s. If, however, your reception will be a smaller, more intimate gathering with less fanfare, then perhaps you might wish for a single pianist to play ballads and classical tunes. Think now about the kinds of entertainers who might be right for the tone of your event. Do you want to dance all night long? Do you want the flashing lights, the party props, the conga line, and the Electric Slide? Or do you simply want some Chopin playing unobtrusively in the background as you enjoy your elegant dessert-and-champagne soiree? The choices are up to you.

The first question that will arise as you start researching entertainers is, do you want a DJ or a band? Some couples prefer the sound and energy of a live band, with talented musicians and vocalists in concert just for them. Others prefer the unmistakable and flawless versions of songs performed on a CD by the original artists. For many, the budget makes the decision for them. DJs are often less expensive than full bands, both in package price and as a consideration for the caterer's head count.

Disappointed? If part of your ideal wedding vision includes live performances by a talented singer or the personalization of "your song" as you dance your first dance, *you can still have that moment*. A great many entertainment companies have listened to the wants and needs of marrying couples who want live song performances *and* the money-saver of a DJ. These companies now offer a split package, in which you can hire a DJ to work your party and also have several songs performed by a vocalist, duo, or small singing group as an accent and personalized act for your event. Adding this special touch to your DJ package might only cost you a fraction more than you'd pay just for the CD-spinner and far less than the cost of a full band. If this on-demand performance is something you desire, ask the entertainment company about their mixed offerings and work your budget to fit your reception vision. As you know by now, you can prioritize your wedding budget to include special touches like this one.

Where Are All the Entertainers?

You guessed it. Start by asking your recently married friends who they hired to entertain at their weddings. This is by far the best way to judge the performance level, personalities, and professionalism of any DJ or band. As great as a sample videotape might seem, especially with clever editing and production, you can't beat the real life validation from a couple who loved their entertainers. Remember that DJs and bands don't just play weddings. So ask your corporate buddies, family, friends, and neighbors who have recently hosted great parties for anniversaries, bar and bat mitzvahs, and corporate or charity events for the business card of the DJ who made their parties a great success.

If you've checked your address book twice, and no one has a contact for you, then check with the American Disc Jockey Association (301-705-5150, www.adja.org) for the names of reputable professionals in your area. You might also garner a collection of great recommendations from your wedding coordinator, the manager of the reception hall (who remembers the bands that have knocked her socks off at previous weddings), your florist, and other wedding professionals. Just be careful of kickback schemes between vendors, and hire only on the basis of a group's wonderful audition and professionalism, not a caterer's big thumbs-up.

At the next level of your research, check out various Web sites for a look at the entertainers in action, and use these referrals *only* as ways to collect names for your interview list. Not taking the time now to do solid research on entertainers, and choosing discounts over quality as your main criteria is the best way to ruin your wedding's chances of success. You want your wedding to be unforgettable, but not because your band showed up in purple ruffle-collar suits and the lead singer was too drunk to remember the words to "That's Amore."

Be especially careful to hire on the basis of *live* performances *not* a well-edited videotape that makes the group look and sound terrific.

Always schedule an audition of your professional musicians or DJ before you sign any contract. Since the quality of your entertainment can make or break your entire reception, don't take shortcuts here. Don't hire a band because their sample tape was the best one of the bunch, and don't hire a band you saw at a wedding last year without putting them through the full interview process now. That band may have changed lead singers and their entire song list since then.

QUESTIONS TO ASK YOUR POTENTIAL ENTERTAINERS

Ready to interview your contenders? First, ask your general questions, and then ask the following specific questions of the *entertainer you'll be hiring for your day.* I emphasize this because many entertainers work as part of a stable owned by a larger entertainment services company. When you call that 800-number, you might be connected to a sales manager or receptionist who is ready to fax you whatever information you request. Take it a step further. Ask to speak to the DJ or band leader himself. This is often a great way to get a real feel for your entertainer's level of rapport and enthusiasm for his job.

1. How long have you been together as a group?

2. Do you work our style of wedding? (Important if you're holding an outdoor, beach, informal, or specialty wedding.)

3. What's your style of music? Do you specialize in Top 40 only, or do you have a wide range of styles from jazz to rock?

4. May we see your song list?

5. Will you take requests from our wedding guests during the event?

6. Can we hear you perform live at a scheduled audition?

7. Are you familiar with the kinds of music we'd like played at our reception?

8. Can we request songs you do not have included on your play list?

9. Are you willing to learn any special songs we'd like played at our reception? (Allow plenty of time, provide sheet music, and expect to pay extra.)

10. Do you charge an additional fee for the band leader or DJ to act as master of ceremonies during the reception?

11. For how many hours will you be playing?

12. How many breaks do you plan to take and how long will the breaks be?

13. Will you play recorded music during your breaks?

14. Will your group dress in tuxedoes to match our formality? What is your standard dress style during your act?

15. What are the special elements of your performance? (In other words, "We don't want any cheesy surprises, so let us know if you plan to break out the sequined dinner jacket, the Hawaiian leis, and the fog machine.")

16. Do you include props in your performance, such as inflated guitars? If we don't want the props, can we negotiate a discount?

17. How much space will you need for your equipment and performance area?

18. Will you need us to supply a table to hold your equipment? (If so, get the measurements of the needed table and how much weight the table needs to hold.)

19. How many power outlets will you need in the area? (Important if you're holding your wedding outdoors, at home, or in an alternate wedding location.)

20. How long will it take you to set up and be ready for the beginning of the event?

21. What extras can we purchase with your basic package? (Such as, live singer, special lighting effects, etc.)

22. Are you willing to stay later than contracted if the party's still going strong? (Important: Especially if you're planning your reception for the afternoon or earlier evening hours, your DJ may have another event booked for an hour after yours was originally scheduled to end. If your guests want to keep dancing, will your DJ be able to stay?)

23. What are your overtime fees? Do you charge overtime by the hour or by the half-hour? (Very important: Get this little tidbit in writing in your contract. You don't want any harsh surprises when you get the final bill.)

CREATING YOUR PLAY LIST

Surely, you have a wish list of songs you'd like to hear at your wedding. It may be that you'd like "Amazed" to be your wedding song, or you have a lineup of Motown songs you know your guests would love to dance to. Sit down with your fiancé and draw up a list of your favorite tunes. Check your most-played CDs, or look at the often-updated list of most popular wedding songs at www .weddingtips.com, to get the ideas flowing. You'll need songs for the following as well:

- Your first dance as husband and wife
- Father-daughter dance
- Mother-son dance
- Special tribute dances, such as a song you dedicate to your parents, your bridal party, the longest-married couple in the room, and even to each other

---

Simplify It

*W*hen hiring a band or performer, be sure to get the names of the band members *in writing.* Since you will hire your entertainers far in advance of your wedding, you run the risk of your band changing their look and style completely before your Big Day. Too many brides and grooms have written to me to share a warning about their bands showing up on the wedding day as a completely different band from the one they hired. Ask your entertainer to notify you of any changes in the band's makeup, personnel, style, or repertoire at the time of the change, so that you will be informed of any impact on your day.

- Ethnic dances
- Line dances
- The last dance of the evening

Your Entertainer As Master of Ceremonies

In many instances, your entertainer will also act as the master of ceremonies and will thus be the one to introduce you and your bridal party as you enter the room at the start of the reception and notify your guests when dinner is about to be served or the Viennese table opens for their enjoyment. These announcements and speeches are an important part of your event, so you'll want to make sure your entertainer has the necessary information.

I highly suggest that you take the time to provide your entertainer with a written schedule for the flow of your event. Of course, an experienced DJ will know by instinct when it's time to make his announcements, and he may even be prompted by the maître d' or wedding coordinator at each stage of the reception. For your part, you can provide a complete list of the names to be announced, such as the correct pronunciation of your bridesmaids' and ushers' names (do it phonetically, if you must, for those trickier names—remember, this is all captured on video for posterity), plus the way you'd like to have special guests announced, by title or with a funny anecdote ("The couple who introduced the bride to the groom . . ." etc.). Spell out your wishes about audience

Simplify It

*A*nother smart move is to make a "Do Not Play" list of songs you *don't* want to hear at your reception. Perhaps you don't want to hear the song that always reminds you of your ex-boyfriend (or worse, reminds your fiancé of his ex-girlfriend). Your recently divorced sister might not want to hear her wedding song, and maybe you'd rather die than have your guests doing the chicken dance or the Macarena. Provide your entertainers with a warning to remove any risk of discomfort.

interaction. Some couples love having an entertainer who involves the crowd and even displays a great comedic sense of timing. Other couples want their entertainer to skip the cheesy party games (if that's how they see them) and just play the darn music. You're the boss, so feel free to let your entertainer know exactly what you expect from his performance on your day.

Additional Money-Saving Tips

Simplify It

*Y*our entertainment contract should spell out all of the details, right down to what the entertainers will wear to your event. Be sure your contract specifies the exact duration of their service, your fee agreement, overtime rates, and a clear payment schedule for deposits and final checks. Check for clear wording on the refund policy in case of cancellation or plan changes. Have changes to this contract written out and initialed by the entertainer or manager. Then, get the musician to sign the contract and keep a copy for yourselves.

• If you really want a band, choose one with fewer members (but still with a great sound).

• Have the DJ perform for fewer hours during the reception. You might choose to have easy-listening music piped into the room during the dinner hours, for instance, and *then* the DJ can start his clock running for the three hours after dinner is over. It's far cheaper than a five-hour entertainment package.

• Hire a pianist or instrumental artist for the dinner hour, rather than keep the clock running for a band or DJ.

• Consider hiring nonwedding bands and groups, such as jazz ensembles found at a local jazz club or music union. These groups often don't command exorbitant fees, and you may find a stellar group with a fine sound for less.

• If you're really low on cash and if your reception will be less formal, make your own music-mix CDs to be played by a responsible guest. You can use your own CDs or download MP3s from the Internet to burn your own music-mix CDs (a talented friend can help you with this one, if you don't have the techno-savvy to burn CDs). For a better job matching appropriate music to, say, the dinner hour, the early dancing hours when your older guests are likely to dance, and then to the wild, later hours of the party, make separate CDs with suitable music for each stage of your party.

• Ask the reception hall to pipe-in classical or easy-listening music during the dinner hour for a savings of up to 30% on your entertainment fee. If you're not having any dancing at your reception, as some couples choose for religious or personal reasons, using this piped-in music will make your entertainment budget a great big $0.

Money on Wheels

Limousines, Classic Cars, and Horse & Carriage Rides

WHAT COULD be better than gliding up to your wedding in a sleek black limousine, with all eyes on you? It's quite a scene when the bride steps out of the car, granting a first, striking glance at her in her gown. Actually, now that I think about it, one thing could be better . . . not paying a lot for that limousine.

Hiring glamorous transportation is often one of the most indulgent portions of a wedding budget. Today's brides and grooms are dropping hundreds of dollars for the use of Excaliburs, Porsches, and stretch Lincoln Navigators to transport themselves and their bridal parties in style, while other couples are going with the fairy-tale look of a horse-drawn carriage. If you're on a budget, you might be wondering just how much that horse and carriage costs or whether or not you can shave a few hundred from your flower order to grab up that stretch Humvee for just an hour. Yes, wedding-day transportation does run a pretty penny, but you *can* hire a car for far less than the

average couple spends. This is one area where you will not have to sacrifice your dreams to save a buck—here's where you'll learn how and
where to rent your conveyance without spending a fortune. It's all in
the choices you make, and your timing.

What Do You Want?

Does your wedding dream include the shiny black stretch limousine?
Or do you love the more exquisite Rolls-Royce for your grand arrival?
Don't think for a minute that you can't hire a classic car for your day.
With the right planning, such as knowing how long you'll need the
car, you can procure the use of just about any exciting model of car,
from a ten-passenger Lexus GX 400 to a thirty-passenger limo bus
(complete with mood lighting and a great sound system for a contin-
uation of the party atmosphere).

The following options are often more expensive than the usual
rented cars, but you might be so drawn to them (and the great photo
ops!) that you'll make room in your budget:

- Horse-drawn carriage (check with the Carriage Association of
  America at www.caaonline.com or Carriage Operators of North
  America at www.cona.org to find reputable carriage rental com-
  panies and additional state associations in your area)
- Gondola or chartered boat
- Hot air balloon
- Trolley
- Horseback

You're only limited by your imagination when it comes to your
mode of transportation. As you'll learn later in this chapter, you'll
handle the expense with the right planning procedure.

Finding Your Transportation Company

I can't tell you how important it is to spend time researching limousine rental companies, comparing price packages, and getting a firsthand look at the vehicle you're ordering. I called up four reputable limousine companies in one town, asked for their basic wedding-day price plans for a standard four-hours' use of a black stretch limousine, and here's what I found:

Limo Company #1: $75 per hour
Limo Company #2: $70 per hour
Limo Company #3: $60 per hour
Limo Company #4: $55 per hour

Clearly, price ranges vary tremendously from company to company, so you can almost certainly find a great deal just by investing more of your time in the search. Start by asking friends who they hired for their wedding day, and then ask, "Were they good?" Ask if the drivers were courteous, ask if the limousines showed up on time, ask if the cars were clean and in great condition. Again, it's this firsthand report that means the most in your research process.

Also, check with friends who do a lot of corporate entertaining to find out their favorite limousine company, and call up a nearby four or five-star hotel to ask the concierge for a referral. These upscale hotels don't mess around with inferior vendors, as they want to provide only the best for their big-name guests, so look for a kind concierge who will be happy to refer you to a great company.

Wedding Day Reflections

We could have done the limousine thing, but we wanted to make more of an entrance. So, we decided to use our wedding setting in a unique and wonderful way, for far less than if we had hired a bunch of limousines. We had our wedding at a marina, with the ceremony and reception taking place on the bayside terrace of a lovely restaurant. Instead of renting limos, we arrived by boat. Friends of ours offered to let us decorate their great little motorboats with flowers and strung lights, and we glided up to the ceremony in style. Our guests loved the entrance, and it made for great pictures and video. Better yet, it cost us nothing!

—Emily and Brad

Check any company names you receive through referrals or read about in the Sunday wedding section of your local paper for professional association membership with the National Limousine Association (800-NLA-7007, www.limo.org). Members of professional associations like this one have earned a good name in the industry, and possess years of reliable service.

Questions to Ask Transportation Companies

1. Do you have our requested type of cars available on our wedding date?
2. What kinds of cars do you have? What are the prices for each of these types?
3. Do you have the model we desire? (i.e., Rolls-Royce, stretch Navigator, etc.)
4. What colors are available for us to select from?
5. What are your available car sizes? Eight-seaters? Ten? Twelve? Larger?
6. What are the basic features of your standard limousine? Champagne glass rack? Sunroof? Television?
7. Can we secure a discount if we hire a more basic car *without* the sunroof, champagne glass setup, etc.?
8. Do you offer the standard wedding package extras, such as a champagne stand and red carpet? Can we negotiate a discount if we don't want them?
9. What kind of experience and training do your drivers receive? (Important: Ask for their most experienced drivers for your day—this isn't the time for a beginner's first trip. Know that drivers need to have special training and certification to drive limousines and stretch luxury cars as well.)
10. What will the drivers be wearing? (For a formal wedding, ask that the drivers wear a tuxedo or appropriate dark suit.)
11. What are your standard wedding package rates?
12. Do you offer a budget wedding package? What is included?
13. What are your rates for a party van or bus for our guests?

However, don't just take an association's word on a company's caliber. Always submit your potential transportation companies to a battery of questions and, remember, you're not just looking for the lowest prices around. Very often, going with the low-ball figure is the best way to cause a wedding-day nightmare, like being stuck on the side of the road on the way to the church. Your hunt for the best

14. Do you have insurance? (Ask to see a copy of the certificate.)

15. Are you a member of a professional association, like the NLA? (Ask to see a copy of the certificate.)

16. What are your overtime rates? Are they configured by the hour, or by the half-hour?

17. Do you charge by the hour or a set fee for a length of time?

18. What is your refund/cancellation policy?

19. Do your drivers carry two-way radios? (This is *important!* Cell phones sometimes do not work in some areas. A two-way radio will connect the driver with the main office, so that contact is always assured in case of emergencies.)

20. Do you have a liquor license, so that we can have a champagne toast in the car? (Be clear on this. Rules vary by state for the types of cars that are allowed to hold drinking passengers, and some companies hold a strict policy that *no* drinking is allowed in their cars.)

21. Are you aware of any local conventions or events that will be going on at the time of our wedding that might make car availability scarce?

22. Do you offer any special seasonal rates or specials, such as 25% off during the winter holidays? (Some companies run specials to coincide with big travel or special event times in their areas. Ask for the company's upcoming special deals and jump in if the numbers and packages are attractive.)

23. Will the cars be washed and waxed before use on our wedding day?

transportation service will consider price *and* service. After all, your driver has a vitally important responsibility on your wedding day: getting you to the ceremony and reception on time.

These are just your fact-gathering questions. The real test comes when you've narrowed down your field of contenders and it's time to visit their offices. Schedule a meeting with the transportation company owner, look over complete price lists, and check out their fleet of cars. Don't just look at pictures of their fine lineup of shiny black limousines. Ask to step into them, check them out, look at the quality of the interior. Is this a new car? Is it well-maintained? Are the ashtrays clean? The rug vaccumed? The windows streak-free? Does it smell of cigarette smoke from recent passengers? (If so, and if the scent offends you, request a nonsmoking car for your wedding day.)

This firsthand inspection is a great way to tell the kind of company you're dealing with. Simply ask for an appointment to view several of his cars, and a quality manager will set up a meeting with you. A shady one, however, will push glossy pictures at you and tell you that you don't need to see his cars. If you get the brush-off, walk away. Don't hire a company that wants you to order sight unseen. No savings of money is worth that risk, especially when—as one couple reported in anguish—a *burgundy-colored* limo pulls up in front of your house on the wedding day.

Don't be afraid to make the transportation company manager write down specifics on your order form. If, for instance, you look at a lovely black stretch limousine in the parking lot, and you love its elegant interior, then specify that you are booking that particular car, by model and license plate. A quality company will grant you that request. The same deal applies if you would like to request a specific driver, as recommended by a former customer or from your own experience with the company.

As always, draw up a complete contract with the company, specifying not only the specifics of the car, but the times and exact street locations of all pickup and drop-off particulars. Especially if you're hiring several cars, you will need to present organized and comprehensive instructions for the drivers, to ensure timely and efficient delivery of all your major players.

Save Money with Your Schedule

Here's where you take that gleaming Excalibur and make it fit into your day in the most economical and efficient way possible. The key is to shorten the amount of time you'll use the car. Simple as that. Start now by writing out the time durations of when you'll need the car. Your beginning list might look like this:

- First car picks up bride, bride's father, and bridal party at bride's house and drives them to ceremony site.
- Second car picks up groom, ushers, and groom's family and drives them to ceremony site.
- Cars wait through the ceremony and then transport everyone to the reception.
- Cars come back at end of reception to pick everyone up and drive them home.

I can tell you right now that this is *not* the most economical plan for your transport expenses. First of all, you can save on your transportation bill by knocking out the first and last items on the list. One of the best ways to cut down your transportation bill is to eliminate transporting a large number of guests to and from the wedding. Many couples I've spoken to said that they either hired a van or bus to take their bridal party, family members, and guests to and from the wedding. They did *not* hire three or four limousines to deliver everyone in style. They ordered one limousine for the bride and groom only.

Another budget slash is to skip the limousine rides to the ceremony site. If you're marrying at a place where you can dress in a side room or other building on site, then you will not need to rent a ride to the wedding at all. In this case, the limousine is scheduled to transport you only to the reception site. When you consider that the meter starts running as the limousines leave their own parking lot, you can eliminate one to two hours of service by having the cars arrive *after your ceremony is over.* In some cases, this can save you $200 to $400, if not more.

Another smart planning strategy is to choose a town car rather than a limousine to take you home once the reception is over. Since the bride and groom often leave the reception before the event is over, it's a wise move to make that safe, designated-driver-ride home be one of less fanfare and more financially feasible. Selecting a town car is often $20 to $50 less per hour than a limousine. If you have a long ride to the airport hotel after the reception, your best choice is a more economical car such as this one.

Wedding Day Reflections

*W*e saved over $300 by just having one limousine take the two of us around on the wedding day. Our family members and bridal party members took the shuttle van provided by our hotel . . . for free! And the driver turned on the music so they could all enjoy the ride.
—Allison and John

While it's always wonderful to eliminate hours of service from your bill, please do not cut too deeply. Be sure that you've acquired solid and dependable transportation for your guests, whether it be a free hotel shuttle bus, a rented party van, or even nondrinking guests who might volunteer rides in their minivans. Be sure that you've protected your guests' well-being by taking these steps, even at a cost.

Look at your location and at the planning of your day to see where you can cut some transportation expenses. The flow of your day, according to your ceremony and reception timing, is going to be a big factor in this portion of your budget. Think about that meter whirring away during the two-hour break between your ceremony and reception. Sure, that breather gives you time to take plenty of pictures and relax with your bridal party, but you've also just tossed $150 to $200 out the window for each limo that's parked, unused, in front of your house. This may not be an issue if you've found a company that charges an acceptable flat rate for their four-hour wedding package, but if you're paying by the hour, this wasted time is wasted cash.

Valet Service

Another element of your transportation plans might be the hiring of valets to park your guests' cars. At some reception establishments, of course, valet service is included, and parking is free. Some sites do charge you a nominal fee for the use of their professional parking staff, and others do charge a per-car expense for parking in their lots. Practices vary from site to site and state to state.

If you have planned your wedding at a nonwedding site such as a state park, an arboretum, a permit-secured spot on a beach, or even at your own home, then you have some additional work to do. While not all couples hire valets for their parking needs, it is a considerate service to provide for guests, especially if a number of your guests are elderly or infirm. Some wonderful sites feature lovely grounds for outdoor or enclosed weddings, but they are accessed by long, winding paths or roads from an established and far-off parking lot. These settings will require parking help as a service to your guests.

Where do you find a team of good valets? Check with your wedding coordinator, the manager of your reception site, and recently married friends for the name of a reputable service. In some cases, you

Penny-Wise

You can call on your kind, helpful friends and relatives who've offered to help by asking them to be drivers for the day. Perhaps a friend has a beautiful convertible, antique car, or classic car that he might be willing to let you use. This valuable service can be counted as his wedding gift to you. Many couples arrange to have friends and relatives line up their convertibles for the wedding-day procession, saving a fortune in the process!

Don't Hire the Neighborhood Teens!

You can go too far in trying to save money on your wedding. It may seem to you that parking cars is an easy job, one that you can get help with from neighborhood teens who can use a bit of extra pocket money. *Don't do it!* Valet parking is a complicated job, with so many cars and keys to keep track of. Expert valet attendants have much experience with this important and unsung task, so do spend the money on a team of pros in order to avoid snarl-ups and nightmares that come from hiring amateurs.

might be able to find a great valet service company through the Internet or Yellow Pages by looking up Valet, Parking Services, or Special Event Services. These companies will assess your parking needs for your site and for your guest head count, and they will arrange for a suitable number of valets to be in attendance. Some more reputable valet companies will even apply for your parking permits for you, when such documentation is necessary for your site or your own street area. (If they don't, be sure you get your own permits ahead of time, following the tips in chapter 3.)

The experts say that the appropriate number of parking attendants is one for every seven or eight cars. It is important to hire enough valet parkers for your guest list, as you certainly don't want to cause a traffic jam at the start of your event or frustrate your guests with a long wait in line at the end of the night. I've been to several parties where the hosts tried to cut corners, hiring only three valets for their 150 guests. Many guests grumbled in line, and some jumped out of line to grab the attendant and locate their cars ahead of more patient guests. The scene was one of utter chaos, and it cast a pall over the delightful time all had enjoyed earlier that evening. So don't cheapen out on this expense, even though valet fees may run as much as $100 to $150 per attendant.

When hiring a valet company, be sure to secure a solid contract for hours and terms of service, specify the times the workers should arrive, what they should be wearing to work your event (shorts and windbreakers don't work for a more formal wedding!), the times and amounts of deposits, and whether tips are included in the valets' payment. Also, ask to see the company's liability insurance policies to be sure that the drivers are covered for any damage to your guests' cars.

Directions

Most couples do include a detailed map or list of directions to the ceremony and reception sites with their invitations or pre-wedding packages. If your event will be held at an established banquet site, hotel, or restaurant, the manager might be able to provide you with preprinted directions cards. These handy little tools are a great organizational time and stress saver, as they remove you and your family from the burden of sending directions through e-mail, mail, or over the phone a few hundred times.

Of course, you can ask a talented friend to draw up a map or write out the directions (after checking them carefully during a practice

Put Those Dollar Bills Away!

A good host will make sure that the valet workers are adequately tipped at the end of the evening. Instruct the valet manager and individual valets that they are not to accept tips from your guests. Your classier guests will almost certainly pull out a tip for the parking attendants, but their offers should be denied by the workers as a matter of policy. Just as you wouldn't offer a cash bar to your guests, you should release your guests from any financial responsibility related to your event.

drive and landmark-spotting expedition). If you create your own maps—which can be a fun and creative endeavor and a great task for a groom who wishes to help but doesn't want to pick out tablecloth colors—don't just depend upon your memory of the route, even if you've lived in the area for years. Several couples have told me to warn you about unforeseen construction and detours in your site area, so always check ahead of time and provide a contact phone number on the maps themselves. Perhaps your site manager, wedding coordinator, or a parent will volunteer to accept calls from hopelessly lost guests.

Additional Money-Saving Tips

• Book your cars early! Last-minute orders can cost you big money in rush fees, and you might not get the greatest selection of cars at a later date.

Simplify It

MapQuest (www.mapquest.com) is a common Web site used by couples who wish to print out their own maps for their guests' use. Just enter your site's specifics and print out a usable map or directions list.

• Go local. Hiring a local rental company can save you a bundle. Remember that the meter starts running from the time the car pulls out of its lot until the time it checks in again at the end of its shift. A local outfit can often mean less driving time and less expense. (Of course, be sure you're hiring for price value and not just for proximity!)

• Know how many cars you'll need. Too many couples book too many cars, generously allowing more space than necessary for their bridal party or for extra guests. On a budget, you might be better off just hiring one or two cars. Talk with your transportation manager to find the best rides possible for the people on your list. One party van might cost less than the three or four limos you've been considering. Price different colors of cars. You're not limited to the standard all-white wedding limousines, and black limousines often make a wonderful, striking contrast with you in your wedding gown. So ask your transportation manager for the prices of black or gray models for even greater savings.

• Don't stretch. Hiring a *regular* limousine, as opposed to a luxury stretch limousine, can be a greater savings.

• Compare costs of classic or exotic car rentals. You might be more the Jaguar type anyway. Sometimes, these non-bridal choices can cost less per hour than the types of cars other brides and grooms rent in great volume.

• Check out historical societies or classic car associations in your area. These clubs might be able to refer you to a member who rents out his 1930s-era, mint-condition antique car for a pittance.

• See what's for free. Your hotel might offer free use of its airport shuttle bus for you and for your guests as a thank-you for planning your reception at their establishment. If you're reserving a block of rooms at the hotel as well, ask for free use of the shuttle on the wedding day and for your guests to get to and from the rehearsal, other wedding weekend activities, and for their trips back to the airport or train stations.

• Hire a driver to be the sober, responsible chauffeur of your own car or cars you've borrowed from friends for the day. Your rental company should be able to quote you hourly prices for the use of their well-trained and experienced drivers. This option can run you $15 to $25 an hour, as opposed to $70 an hour for the driver and limo.

• Look into that party bus! Many companies now rent out clubs-on-wheels, which have elegant leather seats, mood lighting, great sound systems, and restrooms. These party buses might be just the ticket for your larger transportation needs—especially if you'll transport your guests for some distance to the wedding site.

• Take the trolley! In some areas of the country, you all might be able to hop on board a trolley (rent one or catch public transportation) for a fun and photo-friendly ride.

• Skip the champagne as offered by the company. Especially if your ride to the reception will be a short one, you really don't need this expense. If the champagne is already included, see if you can trade this add-on for another, or negotiate a small cut in your bill.

• Find out what the contracted mandatory tip amount is, and, if it's included in the bill, don't tip the driver again on the wedding night.

• If the reception site is within walking distance of the ceremony site, plan a walking procession for your guests! At some locations, your hall might be only a few blocks from the church, so why not line up your bridal party and other guests who are willing to walk the safe route with you? This often becomes a moving celebration, noticed by all passersby. Elderly and infirm guests may be driven instead.

• Have a reliable friend drive you to the hotel after the reception, instead of hiring a ride.

• Ask your bridal party members to drive family members to and from wedding events, such as the rehearsal and rehearsal dinner, to and from beauty salons on the wedding morning, and to and from the airport.

Put It in Print for Less

Invitations, Programs, and Other Printed Items

INVITATIONS MAY not always appear expensive, but when you add up the cost of inserts, envelopes, and the design and printing of those pretty cards, the result is often a jaw-dropping total. With the wealth of styles and designs to choose from, you'll find a wide range of prices on the market. This chapter will help you wade through the intricate details of invitation selection and design to create the print package that's perfect for your wedding . . . and for your budget!

The Hidden Language of Invitations

Your invitations tell your guests far more than just the date and place of your wedding. They're actually the first indicator of the style and formality of your event—the wording and design of the invitation imparts a great deal of information.

261

Through your invitations, your guests will learn the appropriate dress code (an ultraformal invitation will state that it is a "black tie" event), and who is invited (via the inclusion or exclusion of children's names). The stated location, such as a marina or your own home address, will also tell your guests what to wear and what to expect as far as exposure to weather. That's a lot of info packed into one little invitation, so keep the hidden messages in mind as you choose the style and arrangement of your invitation packages.

The First Steps

Quite obviously, you can only set out to choose and order your invitations once you have all the details of your wedding set. Before you flip through one page of those enormous invitation sample books and before you start cruising the online invitation sites, be sure you know every detail your invitation will impart, from the date, day, time, and exact street addresses of your ceremony and reception locations to the style of your wedding. Before you venture into your search, write down the exact spelling of the names of all the people who will be listed as hosts on your invitation and how you'd like them listed. This is particularly important when your parents are divorced and remarried but are hosting the wedding as a team. Most important, of course, you'll need to know how many invitations you will need.

This last item is a crucial one, as too many couples waste a ton of money by ordering way too many invitations, often up to 50% more than necessary. Remember that you're sending invitations to couples or families at one address, not to each individual. So arrange your mailing list by grouping your guest-list names according to who is included in each invitation package.

With the basic information in hand, you're all set to start browsing the various styles and materials on the market and find the perfect invitations for you.

Invitation Etiquette

Rules of etiquette still strongly apply to invitations. This is the one area where have-to's still reign, so do follow these general rules of thumb to figure out who gets their own invitations:

- Married couples receive one invitation, addressed as Mr. and Mrs.
- Children over age eighteen living at home get their own individual invitations as well. (Some couples choose to list children age sixteen and over, to signify the child's status as an adult, particularly if that child is allowed to bring a date.)
- Children under age eighteen are listed by name on their parents' invitations.
- Send bridal party members their own official invitations, even though you know that they're aware of the date, time, and place. They still have to be officially invited and informed of their ability to bring a guest to the wedding, if they are not married.
- Send an invitation to the officiant, if you have decided to invite the officiant as a guest to the reception.
- Always order 15% to 20% more invitations than you'll need for your set guest list. Having this amount of extras on hand allows you to send out more invitations if your first tier guests cannot make it to the wedding, and it will also prevent rush fees or extra order charges later in the process. These extras will not go to waste—you can include them as keepsakes in photo albums, as gifts to guests who could not attend the wedding, even as framed mementos.

What's Your Style and Formality?

The style and formality of your wedding will determine the design, layout, and even colors of the invitations you choose. A classic, formal wedding calls for a more elegant and proper design, such as a simple white or ecru invitation with black italic lettering. A more informal wedding might allow for a more whimsical design and borders on your invitation, printed on cream or a more fun blush-colored paper. The style of invitation you choose not only conveys the tone of your wedding, but it also shows your own sense of personal style.

Allow plenty of time to peruse the many collections of invitation styles out there. Whether you're looking through giant portfolio albums or point-and-clicking your way through the thousands of offerings on an invitation Web site, know that this job is an enormous undertaking and a veritable treasure hunt to find the right combination of elements for the design you desire. Etiquette plays a big role in the design and wording of your invitations, but there are additional crucial issues to tackle when choosing invitations with your budget in mind.

It's All in the Material

Did you know that the type of material, or card stock, your invitation comes in can affect your price by 30% or more? You'll see listings for 100% cotton paper invitations. Sounds like that would be an economical choice, right? Wrong. One hundred percent cotton is among the most expensive card stocks out there. As you explore the world of invitations, you'll discover a great variety of card stock materials: textured papers, thicker cards with that homemade look, papers with flowers or clovers pressed into the material, filmy and transparent card covers . . . the list goes on and on. Paper creation is an art these days, and nowhere is it more lavishly and plentifully offered than in the world of wedding invitations.

If you're looking through sample invitation albums, you will be able to see and touch the many different types of papers. Some are smoother, shinier, ridged, or accented with attractive see-through overlays. These elements of paper design should complement your level of formality and provide just the look you had in mind. A hot trend in wedding invitations today is the invitation that folds in an intricate pattern, held together by a delicate bow of satin or chiffon ribbon. By far, this ribbon-clasp choice is a favorite of brides and grooms who want a unique look for their invitations.

It's Just Your Type

Next comes the issue of which type style you will choose to print the wording of your invitations. Type process affects the pricing tremendously, as some methods are far more expensive than others.

• Engraved. The most expensive and formal of options—and a favorite of "the sky's-the-limit" brides and grooms—this style creates raised lettering and letter indentations on the back of the card stock.

• Thermographed. By far the most popular type style, thermographed invitations offer the look of engraved invitations, only there are no indentations on the back. The simpler printing process means the product is less expensive, and it may even take less time to receive the finished versions.

• Calligraphy. Hand-written in lovely script, calligraphy invitations are especially stylish. If you have a talent for decorative writing, tackle this job yourself, or hire a professional. This option is best if you only require a smaller number of invitations and envelopes. Another option without the expense of hiring an expert: Use a calligraphy font on your home computer.

Penny-Wise

*F*or greater savings, go with lighter weight papers as opposed to heavier card stocks. When you assemble heavier cards, papers, and envelopes into each invitation package, you will double or triple your postal bill for your entire invitation mailing. (Just don't go paper-thin in an effort to save a buck. A flimsy invitation reflects poorly on you.)

Thermography vs. Engraved Invitations . . . What's the Bottom Line?

I spoke with Linda Zec-Prajka of An Invitation to Buy—Nationwide (www.invitations 4sale.com) and got a price-comparison sheet between these two printing processes. For a popular wedding-invitation style that includes an ecru card in black print with a handmade paper wrap, chiffon ribbon-tie, and blank double envelopes, the price differentials for an order of 100 invitations are as follows:

For Engraved Invitations
Invitation card: $361.00
Return address: $75.00
Reception cards: $115.00
Response card set: $175.00
Informal notes (blank inside): $100.00
Four rolls of ribbon (to tie the invitations): $140.00
Total: $966.00

Font Styles

In most invitation catalogs, and at invitation Web sites, you will find a list or display of beautiful fonts for the wording on your cards. These options may range from traditional wedding italics to more ornate Gothic lettering to a range of block, swirly, even fun and whimsical styles. Check the price listings for each type of font—most are broken down into type classifications by expense—and stick with the more standard choices at lower prices. Very often, basic fonts are easier to read than the fancier, more artistic designs. These "simple font" styles are a great buy, but you should be aware that printers often *cannot* adjust the size of this

For Thermographed Invitations

Invitation card: $296.00

Return address: $31.00

Reception cards: $75.00

Response card set: $100.00

Informal notes (blank inside): $75.00

Four rolls of ribbon: $140.00

Total: $717.00

A less detailed invitation of a standard white card with pearlized paneling, no ribbon tie, in black thermographed print is priced as follows

Invitation cards: $129.00

Return address: $30.90

Reception cards: $53.90

Response card set: $63.90

Informal notes: $54.90

Total: $333.50

type for a more centered and attractive layout on the invitation card. So, the savings can affect the look of the finished product here.

A Touch of Color

While colored print is a way to make wedding invitations more decorative, original, and personalized to the style of the wedding, you should know that standard black ink will usually cost you less. Sure, you can create a lovely invitation with hunter green print on an ecru card, beautifully reflecting your outdoor wedding, but you will certainly pay a bit more for the use of color. The same rules apply to

Professionally Speaking

I searched several calligraphy services on the Internet and in my home state, and I found the wonderful and affordable Calligraphy by Kristen (www.calligraphybykristen.com). On the average, owner Kristen Urhausen charges $2 per invitation set for more ornate italic writing, and $1.50 for penning in a standard script style. Kristen suggests the following tips for your ideal calligraphy order:

• If you're on a budget, choose regular script options over the more expensive italic style, which is more time-consuming for the artist to produce.

• Hire a calligrapher who does *not* charge you for delivery of samples of her work. Some companies will charge you if you want to see their work firsthand, and Kristen's company is one that will send you samples for free.

• Book your calligrapher far in advance. Remember that this is painstaking work, and it will take the artist time to complete your order. Last-minute rush jobs can often mean an extra $1 charge per invitation set.

• If you'll have your calligrapher write out your place cards as well, choose a less ornate script over a fancier italic one. Kristen charges fifty cents per place card for standard script and seventy-five cents per place card for italic.

• Always provide your calligrapher with a complete, computer printout of your guests' names and addresses, including zip codes. The correct titles of your guests— as in Miss, Ms., Dr., Captain, and others—should be provided as well.

• Create a solid, complete contract stating the date of guaranteed delivery, and pay with a credit card for tracking of your order.

color-imbued papers, with those blush and multi-hued styles more likely to run at higher prices than traditional white or ecru papers.

Color within invitations does adhere to the rules of formality, with ecru and black print reflecting a formal wedding. If your wedding will be more informal, or breaks somehow from the traditional celebration, then consider color to reflect the style of your day.

Save with Style Choices

Your choices with regard to style can save you a fortune on your invitations, without sacrificing a beautiful and formality-appropriate look. Here are some tips to help you choose:

• Go simpler. A plain invitation with a delicate border for accent, rather than a busier design with lots of embossed graphics, will cost less and reflects a classier style.

• Go smaller. Some invitations are larger than others, and these bigger selections will only cost more to mail. Choosing a smaller style will save you in the long run.

• Reflect your theme. So many invitation companies and catalogs offer beautiful styles that reflect the floral theme of a garden wedding or the beach theme of a seaside wedding. Comparison-shop among these wonderful graphic-laden styles to find the one that best announces to your guests what they can expect for your day.

• Go easy on the borders. Of the many styles to ponder, consider those with simpler borders. Today's styles feature everything from a classy thin black scroll line to simpler pearlized shaded edging to tiny roses or

Wedding Day Reflections

We chose a pale pink invitation with a deeper rose lettering for our formal wedding, and we received a lot of phone calls from guests who weren't sure about the dress code for the wedding. Since they were mostly from out of town and not familiar with the popular name of the great reception site we chose, we spent a lot of time calling everyone and letting them know that we had planned a formal wedding. We had no idea that the rose-colored lettering would make our guests think the wedding was informal.

—Emily and Austin

daisies. Consider the offerings, and choose a simpler border over a more ornate (and sometimes gaudy) one.

Extras, Extras!

No invitation packet is complete with just the invitation. Several extra items are also included for the guests' information, use, and return:

• Response cards, which are crucial for your organization process and guest head-count for the caterer and site.

• Reception cards, if only some of your guests will be invited to both your ceremony and your reception. (Your official invitation for this split guest list, then, is only to the ceremony itself.)

• Hotel information cards. These handy cards inform your guests of where they can book their hotel rooms (or provide confirmation numbers for the rooms you have booked on their behalf); hotel room prices; the reservations phone line; and the availability of non-smoking and handicap access rooms, cribs, cots, and parking information.

• Printed directions to your locations.

• An at-home card, giving your new residence and phone number and perhaps the announcement of your new, married name.

• Invitation cards to additional wedding-weekend events, such as brunches, barbecues, family softball tournaments, and other outings.

Simplify It

*A*sk your wedding site manager for printed directions. Most establishments do provide free a preprinted map or clear directions for visitors and guests. If the manager does not have such directions, create a map or printed directions yourselves using mapquest .com or Go.com's easy directions tools.

Envelopes

Most invitation packages come with matching inner and outer envelopes, and you should discuss the size of your envelopes with your invitation salesperson. Especially if you will have a large number of enclosures, a too small envelope may bulge at the seams or not even hold all the items.

Most formal and informal invitation packages include inner and outer envelopes to hold the entire invitations package. While some couples are now choosing to skip the inner envelope in an effort to save on ordering costs and postage, I do advise you to stick with tradition and use those inner envelopes. They are, after all, a useful indicator to your guests when they see the names of those invited written again on the inner envelope. This is where your friends get the clear message that it is only they, and *not* their three children, who are invited to the wedding. If you omit this envelope, you do not get the chance to reiterate your guest list decision.

You may also find that your chosen style of invitation comes with the option of lined or unlined inner envelopes. Invitations expert Linda Zec-Prajka warns that some liners don't really match the invitation and are therefore an unnecessary expense. Thick and glossy linings often just add to the weight of the package and make a very small impression on your guests.

When looking for ways to trim your invitations budget, do not even think about ordering fewer invitations and envelopes. Just as you'll need extra invitations, you will definitely need those extra envelopes. After all, you and your team of helpful assistants may make a mistake or two while writing out so many invitations late at night, so it's best to order extras now, rather than pay for replacements later. A good rule of thumb is to order thirty to fifty more envelopes than you think you'll need. Sounds like a lot of extras, but you'll find that it doesn't add up to much, and it's money well spent.

Avoid Hand Cramps

Do we have to write out the envelopes by hand? I have a great computer graphics program, and I can use that to print up the envelopes. It would take up so much less time.

Ideally, and according to wedding etiquette, all invitation envelopes should be written out by hand. Many couples are, however, using their home computers to print fine and attractive italics directly onto the envelopes. These envelope-addressing mail merge programs often produce a wonderful look at a great savings of time. Just be sure to stick close to your computer's printer as each envelope comes through so that you can gently unstick the envelope flaps that may have been heated by the printer's inner mechanisms. Not tending to this job might result in the horrible nightmare of having all your envelopes sealed shut and therefore wasted.

What about printing out addresses on pretty wedding-themed labels?

Absolutely not. While etiquette allows computers to print directly onto envelopes, owing to the wonderful quality of laser printers and lovely fonts in computer word-processing programs, it is never okay to use self-stick address labels on your wedding invitations. Tacky, tacky, tacky.

Go with a plain outer envelope. Styles with raised décor, borders, design prints, and (shudder) glitter on the outside are not only in less-than-stellar taste, they can also cause delays and problems at the post office. Thicker, more detailed envelopes might jam up postal processing machines or even challenge automated routing machines with lettering that cannot be recognized by scanners. Don't risk lost or destroyed invitations by choosing dark or detailed envelopes. Stick with something less embellished, for savings and sanity's sake.

When writing out envelopes, be sure you adhere to formal wording for your guests' names and addresses. All abbreviations are spelled out, guests are addressed by their correct titles, and state names are not abbreviated. If you don't have a guest's plus-four zip code handy, simply use the zip code finder at the U.S. Postal Services Web site www.usps.gov.

How to Write It

Again, etiquette rules stand firmly in the realm of invitation wording. Everything from the spelling of certain words to the names listed in the correct order on the invitation imparts vital information and honors through the careful wording of your invitation. In this section, you'll learn the basics for getting the wording right the first time, and keeping everyone happy in the process. The invitation is the first and greatest family diplomacy hotspot, as parents, step-parents, your future in-laws, and even your divorced parents' new spouses can chime in with a firm request to be listed as a host on the invitation. Couples who have not carefully considered the names on their invitations have set off firestorms and lifelong resentments just by using the wrong wording. You'd be surprised at how seriously this one element of your wedding plans can affect future relationships, so get the details in

Simplify It

*B*efore you purchase those pretty Love stamps at the post office, or any other stamp that works with your wedding's theme, take one completed invitation packet, with all extras enclosed, to be weighed officially by a postal agent. Find out the true weight of the package and then select one stamp that covers the total postage amount. The extra weight might require a higher denomination of stamp or perhaps two Love stamps. When figuring your postal needs, use this figure to multiply up the number of packets you'll be mailing and don't forget to add that standard first-class Love stamp for your response card. While you can order your stamps through the U.S. Postal Service's Web site at www .usps.gov, keep in mind that this timesaver costs you a bit extra in shipping charges. It might be better to stand in line at the post office.

That's Honour with an " . . . Our"

Before we get into who gets listed where on the invitation, keep these general wording rules in mind as you begin lettering out your page:

- For formal weddings, use the old English spellings of words like *honour* instead of honor, and *favour*, instead of favor.
- For informal weddings, use the wording *request the pleasure of your company* in the invitation, rather than the more formal *request the honour of your presence*.
- Spell out all abbreviated words, such as Street, Avenue, Boulevard, Circle, Drive, and the like.
- Spell out the times of day. For instance, 4:00 P.M. would be spelled out as *four o'clock in the afternoon,* and 7:00 P.M. would be *seven o'clock in the evening.*
- Provide an exact street location and town for all wedding day sites. No zip code is necessary for a formal invitation.
- Spell out all names in full, formal spelling, such as James Smith for your cousin Jim Smith.
- Use appropriate titles where necessary, such as Doctor Mary Jones or Captain Andrew Smith.
- Avoid using bold lettering or using two different sizes of lettering. All print should be the same pitch.
- Double-check all information for accuracy. Leave nothing to memory; get it right the first time, and avoid having to re-order invitations at rush fees.

order now, and design the wording of your invitations with full respect and future peace in mind.

WHO GETS LISTED ON THE INVITATION?

Back when it was the norm for the bride's parents to pay for the wedding, even if the groom's parents kicked in for their prescribed expense categories, only the bride's parents were listed as the first names on the invitation. Now, with both sets of parents splitting the duties, and with step-parents joining in as hosts, the roster of names listed can take up half the invitation page! And now, many couples are paying for and planning their own weddings, leaving their parents' names completely off the invitation. Which listing style works best for your particular family and situation? Look here at the basic samples I've provided to see which model best suits your situation, and then copy the formula for the wording of your own invitations.

If the bride's parents are hosting the wedding:

Mr. and Mrs. Henry Anderson
request the honour of your presence
at the marriage of their daughter
Amelia Suzanne
and
Timothy James Reese
son of
Mr. and Mrs. Thomas Reese
Saturday, the fourteenth of August
at four o'clock in the afternoon
Saint Augustine Church
1 Main Street
Bangor, Maine

If both sets of parents are sharing hosting responsibilities equally:

Mr. and Mrs. Henry Anderson
and
Mr. and Mrs. Thomas Reese
request the honour of your presence
at the marriage of their children

Amelia Suzanne
and
Timothy James . . .

When divorced parents are hosting:

Mr. Lawrence Jerrolds
and
Mrs. Jennifer Jerrolds
request the honour of your presence
at the wedding of their daughter
Stephanie Elise
to
Mr. David Anthony Harme . . .

When multiple sets of the bride's parents are hosting, such is often the case with divorced and remarried parents, a group title is often used in place of the more time-consuming list of four or more names:

The loving parents of
Stephanie Elise Jerrolds
request the honour of your presence
as their daughter unites in marriage with
Mr. David Anthony Harme . . .

When the couple is planning, paying for, and hosting their own wedding:

Ms. Stephanie Elise Jerrolds
and
Mr. David Anthony Harme

Request the honour of your presence
as they unite in marriage . . .

When the couple is planning, paying for, and hosting their own wedding, but they still want to pay tribute to their parents on the invitation, they might create the following template:

Ms. Stephanie Elise Jerrolds
and
Mr. David Anthony Harme,
together with their families,
Request the honour of your presence
as they unite in marriage . . .

These samples, of course, are simply representative of the most common familial situations as reflected in wedding invitations. Today's more informal invitation styles have wording that is significantly more relaxed, playful, and personalized and reflects the personalities of the bride and groom. Take, for instance:

We're finally tying the knot!
You're invited to join us
As we take our vows,
Drink a toast (or two or three),
And dance all night
At the
Rockshore Pavillion
In Newport, Rhode Island
On Friday the twenty-sixth of September
At 6:00 P.M.

Advice from a Professional

"When you choose the standard lettering on an invitation—which is the more affordable choice—the font stays at one standard size. It may or may not look perfectly proportioned on the card. If you choose 'photo lettering,' for just a small fee more, the printer will determine the proper lettering size to make your wording look perfect on the card."

—LINDA ZEC-PRAJKA, OWNER, AN INVITATION TO BUY—NATIONWIDE (WWW.INVITATIONS4SALE.COM)

Whatever your wording decisions, know that invitation styles determine the number of lines of print that can be attractively and efficiently displayed. Trying to squeeze too much information or too many lines of print onto a smaller-sized invitation will only make the product look cramped and cheap. So keep your wording in line with the available space on the invitation.

Placing Your Order

Once you have your basic design, style, and wording figured out, it's time to place your order. As always, you should allow plenty of time before your mailing date, and you should be sure that your order form is absolutely *perfect,* without a misspelling or mistake in sight. Allow yourself plenty of time to address the envelopes and assemble the packets once the invitations arrive, and check the shipment immediately for errors so they can be fixed in plenty of time.

Where do you want to place your order? You have several options, actually. One of the most common sources is a stationery store. These specialty shops may offer a wall of sample invitation books for you to consider, and their ordering process can be as simple as sitting down with a sales associate while she records your order and wording details. A true professional is well-versed in the terminology and options related to wedding invitations. If your sales associate seems to be stumped when you ask questions about photolettering, thermography, and the like, go somewhere else. A knowledgeable expert will be able to guide you through the selection process, place a correct order, and alert you to any special conditions or delivery procedures.

You can also check out invitation catalogs, in which you flip through a printed catalog, choose your style and model numbers, select the number of invitations you'll need, then either fax, e-mail, mail, or call in your complete order. If you are ordering over the phone, I suggest that you ask the sales associate to read back and spell out each word of your invitation. Over the phone an *s* can sound like an *f*, so be extremely detail-oriented when it comes to placing your order.

Online invitation companies offer you the chance to view thousands of different invitation styles, with the ordering process handled either online or through an affiliated, live service representative. Many of these companies will send you a printed version of their catalog for your review as well.

When ordering online, be sure the site is secure, has a telephone number and street address, and that they offer a complete and solid return and refund policy where appropriate.

Wherever you decide to order your invitations, always practice smart and safe shopping procedures. Secure your investment with a credit card, not a debit card, print out all order confirmation numbers, and get the name of the associate who assisted you. For an even better deal, shop with a company that offers great discounts and

Penny-Wise

*B*elieve it or not, you can find great invitation deals through sources you might not normally expect. Several brides I spoke to said they purchased their invitations at a great discount at a warehouse store, through their houses of worship, through their company's print supply wholesaler, and through family friends with "contacts."

free shipping on all orders. With so much competition out there in the world of invitations, this is a common perk.

Other Printed Items

Your invitations are just one segment of the printed items wish list you may have planned for your day. Also included in your invitation budget might be one or more (or all) of the following:

- Thank-you notes
- Seating cards
- Pew cards
- Maps
- Menu cards
- Invitations to the rehearsal dinner
- Invitations to postwedding events
- Invitations to the bridal brunch
- Printed cards to accompany favors
- Printed cards to accompany guests' hotel room gift baskets
- Directional signs for parking, walking path to the reception, restroom, or parking area
- Additional printed signs
- Wedding programs

Of course, you can order many of these items from an invitations catalog or Web site, but you're best served making these noncrucial print purchases a do-it-yourself job. Perhaps a friend can print up your place cards or menu cards on her home computer, with the completion of this simple task counting as her wedding gift to you. Most couples look for ways to include their family and friends in the wedding plans, and many grooms look for ways they too can contribute to the event. So, make your choices from the list above, and see if you can order them through a less expensive source or create them from scratch for that personal touch.

Do-It-Yourself Invitations

Take a walk through the computer software aisle of any office supply store, and you'll see several Make Your Own Wedding Invitation programs. Some of these kits are worth the $30 to $40 investment, as they provide complete paper, accent materials, and templates to create your own homemade invitations, which can look professionally made if you have good computer and design skills. Many of these kits offer enough paper for twenty-five to thirty invitations, with additional paper needs left up to you. If you only need a few invitations for your small wedding, then these kits might be perfect for you.

Even without a software kit, you can create your own invitations and other printed items using store-bought paper or card stock and the great skills of a computer-savvy friend. It may take a few days to complete the perfect layout, select your wording to fit the paper size, choose the right font, and print out several versions on regular paper until you get everything just right. I have seen wonderful examples of homemade invitations designed and printed on a personal computer, so I can assure you it is possible to create your own invitations at a savings. After you finish, your next task is to find the right size envelopes. Allow plenty of time to create your own invitations, and always print on regular paper first before sliding your more

Simplify It

*Y*our wedding programs are most economical as a do-it-yourself job. Just use your computer's graphic design and word-processor programs to lay out a complete program that's suited to your tastes. You might include an attractive clip art graphic for your cover or incorporate a scanned color picture of the two of you. Page one might list your bridal party, parents, ceremony participants, officiant, and musicians by name. Page two might outline the elements of your ceremony, and page three might include a personal message of thanks from you both. For a more professional look, use glossy or textured paper from an office supply shop, or purchase pretty program covers from a religious bookstore or Web site.

expensive card stock into your printer. With this option, you might just create your own invitations for $15 to $30, rather than several hundred for professionally ordered collections. Just be sure that you have the talent and the time to devote to this important task, as the savings won't matter if the finished product looks amateurish.

RSVPs

Ah, the magic number. Your final guest count—the important figure that will determine your exact expenses with your caterer, your

Can We Skip the Response Card?

I just read an article that says it's okay to ask your guests to e-mail their responses, rather than mail in that little card. Is that a good idea?

No, I can't say that it is. This idea may have come about from someone who takes penny-pinching to the extreme, and I've heard nothing but complaints from the couples who did go high tech for their RSVP process. Remember, not everyone has access to an e-mail account, particularly older relatives. Some messages sent to you might get knocked into cyberspace by a faulty e-mail service, a computer virus, or an incomplete-send by an inexperienced user. Stick with traditional response cards for a reliable head count and to stay organized while tracking guests who have and haven't responded by the due date. For more informal invitations, it's okay to print your RSVP request along with your phone number right on the card.

baker, your florist, and your favors provider—comes to you from the RSVP responses sent in by your guests. When those response cards start arriving daily in the mail, it becomes time to tally up the yeas and nays. So be sure to record an early RSVP date on your invitations with enough lead time for you to determine the final head count.

Additional Money-Saving Tips

• Order single-panel invitations, rather than folded styles.

• Don't even look at the upscale invitation sample books. Some companies are known for their gorgeous, high-priced selections. Tell your invitation sales assistant that you'd only like to see the moderately priced collections. Why torture (or tempt) yourself by looking through invitations that are out of your budget?

• Don't fall for discount scams. Always comparison-shop for prices. It's a common wedding industry scam to offer 50% discounts on invitations with, say, the rental of your tuxes through a certain shop. That 50% discount isn't much of a bargain when the prices of the invitations have been marked way up.

• Use a decorative rubber stamp tool to imprint your homemade invitations, place cards, and programs with your initials, a heart motif, or any other design you favor. An embossing set (inexpensive at craft stores!) will add to the do-it-yourself fun . . . and to great effect.

Simplify It

*T*o find well-priced and high-quality papers, check your local office supply stores or the following paper supply Web sites:

PaperDirect.com,
    800-272-7377
PaperShowcase.com,
    800-287-8163

Wedding Day Reflections

We created our own invitation using a canvas and my own painted lotus flower design. Once I was done with my painting, we took it to a local copy shop along with a print-out of our invitation's text. Their graphic design department laid out the text next to my flower design, and then they copied the result for just $50 in total. We had a gorgeous representation of exactly what we wanted, and it meant more because it was my artwork featured on the invitation.

—Lina

• Don't order your thank-you notes as part of your wedding invitation order, or "at discount" through your photographer. Instead, buy blank-inside thank-you cards or notes from a card store—preferably during a big sale. (No, it's not okay to e-mail your thank-yous with a graphic of you from your wedding day.)

• Send maps only to those guests who request them. Not everyone needs to get one.

Giving Is Better Than Receiving

Favors and Gifts

T HROUGHOUT THE course of your entire wedding planning process, you're sure to receive many wonderful gifts—both the kind you unwrap and the more priceless kind such as words of praise from a parent, sage relationship advice from a long-married couple, and the reassuring presence of your friends. Now, it's time to show your appreciation for your guests, your family, your friends, your bridal party, and each other with gifts and favors you've chosen especially for them.

This section will send you on a wonderful, guilt-free shopping spree as you seek out the perfect items for all of the people on your list. While some couples may have cash to burn and can bestow upon their guests expensive items such as tickets to a Broadway show and Lalique vases, your more modest budget will limit your options a bit. This does not mean you can't find great gifts that will thrill your recipients. In fact, it simply means that you'll find wonderful presents at reasonable prices that *look* more extravagant than they are.

Let's start with your wedding favors.

Wedding Favors

Let's say you have 100 guests coming to your wedding. Those wonderful silver heart-shaped frames you saw at the mall cost $15 apiece. If you were to choose to buy one for each of your guests, your total budget for favors would be $1,500! If you use a common budget-saving tip and buy only one favor per couple, you're still looking at a price tag in the neighborhood of $750 to $900 (including single guests who aren't part of a couple).

I looked through hundreds of favor options at wedding Web sites, bridal stores, department store sales, craft shops, even warehouse stores, and I've assembled a list of the best favor choices for couples on a budget. These items can be found for just a few dollars apiece and at even greater savings when bought in bulk. A big key to finding great favors is exercising your own handicraft talents or asking creative relatives to make favors using items you've found at wholesale or sale prices. For instance, a plain pillar candle can be wrapped up beautifully in a large square of color-coordinated tulle, tied with a pretty ribbon, and tagged with a personal note of thanks from the two of you. A fifty-cent basket with a handle can be filled with small packets of bath salts, votive candles, and a few wrapped chocolates for a decadent bath experience. The options are endless, and your modest budget will be wonderfully served by your own imagination. So read on for some inexpensive favor ideas, think about what you can do with them, and then search out the best resources near you:

• Candles and candleholders (as low as $1.50 each at some craft stores).

• Glass hurricane lamps with color-coordinated pillar candles.

• Glass potpourri bowls with a signature scent of potpourri, such as rose or gardenia. (Buy potpourri in bulk bags at a warehouse store or craft store for even greater savings.)

• Silver frames, found in craft stores or in bulk from great low-priced sources such as Pier 1 (www.pier1.com) where I found adorable butterfly-themed silver frames for just $4 to $10 apiece.

• Engraved silver bells. Find them for under $10 each at www.thingsremembered.com

• Glass bowls filled with sand, seashells, and a silver starfish necklace on a string.

• Wrapped chocolates or truffles. (Nothing beats the elegance of those little gold Godiva two-piece or four-piece chocolate boxes with theme ribbon or imprinted ribbon at www.godiva.com. The prices are quite reasonable for the resulting classy effect!)

• Homemade candies. Use chocolate candy-making or lollipop kits found at your local craft store to melt your own chocolate and custom-design your own creations. This particular creative endeavor is so easy even children can do it. The chocolate molds and lollipop sticks cost little more than a dollar apiece. Pretty patterned candy bags to hold your creations cost just $3 for a bag of twenty or so.

• Homemade cookies. Break out your holiday sugar-cookie recipe, buy a few inexpensive gown-, shoe-, dove-, or bell-shaped cookie cutters, and bake adorable wedding-themed cookies to frost and decorate as you wish. Wrap each picture-perfect cookie in cellophane, tie with a ribbon, and attach a note. If you're holding an informal or outdoor wedding, choose cookie cutters in other appropriate theme designs, such as starfish, flowers, beach balls, or the sun and moon.

• Books. Buy books of romantic poetry, a favorite inspirational author's newest work, or the best quotes about love and marriage, and share the wealth with your guests. A little tip to get greater savings: Call the publisher of the book directly and ask to speak to the special sales department. You might be able to negotiate a large discount or perhaps free shipping on your order of fifty books. For an added personal touch, include a homemade bookmark imprinted with your names and wedding date.

• Videotapes or DVDs. I *love* this idea from a couple in San Francisco who gave their guests copies of the first romantic movie the couple ever saw together. Choose a variety of romantic movies your guests might not already own, providing a mix of VHS tapes and DVDs, and let your guests choose their own favorites.

• Bottles of wine. You can find great suggestions for vintages that cost less than $10 or $15, without them tasting like a bottle of vinegar. If you want to give your guests wine or champagne, check www.wine spectator.com for detailed reviews and suggestions, and then contact your local liquor wholesaler, discount store, or nearby winery for a bulk discount purchase. Cut costs even more by giving each couple one bottle of wine to share.

• Ornaments. Buy beautiful, color-coordinated or white ornaments from a local craft store, and either wrap them in tulle or set them in pretty see-through plastic boxes with a personalized note. With thousands of different styles to choose from, you're certain to find a great selection of color, design, and special effects in boxed collections. For even greater savings, if your wedding is a year in the future, shop the after-Christmas sales to get those $10 boxes of white and silver star ornaments for half off. That's twelve to sixteen individual favors for just a little over $5. Perfect for holiday weddings, this gift is something your guests will definitely use again.

• CD mixes. Use your own home computer to burn romantic or memory-laden music-mix CDs for your guests, and then use CD jackets and labels from your local office supply store to personalize the packaging. Again, this is one option your guests will love . . . and use again and again (unlike a brandy snifter with your names inscribed on it).

• Potted plants and seedlings. For just a few dollars each, you can find great collections of potted flowering plants or seedlings that can be wrapped at the base with colored foil and then labeled with directions for growing and a personal note of thanks. Beyond the sometimes laughingly low expense ($3 for a six-pack of seedlings!) this option allows your guests to take a living piece of your day home and watch it grow in the future. Another option is a pretty collection of flower seed packets, preferably the kind that don't take a lot of work. Some wildflower seeds will work well for guests who don't have a natural green thumb.

• Pampering products. Check your local bath and body store for great collections of men's and women's products and then assemble your own gift baskets.

Favors That Make a Difference

I've heard about couples making donations to charity in their guests' names as wedding favors. Is this a good idea, or is it considered tacky?

I've heard a lot about this trend, particularly after the September 11th tragedies. Couples would rather give their $300 favor budget to a wonderful, reputable, and legitimate charity that can make a difference in people's lives than give trinkets that will sit on a shelf somewhere or go right into future garage sales. My best advice is to make your own decision according to what seems right for you. Few guests will scoff at not getting a collection of candied almonds at the end of the night, but you might hear some pros and cons in the feedback hours. If you do decide to pursue this option, be sure to check your chosen charity well with www.give.org, a national clearinghouse and ratings system for registered charities. An even better check would include calling the charity and asking for their IRS reports to prove their legitimacy. A great charity gives most if not all of its earnings directly to the needy or to research.

• Fun items for theme weddings. For your beach wedding, for instance, hand out colorful sand buckets containing sunglasses, sunscreen, lip sunblock, a trashy paperback novel, and a packet of iced tea mix for a fun gift under $25 that will be used again.

Favors for Children

Kids invited to your wedding will look dumbfounded if you hand them a crystal frame as a favor, so be sure to plan delightful gifts for your youngest child guests and your teens. Some ideas for these specialized items:

• Gift certificates to music or toy stores (don't try to choose a popular video or CD, as kids know best what they like).

• Boxes of chocolate or fun snacks in attractive wrapping.

• Prepaid phone cards.

• Child or teen-appropriate baskets of pampering items.

• Toys for the little kids to play with during the reception (these also help keep them occupied and tantrum-free!).

Be sure to label the adults' and children's favors separately, attach a preprinted or handwritten note of thanks to each, and plan your method of disbursement. You might arrange the favors on a special table near the exit for your guests' own selection. Or, arrange them in the centers of the dinner tables as a double-duty, inexpensive alternative to a pricier centerpiece. Those beautifully tulle-wrapped candles will make attractive accents to your table décor.

Great Gifts for the Special People on Your List

Your family, friends, and other loved ones have been there for you throughout your lives, and now they're about to be a part of your Big

Day. Thank them now for their years of love and support, as well as for their help with the wedding by giving them well-chosen gifts that come straight from the heart.

For Your Parents

Okay, so your parents might have battled with you furiously throughout the planning of the wedding, and your mother may have made an off comment about your future mother-in-law. All parents have bad days, especially during such a hectic time, but you still love them. Regardless of whether or not they paid for the wedding or saved the day with a call to a buddy in the wine business, thank your parents for all they've done for you with a personalized gift, something special that's just *them*. Some ideas:

• Special jewelry items, such as a mother's ring or matching watches (found for less during jewelry sales).

• A wonderful bottle of wine or champagne for her; a bottle of fine cognac or port for him.

• Tickets to a concert by their favorite musical or comedy artist.

• Tickets to a sporting event for a team they both love.

• An engraved silver picture frame to hold wedding day portraits of you with your parents.

• A newly designed photo album featuring pictures of them throughout the years, or photos of your family.

• A professionally edited videotape of your family's old home movies, with soundtrack of their favorite songs.

• A professionally edited videotape of your parents' childhood days, or stills of their childhood snapshots, continuing up through the present day. A special idea for parents who might not have had the funds for a professional wedding video for themselves is to have old family reels of that day transferred to video or CD now. Comparison-shop at full service camera stores, or have a videotape-savvy friend do the job as a wedding gift to you.

FOR YOUR BRIDESMAIDS AND MAID OF HONOR

After making them try on all those bridesmaids' gowns and paying for the one you've chosen, your maids deserve a little something special. Thank them now for their years of laughter and love, their help with the wedding, and their comforting words of advice with a special gift:

- Jewelry to wear on the wedding day.

- Engraved silver bracelets, locket necklaces, business card cases, compacts (one of my favorites, found at www.thingsremembered .com), perfume atomizers, silver keychains.

- Tickets to a play or concert.

- A silver picture frame with your favorite picture of the two of you. (Some brides choose a double picture frame that holds a picture of you from when you were little girls and a current photo from the wedding day.)

- Fine perfume and matching-scent lotion kits.

- Personalized jewelry boxes.

- Travel toiletry kits.

- A professionally edited videotape of your years growing up together.

- A music-mix CD with all your favorite songs that remind you of being back in school, vacations, and the handsome men you've left behind over the years!

- A gift certificate to a bookstore or bookstore café.

• A copy of a book she would love, signed by the author (either gotten firsthand at a big city book signing or sent to your local bookstore on order from a store where the author appeared).

• A handmade craft item, such as a needlepoint theme-embroidered pillow with your favorite quote or catchphrase (brides with limited time can ask a creative relative or friend to make the pillows—with plenty of time to complete the task—as her contribution to the wedding).

• Bottles of fine wine or champagne to be shared on a special occasion.

FOR THE GROOMSMEN AND BEST MAN

It's not *all* beer mugs and cuff links anymore. Consider the following options for great guy-oriented gifts:

• Engraved silver flasks, money clips, cuff links, watches, beer mugs, silver key chains, silver business card cases.

• Classic shaving kits.

• Several fine cigars.

• A round of golf at a nearby country club.

• Tokens for a few buckets of golf balls at the nearby driving range, or a few rounds of fast pitches at the batting cages.

• Tickets to a concert or sporting event.

• A framed picture of your group of friends.

• A professionally edited videotape of your best moments together over the years.

• Bottles of fine port, brandy, or cognac to be shared on a special occasion.

FOR OTHER PARTICIPANTS IN YOUR WEDDING CEREMONY OR RECEPTION

They offered their participation in your wedding, will play an important role in your day, and perhaps saved you a fortune by volunteering their efforts. Thank them now with a token of appreciation such as the following:

- A bottle of wine or liqueur.

- A gift certificate to a bookstore or music store.

- A gift certificate for dinner or brunch at a favorite restaurant.

- Tickets to a movie, comedy club, or musical performance.

- A silver picture frame.

- Chocolates or candies.

- Their own personally assembled album of wedding-day pictures.

- A gift certificate for a manicure/pedicure at a local salon or a massage at a local massage or healing center.

FOR CHILDREN

Whether you've asked your nieces and nephews to be your flower girls and ringbearers, or you're blending your two groups of children into one family, it's a wonderful idea to give the children a special gift on the wedding day:

- An engraved silver charm bracelet, ID bracelet, or watch for older children.

- A music box.

- A much-wanted item, such as the promise of a new puppy after the honeymoon. (Just make sure it's *your* child you make this promise to!)

- A much-wanted sports item, such as new skis, or the promise of new sports lessons, such as karate classes.

- Finally! The keys to the old family car or to a new-to-you car.

- Tickets to the hottest teen concert coming through town.

- A shopping trip for a set number of new clothing items, with parental veto power in play.

- A makeover at a salon or department store beauty counter for your teenage girls.

For Each Other

This is likely to be the most memorable gift you give one another. In most cases, the bride and groom exchange special jewelry to be worn on the wedding day, such as pearl earrings for her and an engraved watch for him. As meaningful as this gift is, you don't have to spend a fortune. Sometimes the best gift is the promise of things to come. Here are some ideas:

- His and hers engraved watches.

- Hyphenating both of your names together, officially.

- Professional framing of each other's most esteemed accomplishments, such as a diploma or a letter of acceptance to a prestigious program or club.

- Presentation of all of your saved love letters, tied with a red ribbon.

- A fine bottle of wine to be shared on your first wedding anniversary.

- An item to support each other's professional goals, such as the registration to a high-level conference or course or a leather portfolio.

• An item that reflects and supports your shared interests, such as mountain bikes, a season's worth of ski passes, or tickets to a lavish event you've always wanted to attend.

• A photo album featuring pictures of the two of you during your courtship . . . with the last half of the book empty and waiting for future snapshots of you through the years (add a note to that effect!).

• A wonderful matted and framed picture of the two of you.

Guests' Hotel Room Gift Baskets

While it's a wonderful gesture to provide baskets of snacks and goodies for your guests who have traveled into town for your wedding, this can be considered an extra, nonessential expense allowable only if you have some spare room in your budget. So, if you've found your gown for half what you budgeted, switched to the domestically grown flowers over the pricier imported ones, and saved a bundle by having Uncle Phil drive you in his Porche rather than having to hire a limousine, then spend some money on gift baskets.

In each basket or inexpensive, pretty gift bag found at a dollar store include such "don't hit the minibar" items as these:

• Bottles of spring water.

• Cans of soda or bottles of juice.

• Minibags of crackers or healthy snack mix.

• Gum and breath mints.

• Guidebooks or pamphlets to nearby sites of interest.

• A new magazine for downtime reading.

• Travel-sized pampering items (such as a mini aromatherapy spray, not the standard toiletries that come complimentary with the room) or fuzzy slippers.

- A reminder invitation to the rehearsal, with directions.

- Printed directions to the wedding.

- Games and toys for the kids.

Smile and Say Cheese!

Those throwaway cameras I mentioned in the photography chapter come into play now. While once considered a nonessential for couples on a sky-high budget who can afford to have a professional photographer stay at their reception for hours and capture every shining moment, the throwaway camera is a tremendous advantage for the bride and groom on a budget. Rather than shell out big bucks for the time and service of a pro, these little cameras deliver great shots taken by guests who know you well and know the shots you'd love.

Here are some tips for finding and providing great throwaway cameras at your reception:

- Don't buy throwaway cameras from a camera shop unless you've conducted a detailed comparison price-check between their offerings and those at other sources. I checked a few different sources and found these price variations:

Established camera shop: $12.99 each.
Pharmacy store, such as Drug Fair: $5.99 each.
Beauty supply store: $9.99 each.
Supermarket: $7.99 each.
Warehouse store, such as Costco, Sam's Club, or BJ's: case bought
    in bulk comes to $3.99 each.

- If you visit various wedding Web sites, you'll discover many different types and designs of wedding-day cameras at a wide range of prices. The styles I found recently ranged from $5.99 to $9.99 each, with some important factors figuring into the value of the sale.

- Go for *quality.* You'll want your pictures to come out great, since they are partially taking the place of your official wedding photographer. Those cheapie no-name cameras will take your shots, but you might run the risk of getting too-dark pictures or even pictures with a green or other colored tint. So go for a reliable brand-name camera for a better shot at turning out good pictures, even if you have to pay slightly more.

- Be sure you've chosen a camera with a flash. Check that well-priced model for a built-in flash, as not all wedding-day cameras come with this feature. It would be a waste of money to discover that sad fact when it's too late.

- Decide if you want fifteen or twenty-seven exposures per camera. Comparison-shop by price, factoring in development charges.

- Don't buy the cameras that imprint messages on the bottoms of your photos. The gimmick may be a fun one, but sometimes the quotes are cheesy and inappropriate for a sentimental photograph. On the average, I've found that message-imprinting cameras run $2 to $5 more than standard cameras.

- Don't buy a camera that requires you to mail it in for developing. Very often, you can get a better deal by choosing a model that can be developed at a nearby store.

- When looking into developing options, comparison-shop by price among camera shops, discount stores such as Target, and warehouse stores such as Sam's Club or Costco. You might be surprised that the right location can save you 30% to 40% off the price of developing.

- Don't even think about getting same-day development for your pictures. Be patient and save 30% to 50% off the cost of developing.

- Provide only one camera per table. Some brides put the throwaway cameras on *every other* guest table for greater savings.

• Set a pretty basket or decorated box on a table by the exit, so that your guests will know to deposit the cameras there for you. Some guests, believe it or not, aren't aware that the cameras aren't for them to keep.

Additional Money-Saving Tips

• If you're going traditional with the candy-coated almonds (to signify the sweetness of married life), shop around for better prices on those almonds. Wedding supply sites and stores may charge more for their specialized shoppers, while bakeries and candy shops might offer them for less.

• Choose gifts with more meaning than price. A special framed photograph will mean more to the recipient than an engraved brandy snifter.

• Don't give into your competitive edge. Trying to outdo your recently married cousin by offering better favors or gifts is just a meaningless waste of money.

• Don't skip the favors. Sure, some couples will say that their guests didn't even miss the party favors, and they saved $400 by not buying any, but it's just ungracious not to thank your guests with even a small gift after they've traveled to be with you, shared your day with you, given you great gifts, and even participated as part of your wedding day. The money you spend on favors is worth far more than what you'll pay for them.

24 Hours to Go!

Where It All Comes Together

WHEN THE clock strikes twelve the day before your wedding, so begins your last full day as an engaged couple planning your important ceremony. It's been a long road, and you've accomplished a tremendous amount since the moment of your engagement. All of the plans for your wedding are in place, and all that's left is to complete the finishing touches and preparation for your Big Day. *This* day will be a busy one, a whirlwind of activity, questions and answers, directing your wedding participants and vendors, and preparing yourself for the wonderful things to come.

During the Day

Pour yourself a cup of coffee, grab your planner, and get ready to settle all the fine points of your day. Several of your vendors may need to be called for confirmation, and you may need to get in touch with your coordinator to check on some last-minute details. Once you're sure that the vendors are ready to serve you tomorrow, that they have the right directions to your sites, and that all your guests are in town and ready to go, it's time to get your own agenda in order.

First, lay out all of your wedding wardrobe, including your undergarments, hosiery, shoes, and accessories so that dressing is an enjoyable and stress-free task. Next, be sure you have the wedding rings—along with your marriage license and any other documents, wallets, and IDs—in a carrying case for transport during the wedding day, and make sure someone has the payment and tip envelopes ready for all of your wedding vendors. Your luggage for the honeymoon should be packed (check your list twice), and brought ahead of time by a reliable volunteer to your hotel room or by the door for placement in the trunk of your getaway car.

Assemble your wedding-day emergency bag to include all of the little save-the-day items such as an extra pair of stockings, pressed powder and lipstick for touchups throughout the day, your cell phone, any medications you're taking, breath mints, contact lens solution, or whatever else you might need in a pinch. Hand this bag off to a reliable relative for transport to the ceremony and reception sites.

With everything set, take a deep breath and get ready for your practice walk down the aisle!

Practice Makes Perfect: The Rehearsal

Together with your officiant, your bridal party members, family, and other wedding participants, you will gather to rehearse the ceremony and ask any last-minute questions.

During the rehearsal, everyone in attendance will learn the ins and outs of their jobs for the day, from where to stand to *when* to stand and sit during the ceremony. Your ushers will practice escorting guests to their seats, and they will also learn where special guests will be seated within the first few rows (use pew cards to prevent any seating fiascoes or hurt feelings among your guests.) Then, run through the entire ceremony, including the songs played by your musicians and the readings, clearing up any confusion along the way.

Next, practice the recessional as a group and figure out how you'll position yourselves in your receiving line. Decide then if the men will also be part of the receiving line and look around for great places nearby to pose for your post-ceremony pictures.

Ask plenty of questions and feel free to request last-minute changes, additions, or eliminations to the ceremony. This is *your* wedding, and you will rest easier tonight if you know that everything is prepared fully for the big day ahead.

Let's Relax! The Rehearsal Dinner

After the run-throughs are over, it's time to relax. Traditionally, the parents of the groom host the rehearsal dinner, and it's up to them whether they wish to plan a mini-wedding of sorts, with an upscale buffet or sit-down dinner complete with champagne toasts and a version of a wedding cake, or a more scaled-down affair. Some families enjoy a laid-back (and inexpensive!) dinner such as lasagna, salad, and garlic bread served at home or a meal enjoyed at a family style restaurant or pizza place. With such a busy day set for tomorrow, and with such an elaborate menu schedule for the reception, many groups decide to go more informal and relaxed tonight. The barbecue rehearsal dinner is popular, with hamburgers, hot dogs, and chicken wings roasted on the grill, while guests enjoy frozen margaritas out in the yard.

Simplify It

*B*e sure that your ceremony participants not only attend the rehearsal but learn from it. Your officiant or coordinator will certainly try to keep everyone's attention, but you should discuss with your maids, and have your groom discuss with his buddies, that the time for play is later. Your polite assertiveness will be far more effective than complaining or blowing off your wedding-stress steam to your over-stimulated friends.

Whatever the style (and expense) of the rehearsal dinner, the important thing is to take time to thank everyone who helped during the planning process and throughout your lives. Propose wonderful, endearing toasts to one another and to your bridal party and parents, and then hand out those wonderful gifts you've selected for everyone.

Now is the time for laughter, hugs, and great casual pictures. This is your last chance to relax, so enjoy the party and then turn in early to get some much-needed rest.

The Morning of the Wedding

It might take a minute to hit you when you awaken the next morning . . .

"This is my wedding day!"

Throw off those covers and get ready for the most wonderful day of your life. You might choose to clear your mind with a walk, a jog, some yoga, or even just a cup of coffee in front of the morning news or Saturday morning cartoons (you'll be quite the sight for a surprise snapshot as you kick back on the couch in your fuzzy slippers and robe, watching the *Powerpuff Girls!*). Or, host the ladies at your bridesmaids' brunch, taking care that everyone has a little something in their stomachs for energy that day. There's no need for a lavish brunch spread complete with serving trays of Eggs Benedict and caviar cream-cheese–filled blintzes. Keep it simple and inexpensive, and send some food over to where the men are preparing themselves as well . . . along with a love note for your groom.

Getting Gorgeous

I am *not* going to advise you to save money by doing all your beauty preparations yourself. And I'm *not* going to tell you to dye your hair on your own either, claiming that a box of dye costs $6 and a professional job can cost $60. The way you look on your wedding day is so incredibly important, not just for your pictures or to make a great impression on your groom and your guests, but because looking your absolute best will make you feel beautiful.

Here, I advise you to find great beauty professionals to help you with your hair, makeup, nails, and skin. Wonderful professionals can use the latest shades and techniques of makeup and beautifully sculpted hairstyles to give you a glamorous look for this once-in-a-lifetime day. Of course, you should be smart about where you go and who you hire. Some spa salons offer wedding-day beauty packages that will cost more than your gown. Start "auditioning" makeup artists and hair stylists long before your wedding and choose the professional with the greatest talent and more moderate prices.

This Manicure's on You

I'd like my maids to get their hair, makeup, and nails done at the salon that morning as well. Do I have to pay for all of them to get the royal treatment?

It would be nice if you did pick up the tab for your maids, but it's not a Must-Do. Many brides who want uniform hairstyles and nail polish shades for their attendants simply tell their maids where and when the salon appointment is, and the maids pick up the tab for their own beauty treatments. If you ask your maids to do this, be sure to choose a moderately priced salon, or just have them get their hair and nails done and not their makeup. Many bridesmaids tell me that they'd rather do their own makeup anyway, since they know they're more comfortable with their usual shades and brands of cosmetics.

Many salons do offer wonderful wedding-morning packages for both you and your maids, gathering you together in a relaxing atmosphere and letting their hair and makeup artists transform you. Consider the itemized price breakdowns of these packages carefully, though. In some instances, they offer an extensive lineup of services—including scalp massage, foot massage, hot-rock relaxation therapy, and the like—plus a complimentary champagne breakfast. It may seem like you're getting quite the deal. When you break it down, though, you might decide that all you really need is your hair, makeup, and nails done on the Big Day, for far less than all of those (admittedly wonderful) extras. Shop carefully and sign up only for the essentials.

If you want to have your hair colored or have a facial, visit the salon a few weeks before the wedding to have these processes done. These aren't procedures that are best done the day before (or the day of) the wedding, since some dye shades need a good week or two to oxidize into a more natural color and since some facial methods can cause breakouts. Allow yourself enough time in advance to allow your look to "settle in."

I do advise that you get professionally waxed at a reputable salon two to three days before your wedding. A great waxing job can erase the problem of shaving (and shaving bumps) throughout your wedding and honeymoon, and it will produce a cleaner, smoother look than you might get from an at-home waxing kit. Completing this task a few days before the wedding will help you get rid of any redness or irritation from the procedure so that your skin looks flawless.

Another beauty treatment you might consider is tanning. Unless you have years and years of experience with self-tanning lotions, hire

Simplify It

As for massages, they're wonderful to keep your stress level in check. But don't pay a fortune for them. On the average, massages run a dollar a minute. Save $30 and have your fiancé work your back and shoulders a day or two before the wedding . . . and return the favor for him. Use scented massage oils, light a scented candle, and play some relaxing music to fully melt your tension away.

a professional. Self-tanning requires adept exfoliation and lotion application, and an expert will apply the solution evenly for a better result. I've seen too many tiger-striped brides who forgot to hit the backs of their knees or who didn't get even application across their chests and face. The result is an orange-y pattern that takes a lot of foundation makeup to even out.

White teeth make your smile look brighter, so check out the many different kinds of tooth-whitening products and procedures available. Your dentist can certainly laser the stains out of your teeth, but some of these treatments cost from $600 to $1,000! At-home tooth-bleaching kits and strips are far more affordable, but you may have to experiment to find the kit that works for you. Start months in advance, and always talk to your dentist before using any tooth-bleaching product. Some people with sensitive teeth, gum disease, or cavities can suffer nerve damage if they're not good candidates for these products. If this is your case, stick with a good whitening toothpaste and let it work its magic while you avoid tooth-staining foods and beverages.

For your groom's best wedding-day look, encourage him to get a haircut one week before the wedding, so that he'll have a more natural look as well. If he goes to a bargain hair salon on the morning of the wedding, trying to save a buck at the last minute, that horrible buzz cut will be forever immortalized in your wedding-day pictures and video.

Right Before the Big Event

When you and your maids return home from the salon, it's time to dress and get ready for your photo session. If you've hired your photographer to take pre-wedding photos of you with your maids and with your family, then you may need a good block of time to assemble your group while the photographer snaps a few rolls of priceless shots. Be sure to freshen up your makeup, blot any shiny spots with pressed powder, and reapply your lipstick or gloss, and then step into the car that will whisk you off into your future.

A Note from the Author

Y ou did it! You planned a beautiful wedding for *less than half* the national average, and unless you tell them, no one will know that your gorgeous day was created on a budget.

You've done a wonderful job of planning every element of your wedding, of outsmarting what could have been a restrictive limitation on your wishes, and of making your dream wedding come true. Best of all, you've included many wonderful, personalized accents to your day, making it uniquely your own.

I want to thank you for allowing me to be part of your planning experience, and I wish you an overflowing abundance of love, luck, happiness, and health in your future together!

If you would like to share your budgeting success stories or wonderful planning ideas with me for possible inclusion in my future wedding books, please send me an e-mail message through my Web site: *www.sharonnaylor.net*. If I use your real-life wedding story in an upcoming book, I will quote you by name and send you a copy of the book, plus a fun free gift.

With all best wishes,

—Sharon Naylor

Appendix A: Wedding Budget Worksheet

Item/Service	Who's Paying	Budgeted	Actual
Engagement announcement			
Engagement party			
Ceremony site			
Ceremony décor			
Officiant's fee			
Marriage license			
Blood tests			
Pre-wedding counseling/classes			
Reception site			
Rentals for reception site			
Preparation of reception site (landscaping, cleaning, etc.)			

Item/Service	Who's Paying	Budgeted	Actual
Additional permits for parking, etc.			
Wedding gown			
Wedding gown fittings			
Accessories and shoes			
Bride's manicure, pedicure, and hair			
Groom's clothing			
Groom's accessories			
Wedding coordinator			
Invitations			
Postage			
Programs			
Thank-you notes			
Caterer's menu			
Liquor			
Cake			
Flowers			
Reception décor			
Reception entertainment			
Photography			
Videography			
Wedding cameras			

Item/Service	Who's Paying	Budgeted	Actual
Limousines or classic cars			
Other guest transportation			
Favors			
Gifts			
Toss-its			
Honeymoon			
Tips			
TOTALS			

Appendix B: Wardrobe Worksheets

Bride's Wardrobe

Bridal Gown

Name of store:

    Address:

    Phone:

    Cell Phone:

    E-mail:

Gown Designer and Style Number:

Size:

Shoe Size:

Deposit Payment Amount and Date:

Size Card Received:

Final Payment Amount and Date:

Pickup Date:

Date of Fittings:

    1.

    2.

    3.

    4.

Accessories

Check off any accessories you're using, and use the space provided to write any notes about what stores you found your accessories in and the prices of each, etc.

❑   Headpiece and Veil

❑   Gloves

❑   Jacket or shawl

❑   Jewelry

❑   Hosiery

❑   Undergarments

❑   Crinoline or slip

❑   Other

Bridesmaids' Wardrobes

Name of store:

Address:

Phone:

Cell Phone:

E-mail:

Gown Designer and Style Number:

Size:

Shoe Size:

Deposit Payment Amount and Date:

Size Card Received:

Final Payment Amount and Date:

Pickup Date:

Date of Fittings:

1.

2.

3.

4.

Accessories

Check off any accessories you're using, and use the space provided to write any
notes about what stores you found your accessories in and the prices of each, etc.

❏ Hair accent/décor

❏ Gloves

❑ Jacket or shawl

❑ Jewelry

❑ Hosiery

❑ Undergarments

❑ Crinoline or slip

❑ Other

Men's Wardrobes

Name of store:

Address:

Phone:

Cell Phone:

E-mail:

Tuxedo Designer and Style Number:

Size:

Shoe Size:

Deposit Payment Amount and Date:

Size Card Received:

Final Payment Amount and Date:

Pickup Date:

Drop-off Date:

Accessories

Check off any accessories you're using, and use the space provided to write any notes about what stores you found your accessories in and the prices of each, etc.

❑ Tie

❑ Cummerbund

❑ Vest

❏ Cufflinks

❏ Other

Resources

Please note that the following information is for your research use only. The author and the publisher do not personally endorse any vendor, service, company, or professional.

BRIDAL GOWNS

Alfred Angelo: 800-531-1125, www.alfredangelo.com

Amsale: 212-971-0170, www.amsale.com

Birnbaum and Bullock: 212-242-2914, www.birnbaumandbullock.com

Bonny: 800-528-0030, www.bonny.com

Bridal Originals: 800-876-GOWN, www.bridaloriginals.com

Brideway: 800-598-0685, www.brideway.net

Christos, Inc.: 212-921-0025, www.christosbridal.com

David's Bridal: 888-399-2743, www.DavidsBridal.com

Demetrios: 212-967-5222, www.demetriosbride.com

Diamond Collection: 212-302-0210, www.adiamondbridal.com

Eden: 800-828-8831, www.edenbridal.com (check out their values collection!)

Emme: 281-634-9225, www.emmebridal.com

Forever Yours: 800-USA-BRIDE, www.foreverbridals.com

Galina: 212-564-1020, www.galinabridal.com

Gowns Online: www.gownsonline.com

Group USA: www.groupusaonline.com

Janell Berte: 717-291-9894, www.berte.com

Jasmine: 800-634-0224, www.jasminebridal.com

Jessica McClintock: 800-333-5301, www.jessicamcclintock.com

Jim Hjelm: 800-686-7880, www.jimhjelmvisions.com

Lila Broude: 201-394-2183

Manale: 212-944-6939, www.manale.com

Marisa: 212-944-0022, www.marisabridals.com

Melissa Sweet Bridal Collections: 404-633-4395, www.melissasweet.com

Michelle Roth: 212-245-3390, www.michelleroth.com

Mon Cheri: 609-530-1900, www.mcbridals.com

Mori Lee: 212-840-5070, www.morileeinc.com

Priscilla of Boston: 617-242-2677, www.priscillaofboston.com

Private Label by G: 800-858-3338, www.privatelabelbyg.com

Roaman's Romance (plus sizes): 800-436-0800

Sweetheart: 800-223-6061, www.gowns.com

Tomasina: 412-563-7788, www.tomasinabridal.com

Venus: 800-OH-VENUS, www.lotusorient.com

Vera Wang: 800-VEW-VERA, www.verawang.com

Yumi Katsura: 212-772-3760, www.yumikatsura.com

BRIDESMAIDS' AND MOTHER-OF-THE-BRIDE GOWNS

After Six: 800-444-8304, www.aftersix.com

Alfred Angelo: 800-531-1125, www.alfredangelo.com

Bill Levkoff: 800-LEVKOFF, www.billlevkoff.com

Bridesmates: www.bridesmates.com

Chadwick's of Boston Special Occasions: 800-525-6650

Champagne Formals: 212-302-9162, www.champagneformals.com

David's Bridal: 888-399-2743, www.DavidsBridal.com

Dessy Creations: 800-444-8304, www.dessy.com

Group USA: www.groupusa.com

JCPenney: www.jcpenney.com

Jessica McClintock: 800-333-5301, www.jessicamcclintock.com

Jim Hjelm Occasions: 800-686-7880, www.jimhjelmoccasions.com

Lazaro: 212-764-5781, www.lazarobridal.com

Macy's: 877-622-9274, www.macys.weddingchannel.com

Melissa Sweet Bridal Collection: 404-633-4395, www.melissasweet.com

Mori Lee: 212-840-5070, www.morileeinc.com

Roaman's Romance (plus sizes): 800-436-0800

Sihouettes: www.silhouettesmaids.com

Spiegel: 800-527-1577, www.spiegel.com

Thread Design: 212-414-8844, www.threaddesign.com

Vera Wang: 800-VEW-VERA, www.verawang.com

Watters and Watters: 972-960-9884, www.watters.com

MEN'S WEDDING WEAR

Gingiss: www.gingiss.com

Marrying Man: www.MarryingMan.com

CHILDREN'S WEDDING WEAR

David's Bridal: 888-399-2743, www.DavidsBridal.com

Finetica Child: www.Fineticachild.com

Katie and Co.: www.katieco.com

Posie's: www.posies.com

ACCESSORIES

Shoes and Handbags

David's Bridal: 888-399-2743, www.DavidsBridal.com

Dyeables: 800-431-2000

Fenaroli for Regalia: 617-723-3682

Kenneth Cole: 800-KENCOLE

My Glass Slipper: www.myglassslipper.com

Nina Footwear: 800-23-NINA

Salon Shoes: 650-588-8677, www.salonshoes.com

Shoe Buy: www.shoebuy.com

Watters and Watters: 972-960-9884, www.watters.com

Veils and Headpieces

Bel Aire Bridals: 310-325-8160, www.belaireveils.com

David's Bridal: 888-399-2743, www.DavidsBridal.com

Dream Veils and Accessories: 312-943-9554, www.dreamveilsacc.com

Fenaroli for Regalia: 617-723-3682

Homa: 973-467-5500, homabridal@aol.com

Renee Romano: 312-943-0912, www.Renee-Romano.com

Winters & Rain: 401-848-0868, www.wintersandrain.com

FABRIC SUPPLIERS

Fabric Depot: 800-392-3376, www.fabricdepot.com

Fabric Mart: 800-242-3695

Greenberg and Hammer: 800-955-5135

Sewing Patterns:

Butterick: www.butterick.com

INVITATIONS

An Invitation to Buy—Nationwide: www.invitations4sale.com

Anna Griffin Invitation Design: 404-817-8170, www.annagriffin.com

Botanical PaperWorks: 888-727-3755

Camelot Wedding Stationery: 800-280-2860

Crane and Co.: 800-572-0024, www.crane.com

Evangel Christian Invitations: 800-457-9774, www.evangelwedding.com

Invitations by Dawn: 800-332-3296, www.invitationsbydawn.com

Julie Holcomb Printers: 510-654-6416, www.julieholcombprinters.com

Now and Forever: 800-451-8616, www.now-and-forever.com

PaperStyle.com (ordering invitations online): 770-667-6100, www
.paperstyle.com

Papyrus: 800-886-6700, www.papyrusonline.com

Precious Collection: 800-537-5222, www.preciouscollection.com

Renaissance Writings: 800-246-8483, www.RenaissanceWriting.com

Rexcraft: 800-635-3898, www.rexcraft.com

WER Paper (eco-friendly tree-free invitations): www.werpaper.com

Willow Tree Lane: 800-219-9230, www.willowtreelane.com

Rings

A Diamond Is Forever: www.adiamondisforever.com

American Gem Society: 800-346-8485, www.ags.org

Benchmark: 800-633-5950, www.benchmarkrings.com

Bianca: 213-622-7234, www.BiancaPlatinum.com

Blue Nile: www.BlueNile.com

Cartier: 800-CARTIER

Christian Bauer: 800-228-3724, www.christianbauer.com

EGL Gemological Society: 877-EGL-USA-1, www.egl.co.za

Honora: 888-2HONORA, www.honora.com

Jeff Cooper Platinum: 888-522-6222, www.jeffcooper.com

Keepsake Diamond Jewelry: 888-4-KEEPSAKE

Lazare Diamond: www.lazarediamonds.com

Novell: 888-916-6835, www.novelldesignstudio.com

OGI Wedding Bands Unlimited: 800-578-3846, www.ogi-ltd.com

Paul Klecka: 888-P-KLECKA, www.klecka.com

Rudolf Erdel Platinum: www.rudolferdel.com

Scott Kay Platinum: 800-487-4898, www.scottkay.com

Tiffany: 800-526-0649, www.tiffany.com

Wedding Ring Hotline: 800-985-RING, www.weddingringhotline.com

Zales: 800-311-JEWEL, www.zales.com

Flowers

AboutFlowers.com: www.AboutFlowers.com

Association of Special Cut Flowers: 440-774-2887

Flowersales.com: www.flowersales.com

International Floral Picture Database: www.flowerweb.com

Romantic Flowers: www.romanticflowers.com

TRAVEL

Airlines

Air Canada: www.aircanada.ca

Air France: www.airfrance.fr

Alaska Airlines: 800-426-0333, www.alaskaair.com

Alitalia: www.zenonet.com

Aloha Airlines: 800-367-5250, www.alohaair.com

America West: 800-247-5692, www.americawest.com

American Airlines: 800-433-7300, www.amrcorp.com

British Airways: 800-247-9297, www.british-airways.com

Continental Airlines: 800-525-0280, www.flycontinental.com

Delta Airlines: 800-221-1212, www.delta-air.com

Hawaiian Airlines: 800-367-5320

KLM Royal Dutch Airlines: 800-374-7747

Northwest Airlines: 800-225-2525, www.nwa.com

Southwest Airlines: 800-435-9792, www.southwest.com

TWA: 800-221-2000, www.twa.com

USAir: 800-428-4322, www.usair.com

United Airlines: 800-241-6522, www.ualservices.com

Virgin Atlantic Airways: 800-862-8621, www.fly.virgin.com

DISCOUNT AIRFARES

Air Fare: www.airfare.com

Cheap Fares: www.cheapfares.com

Cheap Seats: 800-MR-CHEAP

Cheap Tickets: 800-377-1000, www.cheaptickets.com

Discount Airfare: www.discount-airfare.com

Priceline: www.priceline.com

Cruises

American Cruise Line (east coast from Florida to Maine): www.american
   cruiselines.com

A Wedding for You: 800-929-4198 (weddings aboard a cruise ship)

Carnival Cruise Lines: 888-CARNIVAL, www.carnival.com

Celebrity Cruises: www.celebrity-cruises.com

Cruise Lines International: www.cruising.org

Cunard: www.cunardline.com

Delta Queen: www.deltaqueen.com

Discount Cruises: www.cruise.com

Disney Cruises: 407-828-3400, www.disneycruise.com

Holland America: www.hollandamerica.com

Norwegian Cruise Lines: www.ncl.com

Princess Cruises: www.princess.com

Radisson Seven Seas Cruises: www.rssc.com

Royal Caribbean: 800-398-9819, www.royalcaribbean.com

Resorts

Beaches: 800-BEACHES, www.beaches.com

Club Med: www.clubmed.com

Couples Resorts: 800-545-7937, www.sweptaway.com/weddings.htm

Disney: www.disneyweddings.com

Hilton Hotels: www.hilton.com

Hyatt Hotels: www.hyatt.com

Marriott Hotels: www.marriott.com

Radisson: www.radisson.com

Sandals: 800-SANDALS, www.sandals.com

Super Clubs: 800-GO-SUPER, www.superclubs.com

Westin Hotels: www.westin.com

Hotels

To find a suitable hotel in your destination, look up the All Hotels Web site
at www.all-hotels.com

Bed and breakfasts, country inns, and small hotels: www.virtualcities.com

Bed and Breakfast – International Guide: www.ibbp.com

Fodors: www.fodors.com

Hilton: www.hilton.com

Hyatt: www.hyatt.com

Leading Hotels of the World: www.lhw.com

Marriott: www.marriott.com

Radisson: www.radison.com

Westin: www.westin.com

Tourism Departments

Tourism Office Worldwide Directory: www.towd.com

Alabama: 800-252-2262

Alaska: 907-465-2010

Arizona: 602-542-8687

Aruba Tourism Department: 201-330-0800

Australian Tourist Commission: www.australia.com

Bahamas: 212-758-2777, www.bahamas.com

Barbados: 212-986-6516

Bermuda: 800-223-6106

British Virgin Islands: 800-888-5563, ext. 559

California: 800-GO-CALIF

Caribbean: 212-682-0435

Colorado: 800-433-2656

Connecticut: 800-282-6863

Delaware: 800-441-8846

Disney Honeymoons: 877-566-0969, www.disneyhoneymoons.com

Florida: 888-7-FLA-USA

France: 310-568-6665

Fiji: 310-568-1616, www.islandsinthesun.com

Georgia: 800-847-4842

Germany: 212-661-7200

Hawaii: 808-923-1811

Idaho: 800-635-7820

Illinois: 312-814-4732

Indiana: 800-289-ONIN

Iowa: 800-345-IOWA

Ireland: 212-418-0800

Italy: 212-245-4961

Jamaica: 800-233-4582

Kansas: 800-2-KANSAS

Kentucky: 800-225-8747

Key West: 800-648-6269

Lake Tahoe: 800-824-6348, www.go-tahoe.com

Las Vegas: 702-892-0711

Lousiana: 800-334-8626

Maine: 207-623-0363

Maryland: 800-543-1036

Massachusetts: 617-727-3201

Mexico: 800-44-MEXICO

Michigan: 800-543-2937

Minnesota: 800-657-3700

Mississippi: 800-WARMEST

Missouri: 800-877-1234

Monaco: 800-753-9696

Montana: 800-541-1447

Nebraska: 800-228-4307

Nevada: 800-638-2328

New Hampshire: 800-FUN-IN-NH

New Jersey: 800-JERSEY-7

New Jersey/Cape May County: 800-227-2297

New Mexico: 800-545-2040

New York: 800-CALL-NYS

Niagara Falls: 800-338-7890

North Carolina: 800-847-4862

North Dakota: 800-HELLO-ND

Oahu, Hawaii: 877-525-OAHU, www.visitoahu.com

Ohio: 800-BUCKEYE

Oklahoma: 800-654-8240

Oregon: 800-547-7842

Pennsylvania: 800-VISIT-PA

Puerto Rico: www.prtourism.com

Quebec: 800-363-7777

Rhode Island: 800-556-2484

St. Lucia: www.stlucia.org

South Carolina: 800-872-3505

South Dakota: 800-S-DAKOTA

Spain: www.tourspain.es

Tahiti: 800-828-6877, www.islandsinthesun.com

Tennessee: 615-741-2158

Texas: 800-8888-TEX

Utah: 800-222-8824

Vermont: 802-828-3236

Virginia: 800-248-4833

Washington: www.tourism.wa.gov

West Virginia: 800-CALL-WVA

Wisconsin: 800-432-TRIP

Wyoming: 800-225-5996

Train Travel

Amtrak: 800-872-7245, www.amtrak.com

Eurailpass: www.eurail.com

Orient Express Hotels, Trains and Cruises: www.orient-express.com

PROFESSIONAL ASSOCIATIONS

Limousines

National Limousine Association: 800-NLA-7007, www.limo.org

Wedding Consultants

Association of Bridal Consultants: 860-355-0464, www.bridalassn.com

Association of Certified Professional Wedding Consultants: 408-528-9000, www.acpwc.com

June Wedding (Consultants in the Western U.S.) 702-474-9558,
www.junewedding.com

Miscellaneous Organizations

American Disc Jockey Association: 301-705-5150, www.adja.org

American Federation of Musicians: 212-869-1330

American Rental Association: 800-334-2177, www.ararental.org

American Society of Travel Agents: 703-739-2782

Association of Professional Videographers: 209-653-8307, www.avp.to

Better Business Bureau: www.bbb.org/bureaus (to find the Better Business
Bureau of your state or locale)

National Association of Catering Executives: www.nace.net

Professional Photographers of America: 800-786-6277, www.ppa.com

Wedding and Portrait Photographers International: www.eventphotogra-
phers.com

Ceremony Sites

City Search: www.CitySearch.com

Digital Cities: www.DigitalCities.com

Field Trip: www.FieldTrip.com

Go.com: www.Go.com

Here Comes the Guide: www.HereComesTheGuide.com

USA Citylink: www.USACitylink.com

Warehouse Stores

BJ's Wholesale: www.bjswholesale.com

Costco: www.costco.com

Sam's Club: www.samsclub.com

WEDDING WEB SITES

The Best Man: www.thebestman.com

Bridal Guide: www.bridalguide.com

Bride Again magazine: www.brideagain.com

Bride's Magazine: www.brides.com

Elegant Bride: www.elegantbride.com

Martha Stewart Living: www.marthastewart.com

Modern Bride: www.ModernBride.com

Premiere Bride: www.premierebride.com

The Knot: www.theknot.com

The Wedding Channel: www.theweddingchannel.com

The Wedding Helpers: www.weddinghelpers.com

Today's Bride: www.todaysbride.com

Town and Country Weddings (upscale): www.tncweddings.com

Ultimate Internet Wedding Guide: www.ultimatewedding.com

Wedding Bells: www.weddingbells.com

Wedding Central: www.weddingcentral.com

Wedding Details: www.weddingdetails.com

Wedding Spot: www.weddingspot.com

Wedding World: www.weddingworld.com

WEDDING REGISTRIES

Bed Bath & Beyond: 800-GO-BEYOND, www.bedbathandbeyond.com

Bloomingdale's: 800-888-2WED, www.bloomingdales.com

Bon Ton: 800-9BONTON

Crate & Barrel: 800-967-6696, www.crateandbarrel.com

Dillards: 800-626-6001, www.dillards.com

Filene's: www.FilenesWeddings.com

Fortunoff: 800-777-2807, www.fortunoff.com

Gump's: www.gumps.com

Hecht's: www.hechts.com

Home Depot: www.homedepot.com

HoneyLuna (honeymoon registry): 800-809-5862

JCPenney: 800-JCP-GIFT, www.jcpgift.com

Kitchen Etc.: 800-232-4070, www.kitchenetc.com

Kohl's: 800-837-1500

Linens 'n Things: www.lnt.com

Macy's Wedding Channel: 888-92-BRIDES, www.macys.weddingchannel.com

Neiman Marcus: www.neimanmarcus.com

Pier 1 Imports: 800-245-4595, www.pier1.com

Sears: www.sears.com

Service Merchandise: www.servicemerchandise.com

Sur La Table: 800-243-0852, www.surlatable.com

Target's Club Wedd Gift Registry: 800-888-9333, www.target.com

Tiffany: 800-526-0649, www.tiffany.com

Ultimate Online Wedding Mall: www.ultimateweddingmall.com

Wedding Channel.com: www.weddingchannel.com

Williams Sonoma: 800-541-2376, www.williams-sonoma.com

WEDDING SUPPLIES AND SERVICES

Books and Planners

Amazon.com: www.amazon.com

Barnes & Noble: www.bn.com

Borders: www.borders.com

Cake Supplies

Wilton: 800-794-5866, www.wilton.com

Calligraphy

Calligraphy by Kristen: www.calligraphybykristen.com

Petals and Ink: 818-509-6783, www.petalsnink.com

Cameras

C&G Disposable Cameras: www.cngdisposablecamera.com

Kodak: 800-242-2424, www.kodak.com

Michaels: www,michaels.com

Wedding Party Pack: 800-242-2424

Favors and Gifts

Beverly Clark Collection: 877-862-3933, www.beverlyclark.com

Chandler's Candle Company: 800-463-7143, www.chandlerscandle.com

Double T Limited: 800-756-6184, www.uniquefavors.com

Exclusively Weddings: 800-759-7666, www.exclusivelyweddings.com

Favors by Serendipity: 800-320-2663, www.favorsbyserendipity.com

Forever and Always Company: 800-404-4025, www.foreverandalways.com

Godiva: 800-9-GODIVA, www.godiva.com

Gratitude: 800-914-4342, www.giftsofgratitude.com

Illuminations: www.illuminations.com

Personal Creations: 800-326-6626

Pier 1: 800-245-4595, www.pier1.com

Seasons: 800-776-9677

Service Merchandise: 800-251-1212; www.servicemerchandise.com

Tamarac (seedlings): www.tamarac.on.ca

Things Remembered: 800-274-7367, www.thingsremembered.com

Tree and Floral Beginnings (seedlings, bulbs, and candles) 800-499-9580,
    www.plantamemory.com; in Canada, www.plantamemory.on.ca

Wireless: 800-669-9999

Paper Products

OfficeMax: www.officemax.com

Paper Access: 800-727-3701, www.paperaccess.com

Paper Direct: 800-A-PAPERS

Staples: 800-333-3330, www.staples.com

The Wedding Store: www.wedguide.com/store

Ultimate Wedding Store: www.ultimatewedding.com/store

Wedmart.com: 888-802-2229, www.wedmart.com

Weather Service

Check the weather at your ceremony, reception, or honeymoon sites, including five-day forecasts and weather bulletins at the following:

AccuWeather: www.accuweather.com

Rain or Shine: Five-day forecasts for anywhere in the world, plus ski and
    boating conditions: www.rainorshine.com

Sunset Time (Precise sunset time for any day of the year): www.usno.navy.mil

Weather Channel: www.weather.com

Wedding Items (toasting flutes, ring pillows, etc.)

Affectionately Yours: www.affectionately-yours.com

Beverly Clark Collection: 877-862-3933, www.beverlyclark.com

Bridalink Store: www.bridalink.com

Butterfly Celebration: 800-548-3284, www.butterflycelebration.com

Celebration Bells: 217-463-2222, www.celebrationbells.com

Chandler's Candle Company: 800-463-7143, www.chandlerscandle.com

Keutbah Ketubah: 888-KETUBAH, www.KETUBAH.com

Magical Beginnings Butterfly Farms: 888-639-9995, www.butterflyevents
.com (live butterflies for release)

Michaels: 800-642-4235, www.michaels.com

The Wedding Shopper: www.theweddingshopper.com/catalog.htm

Wine and Champagne

Wine.com: www.wine.com

Wine Searcher: www.winesearcher.com

Wine Spectator: www.winespectator.com

Beauty And Health

Beauty Products and Services

Check these sites for makeup and skin care products, assessments, and
services:

Avon: www.avon.com

Beauty.com: www.beauty.com

Beauty Jungle: www.beautyjungle.com

Bobbi Brown Essentials: www.bobbibrown.com

Clinique: www.clinique.com

Elizabeth Arden: www.elizabetharden.com (choose the shades and treatment products that are right for you, and find the perfect perfume for
your big day)

Estée Lauder: www.esteelauder.com

Eve: www.eve.com (carries Lorac, Elizabeth Arden, Calvin Klein, etc)

iBeauty: www.ibeauty.com

Lancôme: www.lancome.com

L'Oreal: www.loreal.com

Mac: www.maccosmetics.com

Makeover Studio: www.makeoverstudio.com (choose your face shape and experiment with makeup shades and looks)

Max Factor: www.maxfactor.com

Maybelline: www.maybelline.com

Michelle Roth: 212-245-3390, www.michellerothbeauty.com

Neutrogena: www.neutrogena.com

Pantene: www.pantene.com

Revlon: www.revlon.com

Sephora: www.sephora.com

Sharon Naylor's Web site: www.sharonnaylor.net

Index